Cambridge Handbooks to the Historical Performance of Music

GENERAL EDITORS Colin Lawson and Robin Stowell

During the last three decades historical performance has become part of mainstream musical life. However, there is as yet no one source from which performers and students can find an overview of the significant issues or glean practical information pertinent to a particular instrument. This series of handbooks guides the modern performer towards the investigation and interpretation of evidence found both in early performance treatises and in the mainstream repertory. Books on individual instruments contain chapters on historical background, equipment, technique and musical style and are illustrated by case studies of significant works in the repertoire. An introductory book provides a more general survey of issues common to all areas of historical performance and will also inform a wide range of students and music lovers.

Forthcoming titles

JOHN HUMPHRIES *The Early Horn: A Practical Introduction*
COLIN LAWSON *The Early Clarinet: A Practical Introduction*
DAVID ROWLAND *Early Keyboard Instruments: A Practical Introduction*
ROBIN STOWELL *The Early Violin and Viola: A Practical Introduction*
RACHEL BROWN *The Early Flute: A Practical Introduction*

Contents

Figures

Preface

During the course of little more than a generation historical performance has become part of mainstream musical life in many parts of the world. A number of years have passed since it was subjected to formal scrutiny by Nicholas Kenyon and others in his symposium *Authenticity and Early Music* (Oxford, 1988) and Howard Mayer Brown, Stanley Sadie and their colleagues in *Performance Practice* (London, 1989). The numerous important developments since then have yet to be evaluated thoroughly in print, hence the conception of this volume, which offers a concise, newly considered overview of historical performance. It aims to address largely practical matters rather than theoretical or philosophical issues and to guide readers towards further investigation and interpretation of the evidence provided not only in the various instrumental treatises, but also in examples from the mainstream repertory.

The Historical Performance of Music: An Introduction has been devised to complement the Cambridge Handbooks to the Historical Performance of Music, a series of short volumes on early music performance which are specific to particular instruments. These handbooks present and interpret evidence from significant primary sources on matters such as technique, style and expression, and (like the present volume) offer suggestions for further reading and study. They also offer guidance on other issues pertinent to the instrument under consideration, including repertory and organology, as well as advice regarding the acquisition of appropriate instruments and accessories. The present volume, however, deals with the more general, large-scale practical issues that need to be addressed in connection with the preparation and execution of performances which are historically informed, yet at the same time individual and vivid. As in each handbook, this volume attempts to put many of the issues discussed into practice by relating them to selected major works *c.* 1700 – *c.* 1900, the core period which forms the principal (though not exclusive) focus for all these publications.

xi

Throughout the presentation is descriptive rather than prescriptive, as performing early music involves much more than simply following rules defined in treatises. Appropriately searching questions need to be asked and guidance given as to how and where suitable answers may be sought. Each case study thus demonstrates the application of the technical, interpretative and other principles discussed in different performing situations and in different musical genres. This provides an historical basis for artistic decision-making which has as its goal the re-creation of a performance as close as possible to the composer's original conception.

We have written for all those who are interested in historical performance, whether as professional performers, students, enthusiastic concert-goers, discriminating arm-chair listeners or 'modern' players who seek advice as to those matters of style, approach and general technique that combine to make up a well-grounded, period interpretation. The balance between historical accuracy and practical expediency in early music has varied wildly over the years from one individual and/or ensemble to the next; curiously, however, the general public has remained blissfully unaware of the detail of these variations. Thus, it is hoped that this book will stimulate its readers to contemplate what makes historical performance different, to study the ways and means in which a stylish interpretation may be established and to use them as the historical foundations for artistic decisions in their own performances.

We do not claim that our inevitably broad and summary view of performance practices c. 1700 – c. 1900 incorporates all the answers. But we hope that we have been successful in disseminating important information on various significant issues within the discipline, corrected some misconceptions, shed some light on some grey areas, encouraged further reading on many subjects by way of the copious endnotes and select bibliography, and demonstrated that theoretical data must be interpreted with discrimination and caution in formulating an historically informed performance. Above all, we hope that we have emphasised sufficiently not only that period performance comprises – of necessity – a mixture of factual knowledge and educated guesswork but also that close observance of theorists' rules is no substitute for artistry, taste and musical intelligence in bringing a performance to life; for then, as now, performers have been admired for what they as individuals brought to the music, and it is with them that the final responsibility for convincing historical performance must rest.

Together we bring to this volume a great deal of experience of professional performance on period instruments. We would like to take this opportunity of acknowledging the influence and inspiration of friends, colleagues and students in many walks of life who have assisted us in the study and practical realisation of historical performance. Among those who have been most influential have been scholars such as Peter le Huray and Peter Williams, directors and performers such as Roy Goodman, Christopher Hogwood, Sigiswald Kuijken, Sir Charles Mackerras, Sir Roger Norrington, Trevor Pinnock and Jaap Schröder, as well as several instrument makers and a number of postgraduate students. Notwithstanding the fact that we have been willing and grateful recipients of so much advice and guidance, we hold ourselves responsible for the overall content of the text, whose scope has been constrained by the space available. Indeed, several topics outlined here will be explored more fully within the specialist handbooks themselves.

We must also acknowledge the invaluable help of Penny Souster and her team at Cambridge University Press, particularly our painstaking copy-editor Lucy Carolan; finally, thanks are also due to the Department of Music at Cardiff University for granting one of us a most timely period of study leave.

1 Music as history

Introduction

'In order to do justice to the piece which he is about to perform, the player must first acquaint himself with the conditions under which it originated. For a work by Bach or Tartini demands a different style of delivery from one by Mendelssohn or Spohr. The space of a century that divides the two first mentioned from the last two means in the historical development of our art not only a great difference in regard to form, but even a greater with respect to musical expression.'[1]

This far-sighted advice appeared at the very beginning of the twentieth century in Joseph Joachim's *Violinschule*, written in collaboration with his pupil Andreas Moser. Inevitably, Joachim's historical approach to Bach or Tartini must have been very different from today's and certainly did not involve a change of violin or bow. But one of the remarkable achievements of the following 100 years has been the probing investigation of musical styles of various eras, with stimulating and often surprising results. Tradition and intuition have been increasingly complemented by an unprecedented realisation of the practical value of primary sources.

The perceptive musical mind has indeed emerged as a necessary adjunct to mere technique and artistry. According to one of his pupils, the great pioneer Arnold Dolmetsch once characteristically remarked that he wanted his students to learn principles rather than pieces, so that they could do their own thinking.[2] A similar approach resurfaces in Gustav Leonhardt's recent observation: 'When one is a student one does things consciously, but when one is more experienced one does not play intellectually any more. One doesn't *think*; one *has thought* . . . things are done automatically, depending on what you intend to say.'[3] Other commentators have pointed to the importance of a certain attitude of mind rather than adherence to a set of techniques applied to an arbitrarily delimited body of early music. The real issue is a comprehensive theory of performance covering music from the earliest times we care about up to the present.[4]

In today's musical climate historical performance in theory and practice has truly come to form part of mainstream musical life. Period instruments are routinely encountered in the concert hall and are virtually obligatory in substantial areas of the repertory, notably in music before 1750. Throughout the world there has developed a huge interest in acquiring instrumental techniques of the past. Naturally, this involves not merely searching out relevant equipment, but also investigating earlier styles of performance. Meanwhile, the entire thrust of such endeavours has been subject to stimulating discussion and argument. But it cannot be denied that artistic life today makes demands which are decidedly unhistorical; for example, the microphone introduces a set of parameters which would have been unthinkable in previous generations. Furthermore, air travel has brought such changes that we do not have the option to turn back the clock.

The original expectations of composers in terms of sound and musical style ('performance practice') have become a lively subject for debate, widely reflected within a range of musical journals. In this area scholars and performers are mutually dependent, drawing upon archival, literary, iconographical, analytical and purely philological studies. The score itself is an imprecise mechanism, which by its very nature offers even the most dutiful performer a rich variety of possibilities.[5] There has always been much detail which a composer did not trouble to write in his scores; he simply knew that certain conventions would be observed. Some of these are no longer current, whereas others have undergone significant changes of meaning. Those elements of style which a composer found it unnecessary to notate will always remain for us a foreign language, but eventually we may be able to converse freely within it as musicians, and so bring a greater range of expression to our interpretations, rather than merely pursuing some kind of unattainable 'authenticity'.

Using the resources for which a particular repertory was intended may well make the music sound more expressive and can make more sense of what the composer actually wrote, re-creating something of its initial impact on the listener. But even if we could witness performances of large-scale works by Bach, Beethoven or Brahms, we should not necessarily want to adopt all their features, since to some extent our own taste would almost certainly continue to influence our interpretation. There will always be circumstances in musical history which we may well not want to emulate; on the other hand, the different approaches to articulation and phrasing which obtained in earlier periods are in themselves a reminder that performing styles have changed out of all recognition.

The roots of the historical performance movement were already well in place at the very beginning of the twentieth century.[6] A valuable survey of changing musical attitudes is Harry Haskell's *The Early Music Revival* (London, 1988), an account of the multifarious activities of musicologists, editors, publishers, makers, collectors, curators, dealers, librarians, performers, teachers and record producers. Significantly, even after historical awareness in Baroque and earlier repertories had become an established principle, it continued to be widely believed that there was no benefit in performing Classical or Romantic music on period instruments. In 1955 H. C. Robbins Landon could routinely remark in his otherwise far-sighted book on Haydn's symphonies that 'no-one will want to perform Haydn's music with natural trumpets and ancient woodwind when our modern counterparts are in most cases superior in every way', a viewpoint which held sway for some considerable time.[7] Even in 1980 the article 'performing practice' in *The New Grove* claimed that in contrast to music written before 1750 'there has been no severance of contact with post-Baroque music as a whole, nor with the instruments used in performing it'. Subsequent musical revelations have proved this argument untenable, as period interpretations of Mozart and Beethoven have been followed by a traversal through the nineteenth century and even beyond. In the event, performance practice from Brahms's time has proved to be fraught with ambiguities, which are in some ways as challenging as those relating to earlier periods. These very problems seem to nourish historical enquiry, as witnessed by recording and concert schedules worldwide and the increasing opportunities at conservatoires for principal study of period instruments.

The nature and development of historical awareness

Performances of 'early music' have been a feature of western culture at various times and places and at least one writer has remarked that we have all surely exaggerated the extent to which musicians before the late nineteenth century performed and studied only the music of their own time.[8] Certainly, musical histories often tend to discuss only that repertory contemporary to a particular time, presented as though one is tracing an imaginary journey through a one-way street which might ultimately be found to link compositions of the distant past with those of the present. But in Renaissance England, for example, sacred vocal music often stayed in the repertories of church and cathedral choirs for more than a hundred years. Then in the late eighteenth and early nineteenth centuries, groups such as the Academy of Ancient Music and the Concert of Antient Music in London regularly performed early English church music as well as works by Purcell, Handel and Corelli. England was the first country where old musical works were performed regularly and reverentially, and where the idea of musical classics first arose. In their different ways historians John Hawkins and Charles Burney found newer (especially instrumental) works offensive to their ears and in questioning aspects of contemporary music, legitimised a canon of old works as the source of authority over musical taste.[9] A recent account of this phenomenon investigates the political and social reasons for such developments.[10] The Handel Commemoration of 1784 was the culmination, creating an extraordinary spectacle, massive in scale and splendour.

The crucial realisation gradually developed during the nineteenth century that contemporary performance styles did not necessarily suit music from earlier times. Prominent among advocates of such a viewpoint was François-Joseph Fétis, whose 'historical concerts' began at the Paris Conservatoire as early as 1832. It was this stylistic awareness which sowed the seeds of what was later to be known as authenticity, attempting to view older music in terms of its original period rather than transplanting it to the present. The widespread acceptance of so-called faithfulness to the original is much more recent and has been widely seen as symptomatic of the loss of a truly living contemporary music. At least one commentator believes that we have lost the unselfconsciousness necessary to use the present as the ultimate standard; the composer's intention has become for us the highest authority.[11]

Influential reworkings of Bach and Handel

The updating of earlier music as a matter of course, reflecting mainstream musical culture until a generation ago, owes a great deal to Mozart's arrangements of the music of Bach and Handel. His preoccupation with the Baroque, stimulated in the 1780s by Baron Gottfried van Swieten, subsequently had an enormous impact on later composers. Van Swieten also came into contact with Haydn and Beethoven and made them aware of their Baroque heritage.[12] One of the tangible results was Mozart's six Preludes and Fugues K404a for string trio, where four of the introductory slow movements were of his own composition and the fugues (by J. S. Bach, except for one by W. F. Bach) were subject not merely to re-instrumentation, but to interventionist treatment in terms of embellishment, melodic line, harmony and even tonality. Van Swieten's private oratorio concerts (from 1787) were initially directed by Mozart and subsequently included the premieres of Haydn's *The Creation* and *The Seasons*. A highlight was Mozart's adaptation of Handel's *Messiah* in 1789, which reflected the circumstances of his time.[13] Mozart held Handel in high regard but in accordance with the spirit of his age felt the need for more orchestral colour, so that it was natural for him to bring the music up to date. Solo numbers were interchanged, transposed, inserted or shortened, while there were far-reaching alterations to the instrumentation. Mozart's orchestral tone-painting resembles contexts within his own operas such as *Don Giovanni* and *Die Zauberflöte*, and the additional wind parts in the tutti choruses make Handel's organ continuo redundant. In the arias Mozart added expression and dynamic markings. The art of high trumpet (clarino) playing had died out in the half-century since the date of composition; Mozart's pragmatic solution was to assign much of the obbligato in 'The trumpet shall sound' to the horn.

The importance of Mozart's approach through the nineteenth century is nicely captured in an article of 1879 by Ebenezer Prout, who introduces the topic thus: 'In the published scores of the older masters, especially Bach and Handel, much is to be met with which if performed exactly as printed will fail altogether to realise the intentions of the composer. This arises partly from the difference in the composition of our modern orchestras as compared with those employed a century and a half ago; partly also from the fact that it was formerly the custom to write out in many cases little more than a skeleton of the music, leaving the details to be filled in at performance from the figured bass.'[14] Prout remarks that passages are regularly encountered in Bach whose effect on the modern orchestra will be altogether different from that designed by the composer; in Handel, our ears are so accustomed to a rich and sonorous instrumentation, that this music if played only with strings and oboes, or sometimes with strings alone, would sound so thin as to be distasteful. Reflecting the taste of his own times, he concludes that additional accompaniments must be judged on their own merits, though the question is not whether but how they should be written. Not foreseeing the climate of authenticity a century later, Prout suggests that modernisations of this kind will probably be written until the end of time.

Clearly, this article implies a quite different approach to the ideal of realising the composer's intentions than that of today. Prout notes that Bach in particular employed a number of instruments which had fallen into disuse, such as the viola d'amore, the viola da gamba, the oboe d'amore, the oboe da caccia and several others. He then proceeds to recommend substitution as far as possible with their modern equivalents. This was indeed Mendelssohn's procedure in his celebrated 1829 revival of Bach's *St Matthew Passion*. Mendelssohn claimed to have presented Bach's works exactly as they were written, but he was no purist, approaching Bach's music as a practical musician eager to bring it to life for his contemporaries.

Mendelssohn brought Bach's music into the public domain once and for all, inspiring performances in several German cities in the 1830s and 1840s and soon throughout Europe. He introduced cuts which reduced the work's performing time by a third; there were rescorings and reassignment of solo parts, together with tempo and dynamic markings that placed a premium on dramatic contrasts and the highly charged emotionalism characteristic of his own time.

Historical considerations

Mendelssohn was influenced in his own music by Baroque composers, as is evident from *Elijah* and from his keyboard preludes and fugues. For Brahms, earlier music offered an even more fruitful creative impetus. Michael Musgrave has noted that in his first choral appointment at Detmold (1857–9) Brahms performed two cantatas from the new *Bach-Gesellschaft* edition, as well as Handel's *Messiah*.[15] Later, he was to explore in performance the then obscure worlds of Schütz and Gabrieli. Brahms contributed to Chrysander's Couperin edition and wrote continuo realisations for the Italian duets and trios of Chrysander's Handel edition. Such an establishment of texts from preferred sources in an era of Collected Editions (including Mozart) was soon to make possible the concepts of *Werktreue* (faithfulness to the text), performance practice and authenticity itself.[16] Meanwhile, Brahms made manuscript copies from rare printed editions of old music and gradually assembled for his own library some important treasures, such as the autograph of Mozart's late G minor Symphony.[17] The creative influence of old music is evident throughout Brahms's own work, which shows enormous historical awareness. His friend Joachim directed a Bach festival at Eisenach in 1884, where he performed the B minor Mass using a modern replica of an oboe d'amore and a so-called 'Bach trumpet', prompting the *Monthly Musical Record* to observe that 'the deficiencies in Bach's music, as we commonly hear it, are due, in fact, not to the author, but to the imperfection, in several remarkable respects, of our vaunted modern orchestra'.[18] This project illustrates a growing realisation that in earlier music the modern instruments commonly used for contemporary repertory would simply not do. But how did Joachim's Baroque performances actually sound? In his own words, 'we must certainly admit the view that the compositions of Tartini and of even older musicians will well bear a treatment in the matter of expression which, while in no way spoiling the uniformity of their style, will correspond more to the sentiment of the present day, than if performed with a timid anxiety to be literally correct. For the violin which we now play existed then as an already perfected instrument, on which all the later victories of technique could have been carried out, had anyone known how to do so.'[19] If Joachim appears here to be a touch patronising by today's standards, it is nevertheless important to remember that the degree of expression appropriate to 'early music' was to remain a matter for debate for years to come.

Discussion as to whether musical instruments had improved or merely changed was rife during the great technological developments of the nineteenth century. For example, Wagner was in no doubt that in Beethoven's symphonies valved trumpets and horns should be used rather than their natural precursors; he re-wrote their parts to remove any supposed limitations. On the other hand, Berlioz described the use of valves for stopped notes in Beethoven as a dangerous abuse; this is of special significance because he also enthuses about modern developments, such as Adolphe Sax's improvements to the clarinet and the newly devised Boehm flute.[20] At a similar period Gleich claimed that the use of valves in Weber and

Beethoven was a 'Vandalismus'.[21] *Grove 1* merely noted that both natural and valved instruments had their advantages. Amid all the argument, some felt that the new versatility of wind instruments was indispensable, whereas others believed that something of the individuality of tone-colour was lost as a result of mechanical developments. Regret continued to be expressed that the true qualities of older instruments had been lost. As William Stone observed, 'hardly any instrument, except the flute, has been so altered and modified . . . in its mechanism . . . as the oboe. . . . It has thus become by far the most elaborate and complicated of reed instruments, and it is a question whether a return to an older and simpler pattern, by lessening the weight of the machine, and the number of holes breaking the continuity of the bore, and by increasing the vibratory powers of the wooden tube, would not conduce to an improved quality of tone.'[22] He was even more vehement with regard to the bassoon: 'Various attempts have been made to give greater accuracy and completeness to its singularly capricious scale; but up to the present time all these seem to have diminished the flexibility of the instrument in florid passages, or to have impaired its peculiar but telling and characteristic tone.'[23] From this it seems probable that more than a century ago Stone would have approved of the return to period instruments for Baroque and Classical repertory.

The pioneers: individuals and institutions

Unsurprisingly, the beginnings of the historical performance movement were modest indeed, though from a European perspective it is significant that in 1915 (the year of publication of Dolmetsch's book) Saint-Saëns surveyed the principal issues of style, technique and equipment in a lecture in San Francisco.[24] A huge number of fledgeling institutions developed throughout Europe, such as the Schola Cantorum of Paris, the Chanteurs de St Gervais of Charles Bordes, two Sociétés d'Instruments Anciens, the Deutsche Vereinigung für alte Musik and Safford Cape's Pro Musica Antiqua of Brussels. There had already been a long tradition of early music at Basle when the gambist August Wenzinger co-founded the Schola Cantorum Basiliensis in 1933. Established as a teaching and research institute for early music from the Middle Ages to Mozart, it gave a new prominence to instrumental music, though retaining a sacred and secular vocal syllabus. Its avowed intention was that early music should become an integral part of everyday life, whilst aspiring to professional standards, rather than those of the dilettante.

Dolmetsch's special status in the history of period performance is justified by the wisdom of his book rather than the eccentricities of his career. His restoration of early instruments from the late 1880s had been motivated by his discovery and subsequent performance of the English repertory of fantasies for viols.[25] His great gift was indeed that he had both the imagination and the musicianship to take a work which had become a museum piece and make it speak to the people of his own time. His comments on period instruments are full of insight, arguing for example that the one-keyed flute *can* be played in tune, but that this 'requires constant watchfulness of the ear, which thus becomes more and more sensitive to faults of intonation'.[26] But Dolmetsch's own reconstructions apparently wanted not only to revive the past, but to improve upon it. In 1932 Donington remarked that 'the old harpsichord has certain limitations [and produces] a jangle, slight in the treble but audible in the bass. Use of the damper-raising pedal is rendered impracticable, precluding a number of effects of great musical value . . . The new instruments, which remedy these historical oversights, have proved both purer and more sustained than any previous harpsichord.'[27] Donington's view of these 'improvements' as sound common sense is at least as interesting as Dolmetsch's 'fidelity' to history. The relationship of copies to originals remains a contentious issue to this day. The erratic quality of Dolmetsch's performances was nicely summarised by his pupil Ralph Kirkpatrick, who observed, 'Study is problematical with a man who prides himself on never practising.'[28] Dolmetsch treated recordings and concerts as work in progress rather than as the finished article. In a sense, he was fortunate in having had the opportunity to implement his pioneering work at a time before the pressures of the recording industry were to place such a high premium on technical accuracy at all costs.

The role of musical expression

An important issue debated throughout the twentieth century has been the degree of expression which is appropriate in the context of 'early music'. Dolmetsch had spoken abstractedly about feeling and expression, rejecting the idea 'that expression in music is a modern thing, and that the old music requires nothing beyond mechanical precision'.[29] The harpsichordist Wanda Landowska, the first early music 'personality', regarded the idea of objectivity as utopian, since no interpreter should be restricted to remaining in the shadow of the author. At the same time she was able to assert that she aspired only to serve her composers. Modern scholars have desired to lay down specific rules about interpretation. But the art of music is of course much more difficult to quantify than the craft. This point is well illustrated in Türk's *Clavierschule* of 1789, which lays out various stylistic precepts, but finally admits that some aspects of musicianship cannot be taught and that all one can do is simply to listen to the best singers.[30]

The widespread aversion to 'interpretation' has been widely linked with Stravinskian neo-classicism, as performers shied away, not just from virtuosity and exhibitionism, but from interventionism of any kind. This philosophy occurs in its purest form in a programme note written by Erwin Bodky for the Cambridge Society for Early Music in the 1950s: 'Early Music was a highly aristocratic art and restraint governed even the display of emotion as well as the exhibition of technical virtuosity. This deprives concerts of Early Music of the atmosphere of electricity which, when present, is one of the finest experiences of the modern concert hall. Who seeks but this may stay away from our concert series. We want to take this opportunity, however, to thank our artists for the voluntary restraint in the display of their artistic capabilities which they exercise when recreating with us the atmosphere of equanimity, tranquillity and noble entertainment which is the characteristic feature of Early Music.'[31] Inevitably, this kind of thinking gave authenticity a bad name, making the term 'scholarly' when applied to performance synonymous with dull and unimaginative. Meanwhile, the critic Theodor Adorno wrote of 'impotent nostalgia' during the course of one of his celebrated articles.[32]

Adorno was especially critical of Hindemith, who in fact showed himself well aware of the inevitable subjectivity of interpretation. What he wrote in 1952 in *A Composer's World* eloquently defines the value of an historical approach, in broad agreement with Dolmetsch: 'All the traits that made the music of the past lovable to its contemporary performers and listeners were inextricably associated with the kind of sound then known and appreciated. If we replace this sound by the sounds typical of our modern instruments and their treatment, we are counterfeiting the musical message the original sound was supposed to transmit. Consequently, all music ought to be performed with the means of production that were in use when the composer gave it to his contemporaries. . . '[33] More significantly, he realised the limitations of such an approach: 'Our spirit of life is not identical with that of our ancestors, and therefore their music, even if restored with utter technical perfection, can never have for us precisely the same meaning it had for them. We cannot tear down the barricade that separates the present world from things and deeds past; the symbol and its prototype cannot be made to coincide absolutely.'[34]

Arguments pro and con

Observers from traditional musical culture have consistently contributed to the debate. Some musicians, such as George Grove, first director of London's Royal College of Music, admitted that they had not yet acquired the taste for the instrumental music of 'ancient' composers such as J. S. Bach.[35] Dolmetsch's waywardness and reliance on hunches drew criticism from scholars such as Thurston Dart, but found a kindred spirit in the figure of Percy Grainger, who wrote of his universality and breadth of vision. Meanwhile, Landowska sparked arguments as to the merits of the harpsichord in relation to the piano. An early convert was the Bach scholar and organist Albert Schweitzer.[36]

A prominent critic of historical performance was the conductor Leopold Stokowski, whose orchestral transcriptions of Bach demonstrate his conception of the music in pictorial terms. He contrasted the written and literal aspects of music with its importance in our imagination, emphasising its constant evolution and the never-ending growth of its expression. Stokowski's consistent belief in musical progress, in which he was a true child of the nineteenth century, continued until his death in 1974. Conversely, Arturo Toscanini believed passionately in a literal respect for the score, a position fraught with difficulty in (for example) Baroque repertory, where conventions of notation were subject to substantial change. In an article of 1932 Wilhelm Furtwängler was highly critical of the trend towards small-scale performances of Baroque music, which he regarded as inappropriate in the large concert halls of his time; furthermore, he made the perspicacious point that modern audiences would need their listening habits and perceptions changed.[37] Hindemith and Furtwängler thus enjoyed some measure of agreement about the limitations of authenticity, but responded in somewhat different ways. Essentially, Furtwängler dismissed the practical relevance of historical performance, as did most other major conductors of the time. On the other hand, a number of chamber orchestras (utilising modern instruments) arose to meet the demand. More recently, Laurence Dreyfus found an unprecedented attack on the infamy of early music in the work of the French surgeon and self-proclaimed sexologist Gérard Zwang, a tirade which Dreyfus attributes to 'a process of musical defamiliarisation which has robbed him of prized possessions'. Zwang's 1977 book *A Contre-Bruit* speaks of worthless antiquarianism, anti-art and of 'those old buggies which they have the effrontery to call musical instruments'.[38]

The efficacy of historical performance has continued to divide musical opinion, with trenchant criticism from such diverse characters as Pierre Boulez, Colin Davis and Neville Marriner counterbalanced by its espousal by such notable figures as Mark Elder, Charles Mackerras, Simon Rattle and Edo de Waart. The comparatively recent comments of virtuoso violinist Pinchas Zukerman have already acquired a certain notoriety: historical performance is 'asinine stuff... a complete and absolute farce... nobody wants to hear that stuff. I don't.' [39]

Post-war philosophies

The scene after 1945 centred upon Amsterdam, The Hague, London and Vienna, rather than war-weary France and Germany. In England a new coming together of the performer and musicologist was symbolised by Thurston Dart, who none the less paid tribute to earlier developments in historical performance within his seminal book. 'Players learned, after much hard work, how to handle these [obsolete] instruments – a very difficult task indeed, for though you can learn how to make a harpsichord by taking an old one to pieces, you cannot do the same thing with harpsichord-playing.'[40] In his ensuing perceptive discussion of sonorities and style, Dart conveys above all the feeling that much work remains to be done, taking for granted the axiom that musical instruments have changed over the years but not necessarily improved. At the conclusion of his book he writes: 'The written text must never be regarded as a dead laboratory specimen; it is only sleeping, though both love and time will be needed to awaken it. But love and time will be wasted without a sense of tradition and of historical continuity...'[41]

A couple of decades later, debate over a kaleidoscope of general and specific issues was stimulated by the arrival in 1973 of the lavishly produced journal *Early Music*, a milestone in the proliferation of specialist magazines worldwide, which aimed to forge a link between scholarship and performance. An important practical impetus at this time was the versatile David Munrow (1942–76), who with The Early Music Consort of London brought new life to medieval and Renaissance repertory and acted as a springboard for the careers of its distinguished alumni. A quite different personality and another seminal figure was the Dutch harpsichordist Gustav Leonhardt, whose meticulous care for historical accuracy in his texts and instruments eschewed the trappings of showmanship.[42] Uninterested in accessibility or entertainment, Leonhardt drew in his audiences with a mixture of subtlety and intensity. It is symptomatic of his approach that only with his encyclopaedic knowledge of Baroque repertory and performance practice could he afford to claim such exclusive value for the facsimile as a performing source. Overall, it is no coincidence that England and Holland have continued to preserve such distinctive stylistic approaches to their interpretation of historical evidence.

Period Mozart and beyond

In the post-war period much Baroque music was recorded on period instruments, often for record labels especially created for the purpose. In 1954 Wenzinger co-directed the Cappella Coloniensis, a period-instrument chamber orchestra formed by Westdeutscher Rundfunk to record and tour worldwide. The following year Wenzinger's performance of Monteverdi's *Orfeo* was a notable success; other milestones included Harnoncourt's Brandenburg Concertos for Telefunken in 1964. By 1972 Leonhardt and Harnoncourt were embarking on a monumental Bach cantata series, contemporary with the formation of English ensembles by John Eliot Gardiner, Christopher Hogwood, Roger Norrington and Trevor

Pinnock. At this time some enterprising individuals and chamber groups were venturing into the Classical and even early Romantic periods. But it was the complete cycle of Mozart Symphonies by Hogwood and the Academy of Ancient Music in the early 1980s which gave a particular impetus to the inclusion of Classical and Romantic repertory within the historical movement, inspiring many orchestral players to enter the field.

Meanwhile, Howard Mayer Brown noted in *The New Grove* that a performance of Beethoven's Sonata Op. 17 on the natural horn provided quite a different aural experience from one played on the modern instrument. He continued, 'To hear Beethoven's symphonies played with the same degree of authenticity ... would be no less revealing in sound quality, but the practical difficulties of assembling and equipping such an orchestra are almost insuperable.'[43] But Beethoven symphonies played with historical awareness were soon to prove revelatory, notably in the hands of Norrington, whose recordings aimed 'to make him sound new; to recapture much of the exhilaration and sheer disturbance that his music certainly generated in his day'.[44] Beethoven cycles continued apace, whilst Berlioz, Mendelssohn, Schumann, Brahms, Wagner and Verdi were soon to prove ripe for treatment. Thus historical awareness eventually reached the era of the earliest recordings, bringing a further perspective on its aspirations and limitations.

Recordings of orchestral music up to the 1930s reveal a style of playing which has yet to be truly emulated by period performance, characterised by a tempo flexibility virtually unknown today, as well as liberally applied portamenti in the strings. That early recordings are now widely regarded as a significant part of the evidence is due not least to Robert Philip's *Early Recordings and Musical Style* (Cambridge, 1992). Recorded performances from the earlier twentieth century give a vivid sense of being projected as if to an audience, the precision and clarity of each note less important than the shape and progress of the music as a whole. Nowadays the balance has shifted significantly, so that accurate and clear performance has become the first priority and characterisation is assumed to take care of itself. If pre-war recordings resemble live performance, many of today's concerts show a palpable influence of the recording session, with clarity and control an overriding priority.

The current scene

As 'early music' has become a major part of musical life, its original pioneering spirit has all too easily been eclipsed by a new technical proficiency. In 1985 Kerman could still complain of the toleration of relaxed standards of instrumental and vocal technique, as well as of interpretation.[45] No-one can doubt that mastery of an instrument is invaluable, provided that it is nourished by a continuing stylistic awareness. As the novelty and exhilaration of period performance wears off, it has become inevitable that some practitioners should take as their primary sources the well-read musical directors with whom they collaborate rather than Leopold Mozart or C. P. E. Bach. This has important implications when such musicians are called upon to educate the next generation of historically aware performers. Meanwhile, claims to authenticity or even historical accuracy (e.g. 'the most original Beethoven yet recorded'[46]) have become ever more muted.

Over the last quarter of a century historical performance has developed much of its profile in the recording studio, but this state of affairs has prompted a timely caution from at least one writer. Clive Brown warned in 1992 that the characteristics of some of the instruments and equipment employed in Beethoven cycles by The Hanover Band, Hogwood and Norrington would certainly not have been familiar to the musicians in Beethoven's Vienna, and that the situation with regard to playing techniques was even more complicated. He claimed with some justification that the commercially motivated race to push period-instrument performance ever more rapidly into the nineteenth century did not offer much hope that the musicians, even if they obtained the appropriate instruments, would have the opportunity to find or consolidate appropriate styles of playing them. He rightly notes that there is infinitely more to historically sensitive performance than merely employing the right equipment, and that the public is in danger of being offered attractively packaged but unripe fruit.[47] This criticism is a significant reflection of today's current musical climate, each performer occupying an individual position within a spectrum ranging from historical awareness to practical expediency and not always being fully aware of his own or his colleagues' stance. For the general public the phrase 'on original instruments' does literally cover a multitude of varying practices.

It is largely the ethos rather than the detailed practicalities of period performance which has been debated in the work of Harnoncourt (1982, trans.

1988), Dreyfus (1983), Kerman (1985), Kenyon (1988), Mayer Brown and Sadie (1989), Kivy (1995), Taruskin (1995) and Sherman (1997). The philosophical issues they raise will form the basis of the discussion in Chapter 6. Harnoncourt's perceptive essays relate historical awareness to the current position of music in our lives and our attitude to contemporary culture. Meanwhile, in preparing the feature entitled 'The limits of authenticity' for the February 1984 issue of *Early Music*, Nicholas Kenyon articulated for his contributors a number of pertinent questions, which will be addressed in subsequent chapters. Is the use of period instruments in re-creating the music of the past really a significant factor compared with musical understanding, cultural and social context, acoustical considerations, concert-giving situations? Can a composer expect to have any influence over how his music is performed after he has written it, and what moral obligation is there to fulfil his original intentions? Are we more likely to understand a composer's piece of music by restricting ourselves to the means he had available when he wrote it, or does such a restriction inhibit our full expression of the piece? What is the relation between a performer's and a scholar's work in this area?

2   The application of primary sources

Primary sources are the historical performer's raw material, the surviving evidence of past practices. In addition to composers' original autographs, sketches and drafts, evaluated later in connection with editions, the performer's primary source materials range from instrumental and theoretical treatises to surviving instruments, iconography, historical archives, references in literature, journals, newspaper reports, and sometimes even letters, diaries, catalogues, advertisements and, latterly, early recordings.[1] This list could also be extended to include aspects of other art forms such as dance, some steps of which may have important implications for musical tempo. The relevance and significance of each of these source-groups inevitably varies according to the repertory to be performed, its period and geographical locality.

In order to realise the goal of historically informed performance, musicians need to collect, criticise, arrange, evaluate and interpret such raw material, which may be of very different origin, content, quality and purpose. Problems often arise, for example, in assessing a writer's background, his motives, his relation to his contemporaries, and his intended or actual readership; and it is rarely clear how widely most of any generation's music or treatises were known. The sources themselves are unreliable in varying degrees and may be self-contradictory or contradictory with one another in some respects and tiresomely repetitive in others. Nevertheless, either singly or as a group, they assist in building a picture and, once thoroughly evaluated, normally provide valuable information regarding the context or specifics of historical performance. On the other hand, the body of surviving literature unfortunately leaves several questions unresolved and is no substitute for information communicated in public and private instruction; at most, it offers samples of what successive musicians and teachers themselves read, and, to some extent, practised.

Surviving instruments

Surviving instruments offer much tangible help in forging historically aware performances, providing the vital apparatus for 'laboratory'
experiments in matters of technique, interpretation and style. The foresight
of those who established private and public instrument collections worldwide, particularly in the late nineteenth century, has been of invaluable
assistance to the progress and credibility of the historical performance
movement. One of the oldest institutional collections still prospering is that
of the Gesellschaft der Musikfreunde in Vienna, whose Sammlung alter
Musikinstrumente originated in 1824. The acquisition of Louis Clapisson's
collection by the Paris Conservatoire in 1864, the creation of the Brussels
Conservatoire's museum from the private collections of François-Joseph
Fétis, Victor-Charles Mahillon and others in the 1870s, and the Berlin
Königliche Hochschule für Musik's procurement of Paul de Wit's first collection in 1888 was matched by private collectors such as Auguste Tolbecque
in France, Carl Engel and Alfred Hipkins in Britain, and Morris Steinert in
the USA. The enormous explosion in the number of specialist instrument
collections established since these sparks of interest is attested by the lengthy
list included in *The New Grove*.[2] Photographs, descriptions, construction
plans, measurements and other detailed information included in the catalogues of many of these collections have also proved immensely valuable in
the dissemination of knowledge about organology.

The increased practice of collecting instruments has inevitably raised the
controversy regarding the relative claims of preservation and investigation
through use, and the potential benefits of restoration have had to be weighed
continually against the possible destruction of original evidence. Most
museums and institutions have taken the conservative option and preserved
their instruments in stable conditions and in scientifically monitored envi-
ronments, but some have attempted re-conditioning and some private collectors and conservatoires have taken the bolder step of allowing their
instruments to be loaned to careful users. Leading centres of conservation
include the Germanisches Nationalmuseum, Nuremberg, and the
Smithsonian Institute's National Museum of History and Technology,
Washington, DC. The preservation of early instruments has proved of ines-
timable value to modern makers of reproductions; this is evident in respect
of Nikolaus Harnoncourt's discoveries with regard to the oboe da caccia in

the case of Bach's *St Matthew Passion* outlined in Chapter 5. The replicas gain most of the advantages of restoration without endangering the original instrument and, thanks to organological research, may represent the original state even when the original instrument has been modified.

Examination of exhibits in the various collections worldwide has also provided instrument researchers with some (but often frustratingly insufficient) information about pitch in the period and geographical area of their construction. The use of historically accurate accessories such as reeds, brass mouthpieces and strings is also essential, because it can change entirely the perception of an instrument and its repertory. Musical boxes, musical clocks, barrel organs and other mechanically governed 'instruments' from the eighteenth century onwards also provide fairly accurate information about relative pitch and rhythmic values. Some insight into absolute tempo values can also be gained by timing performances so preserved.

Eleanor Selfridge-Field has drawn attention to some of the advantages and disadvantages of the modern reconstruction of instruments for period performance and demonstrates how the problems that modern makers have attempted to overcome sometimes have a direct effect on scholars and performers. She cites the Charles Fisk Organ (1983) at Stanford University, with its duplicate pipes for 'mean-tone' and 'well-tempered' tunings, pointing out that 'it creates a corresponding need for "push button" adaptability among collaborating instrumentalists and singers that was not a requisite of earlier times'.[3] Similar earlier attempts at conflating past and present to facilitate the performance process, such as the so-called 'Bach bow', various hybrid keyboard instruments and other organological freaks, have not gained currency, even though some have made out a case for modern instruments being superior in design and construction to their predecessors.

Iconographical sources

As a principal aim of historical research is to re-create a picture of the past, it follows that reconstruction of any specific musical occasion will be all the more convincing if it can be related directly to surviving iconographical material, whether in the form of sculpture, paintings, engravings, photographs or film. Iconographical sources have provided us with invaluable information about performance issues, ranging from the history and

construction of instruments to knowledge about composers' and performers' lives and the social and intellectual atmosphere in which they worked.
Howard Mayer Brown comments: 'Pictures not only help to explain the
place of actual sounding music in society, but they also reveal the characteristic ways in which musical subjects were used symbolically or allegorically,
and how music was used to illuminate the mythical, philosophical, theological or educational doctrines of an age.'[4] However, conclusions from such
evidence may need to be corroborated from literary, archival or other
sources, because pictures cannot reveal the impossible regarding, for
example, such details of instrument construction as the materials used, the
size and shape of the bore, the thickness of a soundboard or the tension of a
string.

Pictorial evidence, from newspapers, treatises or other sources, may also
furnish important detail about playing techniques and positions (e.g.
engravings of bow holds, embouchures and fingering charts in treatises), the
various accessories that performers employed (such as music stands, foot-
stools and whether the music employed was written or printed), the social
context and conditions of their performances (whether indoors or out-
doors, whether the performers were seated or standing, and whether or not
an audience was present), the particular groupings of instruments and/or
voices for various types of music at a given place and time,[5] the constitution
and distribution of orchestras and choirs, and whether or not there was a
conductor. It has also proved a rich source of information regarding dance
postures appropriate to particular kinds of pieces, operatic costumes,
scenery and stage settings, the machines used in opera performances, and
the size, proportions and conditions of theatres and concert venues.

Of course, iconographical evidence must be used with some caution and
should not be accepted as a reflection of contemporary reality without
careful evaluation in its artistic and historical context. Investigation into the
artist's original intentions is of paramount importance in such assessment,
and conclusions must be based on a broad sampling of sources in the same
tradition for an appropriate interpretation. The truth may have been distorted to satisfy aesthetic, social or political ends; artistic licence may have
resulted in inaccurate representation of instruments, or even the invention
of completely non-functional instruments for an intellectual or symbolic
reason best known to the artist; and many drawings and engravings of per-

formances had some satirical purpose, incorporating deliberate exaggerations of selected details.

Historical archives

Historical archives of English, French and Austrian courts and of Italian churches and various sacred and secular institutions in Germany and other countries have furnished useful general information about musical activities, occasionally offering extensive details for particular events. Lists of personnel showing dates of hire or retirement, or rates of pay, have assisted in both determining the general dimensions of choral and instrumental groups and providing information about the itineraries of peripatetic musicians. However, such archives often present problems of decipherability or incorporate mistakes regarding the names of personnel. Furthermore, they will not necessarily explain any system of rotation that the musicians may have served or indicate whether the lists include retired musicians and apprentices or 'extras' such as students, amateurs, town waits or military bandsmen. As Eleanor Selfridge-Field observes: 'the names of young musicians who served, but who could not officially be hired until a vacancy was created by the death of a senior musician, were not recorded'; changes in responsibilities were not consistently documented: 'positions were sometimes sold, especially at the court of St James, without official note being made'; and one performer might serve in two distinct roles: 'in 18th-century Venice oboists were often flautists as well, while in Vienna oboists doubled as trombonists and in Paris those who played the horn also played the viola'.[6]

Literary sources

Although they only rarely offer specific advice, journals and diaries, letters and the monthly and weekly forerunners of modern daily newspapers have included significant observations on performance issues such as programme content, the deployment of resources and the reception of particular musical events. Many periodicals of the eighteenth century and thereafter, whether specifically musical or general, apprise us about concert or opera performances and new publications and include performance reviews and other relevant articles. Among the most important eighteenth-century specialist music periodicals were the *Journal de musique* (Paris, 1770–7), the *Magazin der Musik* (Hamburg and Copenhagen, 1783–9) and the *Allgemeine musikalische Zeitung* (Leipzig, from 1798/9), while general publications such as the *Journal de Paris, Mercure de France,* the *Gentleman's Magazine* or the *Wiener Zeitung* have also proved informative. The almost insatiable demand for such music periodicals in the nineteenth century prompted the production of A. B. Marx's *Berliner allgemeine musikalische Zeitung* (1824), Fétis's *Revue musicale* (1827) in Paris, Schumann's celebrated *Neue Zeitschrift für Musik* (1834) in Leipzig and Schlesinger's *Gazette musicale* (1834; amalgamated in 1835 with the *Revue musicale* to become the *Revue et Gazette musicale*), as well as *The Musical World* (1836) and *Musical Times* (1844) in London, the *Gazzetta musicale . . .* (1842) in Milan, and *Dwight's Journal of Music* (1852) in Boston.

Writers in the 'press' often had their own political, rather than aesthetic or musical, agenda when writing their reviews. However, the letters of, for example, C. P. E. Bach, Gluck, Haydn, Beethoven and especially the Mozart family have provided invaluable insights into the musical performance of their times, perhaps highlighting philosophical considerations that influenced musical practices, explaining the reasons behind their or other composers' particular revisions, or making other revelations of practical consequence.

Autobiographies by, for example, Dittersdorf, Spohr, Berlioz or Wagner and the travel diaries of such respected musicians as Burney or Reichardt also incorporate information about performance practice.[7] Memoirs and recollections of distinguished performers have also proved useful sources,[8] and the work of lexicographers such as Rousseau, Koch, Sulzer and Rees are especially informative about their particular national tastes and times.[9] Annual almanacs summarising cultural events in a city or country and providing liturgical and civic calendars for the following year often elucidate details of repertory and personnel,[10] and the minutes and publications of learned societies often incorporate information on performance issues.[11]

Practical treatises – uses and limitations

Instrumental and vocal treatises offer the most direct access to fundamental technical instruction, interpretation and more general matters such as notation, music history, expression, taste and aesthetics. However, their value as sources must not be exaggerated, for most present the fruits of many years of thought, experience and observation and incorporate instructions that may lag well behind actual practice. Care should therefore be taken in the application of Quantz's instructions in his *Versuch* (1752), published when he was fifty-five and beholden to practices fashionable in his formative years, to, say, performances of works by the young Mozart. Burney, when visiting the elderly German, found his music 'truly stationary' and his taste 'that of forty years ago'.[12]

Many treatises have led performers to devise theories mistakenly, make inferences from sources too hastily and use performing conventions erroneously. As Frederick Neumann observes, problems arise from either the use of wrong sources or the wrong use of sources. Neumann believes that authors of treatises should be regarded not as 'prophets who reveal infallible verities', but rather as 'very human witnesses who left us an affidavit about certain things they knew . . . believed in, [and] . . . wished their readers to believe'.[13] He likens the principles required of music researchers to the procedures of evaluating testimony in jurisprudence and claims that sources such as historical treatises cannot be used safely without thorough and satisfactory assessment of the personality, background, knowledge, status and influence of the writer, the credibility, reliability and consistency of both the treatise's textual content and the musical style and aesthetic it propounds, the readership to whom it is addressed, its relationship to other sources, its geographical and temporal limitations, and its relationship to the repertory (and the composers) to which it is applicable.

As few of the rules disseminated by Baroque theorists can be treated as absolute – and opinion about many interpretative issues was rarely unanimous – performers should be wary of allowing primary sources to lead them blindly. They should guard against using specific information from a treatise too generally, thereby assuming that existing conventions were universally valid and venturing beyond its legitimate field or period of pertinence. Most authors of practical manuals travelled little and knew of practices elsewhere only as much as they could deduce them by examining music itself. Treatises should not be assumed to have national, let alone international validity, for there was no universal Baroque convention which regulated performance throughout Europe. Stylistic differences co-existed on a national, regional and personal level, and the many contradictions within historical treatises give the lie to such an assumption. Although Quantz and C. P. E. Bach held similar aesthetic principles and were closely associated for many years at the court of Frederick II of Prussia, they disagree on several performance issues; thus, the rules of a treatise cannot safely be routinely applied to the music of another composer without reliable independent supporting evidence.

The dangers of assuming that conventions described in treatises remain static over a long period must also be heeded. However, certain practices may have a degree of universality, as some incorporate an element of inertia unaffected by changes of taste and style. Therefore, some of Quantz's *Versuch* 'is valid for Quantz alone, some for other *galant* composers as well, some for Bach, some for Mozart . . . some was probably valid a thousand years ago, and some is valid still today'.[14] A treatise will thus most likely be pertinent largely to the music of its writer and his immediate circle of influence, the likelihood decreasing 'in geometric proportion with the crossing of barriers of taste and style, such as the one that separates the musical world of Quantz from the world of Bach, despite the fact that the two men were almost contemporaries'.[15] The ephemeral nature of musical fashion was also such that performers should guard against applying the musical principles of one school or even decade to another.

Another type of fallacy derives from the assumption that performance practices have currency only if specifically authorised by a treatise. Writers never perceived themselves as writing for posterity and often omitted to document various conventions which are not part of current practice – Roger North, for example, writes of techniques 'which may be knowne but not described'.[16] In any case, performance was a less formal art in our main period of focus than it is nowadays, and the vast majority of seventeenth- and eighteenth-century treatises were intended for amateur instruction, often appearing as 'do-it-yourself' or 'self-help' volumes.[17] Many sources tend therefore to be vague rather than specific, doubtless reflecting the importance of the master–pupil relationship, in which technical secrets could be divulged for financial gain. Nevertheless, the elementary level of such sources was not indicative of performance standards attained by professional musicians. Such treatises thus serve collectively as revealing social documents of their times, demonstrating music's attraction to a broader social sector. Instruction was left largely to the teacher and sometimes even to the ingenuity of the pupil – curiously, Daniel Speer's *Grund-richtiger . . . Unterricht* (Ulm, 1687) leaves the matter of holding the violin and bow to the student's discretion and imagination – and very few treatises aimed to be comprehensive.

Further problems may be caused by inconsistencies, qualifications of previous statements and even contradictions within the same treatise or across different publications, reflecting in some cases a change of opinion, attitude or actual practice. And performers should guard against misrepresenting writers' opinions by using incomplete citations, quotations out of context and inaccurate translations in their analyses.

Sometimes a primary source will present a rule or example that is not explicitly qualified, possibly because the work is intended for beginners and its rules as preliminary instructions. To take such a rule at face value may lead to too narrow an interpretation, as Bach's ornament table ('Explicatio') in the *Clavierbüchlein* for eleven-year-old Friedemann demonstrates. This authoritative document is neither comprehensive nor exclusive or precise; it also incorporates oversimplifications, which may result in misunderstandings and faulty interpretation. The nature of artistic performance is so complex, with all it involves in the way of fine shading of rhythm, tempo, nuance and expression, that such ornaments defy exact description or definition. Attempts to do so in tables, words or musical notation will have been intended as rough outlines rather than exact designs, memory aids rather than definite models.

Practical treatises – a summary

Most practical treatises up to the middle of the eighteenth century were addressed largely to educated amateur musicians or provincial music teachers. They focused on matters pertinent to a single instrument or family of instruments and were generally uninformative about instrumental or vocal technique.[18] Simpson's *The Division-Violist* (1659), for example, documents not only the growing interest in consorts and ensembles but also the emerging recognition of instrumental music as a genre distinct from, yet closely associated with, vocal music; Mace's *Musick's Monument* (1676) specialises in the needs of lutenists and theorbo players; and keyboard instruments were the principal focus of attention for early eighteenth-century writers of practical treatises, most of whom incorporated detailed discussion of continuo playing.[19]

On a generally higher technical level were treatises such as François Couperin's *L'art de toucher le clavecin* (1716), which represents a more independent approach to solo keyboard performance, and Hotteterre's *Principes de la flûte traversière*... (1707), which includes instructions for playing the recorder and oboe as well as the flute and is a significant source of information about early woodwind practice in general, particularly tonguing and ornamentation. Meanwhile, Tosi's *Opinioni de' cantori antichi e moderni* (1723) reflects the growth in popularity of opera and incorporates significant instruction about ornamentation and tempo rubato.

After Geminiani's progressive *The Art of Playing on the Violin* (1751), the 1750s witnessed the appearance of three major treatises which combined comparatively advanced technical instruction regarding their specialist instruments with copious details regarding performance practice: Quantz's *Versuch einer Anweisung die Flöte traversiere zu spielen* (1752), C. P. E. Bach's *Versuch über die wahre Art das Clavier zu spielen* (1753 and 1762) and Leopold Mozart's *Versuch einer gründlichen Violinschule* (1756). Leopold Mozart intended to lay 'the foundation of good style', while Quantz's treatise has been described as 'an omnibus of eighteenth-century information'.[20] Quantz aimed to train a skilled and intelligent musician, while Emanuel Bach also valued musical intelligence more highly than mere technique. Consequently, their performance instructions are never an end in themselves; rather, they are intimately linked not only to a theory of interpretation, but also to an entire aesthetic based on the doctrine of the affections.

A comprehensive survey of the most informative instrumental and vocal treatises is beyond the scope of this chapter; their content and significance will be evaluated in this volume's complementary series of handbooks devoted to individual instruments. Prominent among late eighteenth-century examples, however, are Mancini's *Pensieri, e riflessioni pratiche sopra il canto figurato* (1774), Hiller's *Anweisung zum musikalisch-richtigen Gesange* (1774), Türk's *Clavierschule, oder Anweisung zum Clavierspielen* (1789), Milchmeyer's *Die wahre Art das Pianoforte zu spielen* (1797), Tromlitz's *Ausführlicher und gründlicher Unterricht die Flöte zu spielen* (1791), Galeazzi's *Elementi teorico-pratici di musica con un saggio sopra l'arte di suonare il violino analizzata, ed a dimostrabili principi ridotta* ... (1791–6) and Cartier's *L'art du violon* (1798).

The establishment of the Paris Conservatoire (1795) prompted a new development: the production of faculty-based treatises offering systematic courses of technical and interpretative instruction for aspiring professionals. These included Lefèvre's *Méthode de clarinette* (Paris, 1802/R1974), Adam's *Méthode de piano du Conservatoire* (Paris, 1802), Ozi's *Nouvelle Méthode de basson* (1803), Rode, Baillot and Kreutzer's *Méthode de violon* (1803), Hugo and Wunderlich's *Méthode de flûte du Conservatoire* (Paris, 1804/R1975), Baillot, Levasseur, Catel and Baudiot's *Méthode de violoncelle* (1804), Brod's *Grande méthode de hautbois* (Paris, c. 1826–30) and Baillot's *L'art du violon: nouvelle méthode* (1835). Most incorporated mechanical training for advanced players, in the form of exercises and studies, at the expense of philosophy about musical rhetoric and the communication of emotion, and they had a profound influence on technical development in an age in which virtuosity was openly encouraged.

The subsequent explosion in the publication of practical treatises in the nineteenth century included several significant works. Many of the best tutors for orchestral instruments were written by members of the Société des Concerts du Conservatoire, notably Klosé's *Méthode pour servir à l'enseignement de la clarinette à anneaux mobiles* (1843) and Arban's *Grande méthode complète pour cornets à pistons et de saxhorn* (Paris, 1864). In addition, treatises by Corri (1810) and García (1847) represent the evolving *bel canto* school of singing in the wake of Tosi, Mancini and Hiller; Clementi (1801), Hummel (1828) and Czerny (1839) authored influential treatises for the piano; Labarre, Spohr (1832), Habeneck (c. 1840), de Bériot (1858), David, Joachim and Moser (1902–5), Duport (c. 1806), Dotzauer, Kummer, Romberg (1840) and Piatti (1878) were in the forefront of instruction materials for stringed instruments;[21] Sellner, Brod, Müller, Berr, Baermann, Almenraeder and Jancourt were among those who bolstered the market for woodwinds;[22] and Dauprat, Meifred and Gallay were the other principal writers for brass instruments.[23]

Theoretical treatises

In addition to practical tutors, numerous treatises on theoretical musical issues appeared through the centuries, ranging from the writings of

Praetorius, Mersenne, Zacconi and Kircher to those of Mattheson (1739), Avison (1752), Adlung (1758) and Mosel.[24] Such treatises were prepared largely for academicians and tended to explain the rules and aesthetics of composition, to provide inventories or descriptions of existing (or at least of theoretically possible) instruments, or to discuss mathematical and somewhat idealised historical aspects of music. While they help to exclude some avenues regarding interpretative issues, they rarely offer straightforward advice of immediately practical help, since their authors were often closer to the ranks of philosophers than of musicians.

Some of these treatises (e.g. those by Praetorius, Mersenne and Adlung) give vital clues on matters of tuning or pitch, but there were also several specialist publications devoted to such issues.[25] Treatises on orchestration also became fashionable towards the mid-nineteenth century, commencing with the works of Kastner (1837 and 1839) and continuing with those of, among others, Berlioz (1843) and Rimsky-Korsakov.[26] Such publications have proved invaluable works of reference regarding the technique and potential of orchestral instruments, orchestral placement and other performance details, as have also the conducting treatises of Berlioz, Wagner (1869) and Weingartner and many lesser studies.[27]

The importance of communication

The importance of communicating emotion in music was especially emphasised in the seventeenth and eighteenth centuries – indeed, the performer was considered to be an equal creator with the composer (and often, of course, they were one and the same). Praetorius states that a singer should move the heart of the listener and Heinichen claims that the true aim of music is 'to move the feelings'. Geminiani writes constantly about expressing the passions: 'The intention of musick is not only to please the ear,' he claims, 'but to express sentiments, strike the imagination, affect the mind, and command the passions. The art of playing the violin consists in giving that instrument a tone that shall in a manner rival the most perfect human voice.'[28] Such use of speech and singing as models for 'natural' procedure became common in instrumental performance during the eighteenth century, for 'he who performs a composition so that its inherent affect is expressed to the utmost even in every single passage, and the notes become, so to speak, a language of the feelings, is said to have a good execution'.[29] *Forte* and *piano*, for example, were used 'to produce the same effects that an orator does by raising and lowering his voice',[30] and the finer points of articulation, ornamentation and expression, including realisation of a composer's rhetorical approach to the craft of composition, were vital constituents of 'good execution'.

Music was thus bound by similar rules to language, especially those which governed the art of speaking. A piece of music was considered an artistic form of speech, presented according to the orator's art of rhetoric, which involved strict rules rooted in antiquity.[31] Mattheson proposed a rational scheme of musical composition inspired from those sections of rhetorical theory concerned with finding and presenting arguments: *inventio* (invention of an idea), *dispositio* (arrangement of the idea into the parts of an oration), *decoratio* (the elaboration of the idea),[32] and *pronuntiatio* (the performance or delivery of the oration). The *dispositio* was generally subdivided into six sections: *exordium* (introduction), *narratio* (narrative), *divisio* or *propositio* (statement of the content and aim of the sound-speech), *confutatio* (refutation or rebuttal), *confirmatio* (reaffirmation of the *propositio*) and *peroratio* or *conclusio* (conclusion);[33] and the musical 'speech', as composed and performed, was intended to 'affect' the listener in a similar manner as its literary counterpart. Thus, the compositional process (like the literary process) was itself a rhetorical act, the composer generally incorporating appropriate rhetorical figures to convey fairly precise meanings within the relevant affect, and a work's form was either strictly rhetorical (in line with Mattheson's subdivisions above) or at least strongly influenced by rhetoric.

Writings advocating a rhetorical approach to composition were largely addressed initially to composers of vocal music. The Baroque concept of 'affect' – an ideal emotional or moral state such as sadness, hate, love, joy or doubt – arose from the association of rhetoric and music and appeared for the first time in connection with early Italian monody ('di muovere l'affetto dell'animo', as Caccini, among others, terms it).[34] It featured constantly in the prefaces of Caccini and Monteverdi, as well as in the theories of representatives of the new movement, such as Galilei.[35] Even after the growth of independent instrumental music, rhetorical principles continued for some time to be used not only for vocal music but also for instrumental works.[36] The concept, relating to both composition and performance, developed into an extensive system, appreciated throughout Europe, by which music was capable of moving the listener to the extent of transporting him into a new physical and spiritual existence, the outcome varying somewhat from one person to another according to his own blend of the four temperaments – the phlegmatic, sanguine, choleric and melancholic.[37] To achieve this goal, composer and performer utilised a wide range of affects, most common among which were, according to Kircher: *Affectus amoris; Luctus seu Planctus; Laetitiae & Exultationis; Furoris & Indignationis; Commiserationis & Lacrimarum; Timoris & Afflictionis; Praesumptionis & Audaciae; Admirationis.*[38]

In vocal and dramatic music, the affect was usually clear from the words and the dramatic situation; for instrumental music, however, the presentation of such affects for both composer and performer was subject to fairly strict rules. Beginning with Mersenne and Kircher in the mid-seventeenth century,[39] theorists such as Werckmeister, Printz, Mattheson, Marpurg, Scheibe and Quantz devoted large sections of their treatises to categorising and describing types of affect (often referred to as 'passions' or 'sentiments') as well as the affective connotations of keys, time-words, dissonance, scales, intervallic relationships, articulation, dance movements, rhythms, instrumental colour, forms and styles. A major key, for example, expressed gay, bold, serious or sublime sentiments, whereas a minor one was more suited to expressing flattery, melancholy or a tender effect.[40] Thus, for Mattheson C major was 'bold' (Charpentier: 'gay and warlike'), F major was 'beautiful' (but Charpentier said 'furious', and Rameau agreed), A minor was 'calm' (Charpentier: 'tender') and D minor was 'devout' (Charpentier: 'grave and pious').

Mattheson proclaimed that music without praiseworthy affections 'can be considered nothing, does nothing, and means nothing'.[41] Closely associated with rhetoric and the so-called 'doctrine of the affections' were the *loci topici* or *Figuren* (*figurae* or figures), which assisted in the representation of the affections in music. They were recognisable 'codes' according to which music was both composed and understood and thus provided a context and an expressive vocabulary for communication between the composer, the performer and the listener.[42] Joachim Burmeister first proposed a musical-rhetorical system based on musical figures.[43] Though not applied absolutely rigidly, such rhetorical concepts became routine techniques used in the craft

Ex. 2.1 'Niederfallen' ('falling down') figure in 'Der Heiland fällt vor seinem Vater nieder', J. S. Bach, *St Matthew Passion* (I, 22)

Ex. 2.2 H. von Biber, *Rosenkranz* Sonata No. 6, 'Christus am Oelberg'

[tuning]

of composition, influencing structure, style, expression and method. Musicians were effectively orators who normally composed pieces as if they were orations, including all of the sections, divisions and periods appropriate to speech. Just as an orator invented an idea (*inventio*) upon which he elaborated with figures of speech in the *decoratio*, the composer developed his idea within the prevalent affect by using the *loci topici*, mostly fairly short figures such as Ex. 2.1, which represents the 'Niederfallen' ('falling down') in the recitative 'Der Heiland fällt vor seinem Vater nieder' from Bach's *St Matthew Passion* (I, 22), or Ex. 2.2 from Biber's sixth *Rosenkranz* sonata 'Christus am Oelberg', which doubtless was intended to convey a similar meaning. Perhaps the most abrupt was the false relation, which was expressive of sorrow; however, some figures are quite long, especially the so-called 'Lamentobass', expressing grief or pain by means of a chromatic descent through the interval of a fourth, and two or more figures may be juxtaposed in dialogue to constitute an extended 'phrase' or 'sentence'.

Unger has provided the most detailed catalogue of musical figures extracted from a wide range of sources,[44] but efforts to systematise theorists' teachings on *Figuren*, an activity to which much attention was devoted earlier in this century,[45] are now regarded with caution. Buelow provides a convenient list, with examples from the repertory, of the most frequently cited musical figures, divided into seven broad categories: figures of melodic repetition; figures based on fugal imitation; figures formed by dissonance structures; interval figures; hypotyposis figures; sound figures; and figures formed by silence.[46]

Musical-rhetorical concepts continued to feature prominently in the second half of the eighteenth century (and remained part of compositional technique well into the nineteenth century),[47] even though the affections began to lose their objective quality as rationalised emotional states that acted as unifying devices throughout a piece, thanks largely to the desire to introduce the elements of contrast and variety. Forkel states that 'music expresses the "multiple modifications" of feeling through multiple modifications of musical expression', preparing the way for a more individual approach to expression.[48] Consequently, the *pronuntiatio* – that part of rhetorical theory concerning execution and delivery – received increased emphasis, stressing further the performer's important relationship with his audience.

Quantz repeatedly insists that the performer should 'divine the intention of the composer,' to 'seek to enter into the principal and related passions that he is to express' and to 'take on the feeling which the composer intended in writing it';[49] and Emanuel Bach is adamant that if a player is not himself moved by what he plays, he will never move others, which should be his real aim.[50] Performers were thus constantly exhorted to employ the techniques of good delivery, notably clarity, pleasing variety of tone, contrasts of emphasis and appropriate expression, 'to make themselves masters of the hearts of their listeners, to arouse or still their passions, and to transport them now to this sentiment, now to that'.[51] The rhetorical caesura, intelligent sentence structure, emphases (on the model of speech) and meaningful rhetorical figures were all devices which helped the listener to comprehend and be moved by the music.

Nowadays, of course, lost conventions of listening – the average modern concert-goer is not educated in theories of rhetoric – make the performer's goals more difficult to realise; nevertheless, he should attempt to combine in his interpretation a full awareness of, and identification with, the affects of the piece and a close perception of its complete rhetorical pattern of paragraphs, sentences, and phrases, with an impression of that vital performing ingredient, spontaneity. As Geminiani remarks:

> I would besides advise, as well the Composer as the Performer,
> who is ambitious to inspire his Audience, to be first inspired
> himself; which he cannot fail to be if he chuses a Work of Genius, if

he makes himself thoroughly acquainted with all its Beauties; and if while his Imagination is warm and glowing he pours the same exalted Spirit into his own Performance.[52]

Audiences, for their part, must accept that listening to music is an active rather than an inert occupation; accordingly, if they wish to appreciate performances fully, they must familiarise themselves with the aims and objectives of the composer(s) concerned and endeavour to comprehend also the performer's contribution as intermediary.

The role of editions

The principal role of a responsible edition is to present, normally in printed form, an 'established text' that most fully represents the editor's conception of the work as it developed in composition and performance at the hands of the composer. Such a function is simple enough to comprehend, but the editorial processes involved can be extremely complex. Establishing a musical text for Handel's *Messiah*, for example, poses enormous problems, because of its complex performance history,[53] but editors of vocal music are also required to investigate the sources of literary texts set by composers, to edit them and to provide translations where appropriate.

Determined by a critical examination of the music, its textual history, the evidence and filiation of its sources, and its historical context and style, an edition may represent only a snapshot in a work's complex profile; by contrast, it may incorporate all of the work's variant forms as found in the sources or its aim may be, for example, to reproduce the *Fassung letzter Hand* – the composer's final version. Indeed, most modern editors seem to prefer to base a new edition on one good source than to publish a conflation resembling nothing that actually existed during the work's evolution. Difficulties arise if an autograph and an early printed edition supervised or used by the composer both survive and supply contradictory evidence; in such cases some editors (e.g. Georg von Dadelsen and Wilhelm Altmann) have favoured the printed edition, while others (e.g. Heinrich Schenker and Paul Mies) have given preference to the manuscript.

It is therefore vital for performers to understand fully an editor's aims, objectives, working methods and dilemmas before formulating firm ideas regarding matters of interpretation. It is also important that they seek editions for which the various primary sources (autograph sketches, autograph composing scores, autograph fair copies, autograph orchestral parts, secondary copies of orchestral parts corrected by the composer, scores/parts published during the composer's lifetime, autograph arrangements) have been thoroughly examined, dated (using watermarks or other relevant procedures), evaluated and prioritised, and in which due importance has been accorded to any secondary material. Performers must be able to distinguish between editorial suggestions for realising the composer's intentions and those markings found in the musical sources, and correction of errors or inner inconsistencies (whether by conjecture or on the evidence of readings from other sources) must be noted, either in footnotes or, better still, in a critical commentary.

Critical commentaries, however, are often ignored by performers, and sometimes at great cost to the validity and credibility of their interpretations. Here, sources are described (whether autograph, manuscript copy or printed; whether parts or a score; the layout of the source; the titles or vocal/instrumental names it incorporates) and dated (with details of watermarks, rastra, publication dates), and copyists for any secondary manuscripts are identified. Editorial method is explained, identifying the relative priority given to the sources, the notational principles adopted and how these relate to the notational conventions of the original; and a list of particular readings is provided (including editorial corrections), recording essential information which is not apparent from the musical score alone and detailing differences between principal source materials and the reasons for the editorial decisions taken. In fact, the sooner performers appreciate that editors are required to undertake a similar act of interpretation – of making educated, critically informed choices – the more they will value the editor's role. For the discipline of editing, like performance and all critical undertakings, is undergoing continual change in response to the changing critical environment.

Performers can glean much about phrasing, articulation and other interpretative issues from using facsimiles and old prints which have come under an editorial eye, and, in some cases, playing from old notations, an exercise that illuminates many aspects of performing practice by forcing musicians to solve problems in the way their earlier counterparts did. But most modern editions take the form of either scholarly critical editions, complete with critical commentary and other *Revisionsberichte*, or practical editions for performers which present the authoritative texts of those critical editions, but without detailed critical notes and full scholarly apparatus.

Scholarly critical editions, which carefully indicate all or at least the most important variants and reproduce as many of the features of the original notation as the editor supposes are important to an understanding of the composer's intentions, normally present the information necessary for seasoned modern performers to form their own judgements and make appropriate choices regarding performance issues. Arthur Mendel believes: 'If editors really want to help the performer, what they should do is not provide him with ready-made answers to questions that have no definite answers, but encourage him in every way possible (including frequent references in the score to the critical report) to think out answers for himself.'[54] Sound advice this may seem, but the success of such a policy inevitably depends on the status, knowledge, aims and potential of the performer concerned. While some performers are relatively self-sufficient in determining their interpretations, others expect or require editorial guidance on various issues of performance and style that may have supplemented or varied the established text. Such guidance might include the incidence and content of cadenzas and *Eingänge* in Mozart's piano concertos and the implications of the various abbreviations in their solo parts (e.g. simple chords where arpeggios were probably intended, passages in slow movements that should be ornamented, and the realisation of figured basses during tuttis); editorial advice on ornamentation, on the interpretation and implications for performance of annotations, regarding such matters as tempo, dynamics, ornament symbols, articulation and pedalling, that are inconsistently applied, and even on the distribution of text syllables in vocal music, which may be particularly pertinent to a convincing interpretation. As Thurston Dart put it: 'the editor's work is no longer a coat of protective varnish through which the composer's picture shines undimmed, but a whole set of brush-strokes using the same painting technique and materials as the original artist'.[55] But in their zeal for consistency, editors must guard against making interpretative decisions that are properly within the province of the individual performer. Thus he ought not to resolve some kinds of inconsistency that are open to more than one acceptable manner of performance, for example passages in which triplets coincide with dotted figures; nor should he write out passages where overdotting is implied or where *notes inégales* are appropriate. But the wise editor will indicate clearly the possibility of alterations to the printed score either in small notes or rhythmic symbols above the staff, or in a preface or footnotes, and not obscure the original notation.

Although there is a growing body of specialist performers for whom realised continuo parts are 'not merely unnecessary but a provoking irritant',[56] it is normal practice for editors of practical editions to compensate for the fact that most modern performers, unlike their eighteenth-century counterparts, are not routinely used to improvising chords above a bass-line (whether figured, partially figured or completely unfigured) and thus require a full 'realisation'. They may choose to provide a stylish realisation, which may be not only subjective and idiosyncratic, but also possibly inappropriate for some circumstances and misleading to performers who may (mistakenly) take it as definitive. Alternatively, they may prefer to offer a very simple accompaniment, indicating the correct harmonies and arranged in a way to facilitate a more elaborate version by an inventive performer; but this latter solution leaves them open to charges of being lacking in both imagination and sensitivity to musical style. Too many editors prepare thick, full accompaniments in four real parts, which demonstrate their proficiency at academic counterpoint but do not supply an adequate realisation for intelligent performers.

No similar editorial convention about divisions or *passaggi* has been firmly established, but many editors offer their own highly embellished versions of Italianate slow movements (where such divisions were commonly applied, and may even have been obligatory) above the staff. Others suggest in a footnote or preface that such divisions should be added, without making specific suggestions, but some merely print the simple version without comment. Editors of Baroque operas, on the other hand, seldom include proposals for the embellished repeats expected of singers in da capo arias or suggest which phrase-endings in recitatives can or should be sung with appoggiaturas.

If scholarly critical editions are sometimes difficult or impossible to use for performances without more or less extensive re-editing, so-called 'performing editions', which attempt to include all the information necessary for satisfactory performance, but place little emphasis on variant readings and the less obviously practical features of the original notation, often frequently fail to include sufficient information to allow a critical user to challenge editorial decisions. Moreover, 'performing editions' run the risk of introducing the precepts and prejudices of the editor's own time, thus obscuring or obliterating altogether the composer's intentions. The period during which some of the most extravagant 'performing editions' appeared and were most readily accepted was around the middle of the nineteenth century, when many fêted virtuosos and teachers simply up-dated earlier music to suit organological and technical developments. Such heavily edited publications made the music immediately accessible to a wide range of musicians, but the composer's original notation was often obscured by an abundance of undeclared editorial performance annotations (e.g. tempo markings, dynamics, phrasing, fingering and pedalling). The products of such editorial high-handedness more closely approximated arrangements than editions, resulting in performers being deceived into seeing early music through the eyes of someone quite other than the composer. Nevertheless, they constitute valuable sources of information about the technique, style and performing practices of their era.

It was as a reaction to such 'performing editions' that a vogue for *Urtext* ('original text') editions was started in the late nineteenth century. The *Urtext* concept had arguably taken root earlier in the work of such musical antiquarians as Charles Burney and Samuel Arnold, whose unsuccessful attempts to create a complete Handel edition set high standards of source fidelity; but it was doubtless prompted further by a parallel trend set by the *Bach-Gesellschaft* in 1851 with the first of its historical editions devoted to the complete works of J. S. Bach. *Urtexts* became principally associated initially with keyboard music, in which the usurpation of the role of editor by the solo virtuoso had become extreme; and they purported to present the composer's original text, normally using the MS or first printed edition, free of editorial intervention, allowing performers to form their own interpretations from the original notation.

However honourable the intentions of the concept, scholars have found little use for the *Urtext* and even its staunchest proponents, such as Günter Henle and Georg Feder, eventually conceded that an editor's critical intervention was inevitable.[57] As Walter Emery explains: 'There is no such thing as an "original text" of any piece of old music, unless either there is only one source, or all the sources give identical readings. In my experience there are usually more sources than one, and they almost always differ; one has therefore to begin by asking which *is* the original. When there really is an identifiable original (such as a unique MS), it is often manifestly wrong; in which case it cannot be printed as it stands, or in other words, it has to be edited.'[58] Consequently, he argues, an *Urtext* 'represents, as a rule, not what the composer wrote, but an editor's theory about what the composer meant to write; and . . . although the editor's theory may be right, there may be a great difference between the notes the composer meant to write and those he meant to be played'.[59] One need look no further than Bärenreiter's ongoing '*Urtext*' of Beethoven's symphonies, based on Jonathan Del Mar's important manuscript researches, to realise the truth of Emery's assertions. Del Mar's versions incorporate a significant number of emendations to what had previously appeared as accepted 'established' texts.[60]

The term *Urtext* is now largely discredited, hastened by the commercialisation of the concept in the immediately post-Second-World-War period.[61] Other than scholarly critical editions, the obvious compromise for publishers has proved to be a combined-purpose edition, which offers an established text and essential source information for scholars, together with enough practical advice about interpretation for performers, and with every editorial addition, interpolation or interpretation clearly distinguishable.

Every performance is in itself an interpretation, even if original sources are followed as closely as possible; and in order to give a convincing and credible rendition, it is essential for performers to understand not only the text but also its meaning. Editing music and interpreting musical sources are kinds of science; like the real sciences, they progress and develop, posing new questions and problems. As our knowledge of repertories and their sources deepens, and our critical appraisal of that knowledge continues, new editions and approaches are needed to keep pace with, and reflect, the latest developments while preserving the plausible work of the past. Jonathan Del Mar's incorporation of the composer's three pages of corrections (auctioned at Sotheby's in 1988) into his edition of Beethoven's Ninth Symphony, and the practical problems they pose, provide but one example of this ever-developing process.

Musical taste

'Musical taste' serves as the final arbiter in the interpretation of historical evidence. According to Geminiani, this involves 'expressing with Strength and Delicacy the Intention of the Composer', while Mattheson defines taste, in its figurative sense, as 'that internal sensibility, selection, and judgement by which our intellect reveals itself in matters of feeling'.[62] It requires performers to exercise discrimination and judgement concerning issues that will best serve the interests of the music and is informed by a thorough understanding of those issues – 'Nature, reason and the experience of art are our guides', writes Mattheson[63] – including the parameters within which the composer was operating, the consequent national or other stylistic boundaries which should be heeded and a detailed acquaintance with the conventions relevant to the music. For the optimum tempo, for example, taste involves consideration of a range of factors such as the rate of harmonic change, the character of the figures, the type of texture and so on, right down to the acoustics of the performance venue. Similarly, the effective application of dynamics, stylish continuo playing, flexibility of rhythmic nuance and appropriate realisation of matters of expression, phrasing, articulation and ornamentation will often necessarily be dependent on sound judgements made in the light of thorough knowledge and a wealth of experience in the relevant repertory.

Taste is not a twentieth-century phenomenon, even though, of course, interpreting appropriately a wide range of historical styles was not part of a seventeenth- or eighteenth-century performer's brief. Constant reference is made to taste in sources, particularly those of the eighteenth century. Couperin associates playing well with having 'le bon goût' and takes great pains to indicate the appropriate ornaments for his *Pièces de clavecin* in order that they may impress 'persons of real taste'.[64] Quantz considers 'good taste' as the only sure guide to assessing art objects, and music in particular; ever mindful of the principle that the ultimate aim of music is to arouse the listener's emotions, he provides precise directions about taste, stressing the need for a judicious amount of contrasts, balance among the parts and avoidance of excesses, particularly of counterpoint, which is conceived 'more for the eye than for the ear'.[65]

Tosi makes several references to the importance of cultivating taste regarding the performance of appoggiaturas, *messe di voce*, trills, extempore embellishments, cadences and rubato, writing much about the 'Mode' or popular taste of his day.[66] Like Marpurg and others, he exhorts students to listen to and copy the most celebrated singers and instrumentalists and 'get a good taste' through 'the study of others'. He also encourages them often to 'sing the most agreeable compositions of the best authors, and accustom the ear to that which pleases', since through such actions 'the taste in time becomes Art and Art Nature'.[67] In appreciation of national differences, Tosi writes: 'To please universally, reason will tell you that you must always sing well; but if reason does not inform you, interest will persuade you to conform to the taste of that nation (provided it be not too depraved) which pays you.'[68] Tosi includes in the category of bad taste excessive vibrato, the inappropriate incidence of ad libitum cadenzas in final cadences and a surfeit of 'broken cadences' in recitatives.[69]

Francesco Geminiani published two treatises on the subject of taste within about a year of each other.[70] His principal goal in both treatises was to illustrate the best places to introduce trills, mordents, turns, crescendos and diminuendos and to set parameters regarding extempore embellishment in order to 'move the audience' and play 'any Composition in a good Taste'. Geminiani's *Rules* . . . is misleadingly titled, because, apart from advice for thoroughbass playing, it propounds few actual regulations; instead, it illustrates through musical examples (national Airs with variations), the student being required to infer the elements of good taste through observation, intuition and practice. In his *A Treatise of Good Taste* . . . Geminiani explains the meaning of each 'ornament of expression' and its particular sentiment, providing a table 'of the elements of playing and singing in a good taste',[71] and presents the student with a variety of compositions to be practised in order to achieve good taste in performing such 'ornaments'. Interestingly, Burney commented that Geminiani's two treatises appeared 'too soon for the present times. Indeed a treatise on good taste in dress, during the reign of Queen Elizabeth, would now be as useful to a tailor or milliner, as the rules of taste in Music, forty years ago, to a modern musician.'[72]

Mattheson spoke sarcastically about those who said it was 'almost impossible to make rules, under the pretext that it [interpretation] depends on good taste'.[73] At times performers must be technicians, at times interpreters and at times creators, for many rules impinge on the alleged liberty with which they may present the music; conversely, certain works sometimes refute their intellectually grounded precepts. Performers will almost inevitably have to be the final arbiters in such matters and devise tasteful solutions to problems (e.g. of articulation, ornamentation or, in the early Baroque, the treatment of *musica ficta*) for which there are no definitive or widely accepted answers. Furthermore, considered application of musical taste gives interpretations individuality, variety and their intrinsic value within the flexible, though not indefinitely elastic boundaries of style. As Marpurg remarks concerning embellishments, 'it is impossible to derive rules suitable to all possible occasions as long as music remains an inexhaustible sea of change, and one person's feelings differ from another's'; similarly, Quantz observes that, for both performer and listener, 'much depends upon differences in temperament . . . We are not always in the same humour when we hear a piece for the first time'. And Czerny is adamant that each great performance will be a unique experience, for 'much depends on the individuality of the player . . . Hence one may principally cause humour to predominate, another earnestness, a third feeling, a fourth bravura, and so on; but he who is able to unite all these, is evidently the most talented.'[74]

Evidence about early playing styles is almost never complete. While we have to rely substantially on our intuitive response to the expressive implications of early music, our purpose in educating ourselves as musicians is to enable us to play instinctively and express ourselves within a given stylistic framework. We must always be mindful of the dangers of allowing our attempts at stylish interpretation of seventeenth- or eighteenth-century music, for example, to be governed too much by rules and to be conditioned by the styles and tastes of the intervening years; but in our efforts to express ourselves within a style, we must attune our imaginations as closely as possible to the taste of the period of the music. In the final analysis, although intuition is one of a musician's most valuable attributes, it is no substitute for knowledge; and historical research has an extremely important part to play in the performance process.

3   Changes in musical style

The term 'style' has various connotations in music. It may be applied to single works or composers (Mahler's style); to compositional genres (symphonic style); to media (keyboard style); to compositional methods (contrapuntal style); to performance in a particular city or geographical area (Mannheim style); to historical periods (Baroque style); or even to technical demand (virtuoso style). More specifically, it may refer, as here, to the interpretation of a work's component parts such as rhythm, tempo, harmony or ornamentation. In a present world that is becoming increasingly international in outlook and more homogeneous in the study and performance of music, distinctive styles are disappearing. But the diversity of idioms prevalent during the period under discussion, conditioned largely by national or regional conventions and individual taste, must be assimilated by historical performers when formulating their interpretations. How else would it be possible to differentiate between performances of works by, say, Cherubini, Beethoven and Rossini, three roughly contemporary composers whose music emanated from very different European centres?

National idioms

Three principal national idioms can be distinguished during the Baroque period – Italian, French and German.[1] The concept of national style concerns not only the ways in which composers wrote their music, influenced by considerations such as tradition, function, social context and even language, but also its performance; it also extends to aspects of instrument construction and sound ideal.

The representation and excitation of the emotions in music, fostered in Italy around the beginning of the seventeenth century, were quite contrary to earlier practice, involving emotional expression on the model of speech. Although the Italian language's free, capricious type of expression resulted in the music taking second place to the drama in opera, the unfettered Italian style of presentation encouraged a trend towards virtuosity in instrumental music. Even when Italian music eventually became more formalised, its manner of presentation remained capricious, rich in fantasy, and full of surprises.

The definitive French style was initiated by an Italian, Jean-Baptiste Lully (originally Giovanni Battista Lulli), but its formal severity, refined precision and thoroughly ordered, mannered approach (with ornaments and detailed performance instructions prescribed and the greatest possible nuancing within the smallest range) were in sharp contrast with Italian taste. French music also incorporated a rhythmic system of great subtlety and took over from pre-Lullian times a preference for dance-forms, such that concert-pieces, opera arias and choruses, and even much sacred music, were founded on dance.

Like many writers before him,[2] Quantz compares the two styles at length, directly contrasting their approaches to composition, singing and playing, even though his claims to impartiality seem false:

> In *composition* the *Italians* are unrestrained, sublime, lively, expressive, profound, and majestic in their manner of thinking; they are rather bizarre, free, daring, bold, extravagant, and sometimes negligent in metrics; they are also singing, flattering, tender, moving, and rich in invention. They write more for the connoisseur than the amateur. In *composition* the *French* are indeed lively, expressive, natural, pleasing and comprehensible to the public, and more correct in metrics than the Italians; but they are neither profound nor venturesome. They are very limited and slavish, always imitating themselves, stingy in their manner of thinking, and dry in invention. They always warm up the ideas of their predecessors; and they write more for the amateur than for the connoisseur.
>
> The *Italian manner of singing* is profound and artful; it at once moves and excites admiration; it stimulates the musical intellect; it is pleasing, charming, expressive, rich in taste and expression, and transports the listeners in an agreeable manner from one passion to another. The *French manner of singing* is more simple than artful, more spoken than sung, more forced than natural in the

expression of the passions and in the use of the voice; in style and expression it is poor, and always uniform; it is more for amateurs than for connoisseurs; it is better suited to drinking songs than to serious arias, diverting the senses, but leaving the musical intellect completely idle.

The *Italian manner of playing* is arbitrary, extravagant, artificial, obscure, frequently bold and bizarre, and difficult in execution; it permits many additions of graces, and requires a seemly knowledge of harmony; but among the ignorant it excites more admiration than pleasure. The *French manner of playing* is slavish, yet modest, distinct, neat and true in execution, easy to imitate, neither profound nor obscure, but comprehensible to everyone, and convenient for amateurs; it does not require much knowledge of harmony, since the embellishments are generally prescribed by the composer; but it gives the connoisseurs little to reflect upon. In a word, Italian music is arbitrary, and French is circumscribed. If it is to have a good effect, the French depends more upon the composition than the performance, while the Italian depends upon the performance almost as much as upon the composition, and in some cases almost more.[3]

The differences between the Italian and French styles were not always as clearly defined as Quantz's comparison might imply. For example, some composers, such as J. S. Bach or Telemann, cultivated both French and Italian styles, as well as the distinctive German style, which had developed from a mid-seventeenth-century compositional idiom 'harmonious and rich in full chords, but . . . neither melodious nor charming' and playing and singing described simply as 'bad'.[4] Telemann even incorporated some Slavonic folk influences. Quantz perceives an improvement in the German style from *c.* 1650 onwards and advances the case for a 'mixed' German style which makes 'use of the good things in all types of foreign music'.[5] Although both Couperin and Campra had earlier striven for a *mélange des genres*, it was left to later German composers to arrive at a fully integrated mixture of French 'delicacy' and Italian 'vitality' in Quantz's highly expressive, ornate 'galant' idiom, thereby pointing the way to Quantz's vision of 'a good style that is universal'.[6]

Even with the emergence of a more international style in the Classical era, national preferences are often evident (the music of Haydn, Mozart and Beethoven, for example, involves national traits absorbed in a more cosmopolitan idiom); and there were countless nineteenth-century trends which distinguished the music of one country from another, whether drawing on folk melodies, dance rhythms, extra-musical elements or other characteristics.

National styles and preferences also extended to musical instruments. French organs, for example, had their own clearly defined characteristics, differing markedly from Italian instruments, and French and Italian traditions are observable in German organ design just as they are in German music. However, German organs were no mere syntheses of other national types, Schnitger's instruments being unrivalled in comprehensiveness of pedal departments.[7] Characteristics of harpsichords ranged generally from the smooth, sweet tone of French instruments, to the more direct, brilliant sound of Flemish models, the shallow, more pronounced attack of Italian designs and the powerful, rich English instruments. The light, shallow key action, thin, bright resonance, efficient damping mechanism and clear, 'transparent' sound of Viennese pianos (preferred by Haydn and Mozart) contrasted with 'English action' models (championed by, among others, Clementi), which were capable of greater cantabile and volume.

National or regional characteristics are also discernible in the development of the orchestra, especially the wind section. The sound of, say, eighteenth-century Bohemian and English clarinets was very different, and the Boehm system clarinet developed (c. 1839–43) by Hyacinthe Klosé and Louis-August Buffet gained acceptance almost everywhere except Germany and Britain; the 'Simple System' instrument dominated in Britain well into the twentieth century. The bassoon, like the clarinet and oboe, also took two principal lines of development. But whereas French oboe makers tended to narrow the bore, departing further from the Baroque ideal than the Germans, French bassoons retained for longest, and to a lessening extent still retain, the older bores, more nasal tone colourings, lightness and ease of articulation of the Baroque and Classical bassoons. German bassoon makers strove for a more even and homogeneous tone-quality and Heckel's radical modifications transformed the instrument late in the nineteenth century. American influence has been strong in recent years, particularly with brass instruments, reducing dramatically the range and diversity of available orchestral timbres worldwide.

National (as well as individual) preferences also relate to the reed, mouthpiece or other relevant accessories chosen by players and the technical approaches cultivated (clarinet playing since the eighteenth century, for example, has involved a gradual transition from applying the upper lip to the reed to the present, almost universal, approach with the reed on the lower lip). Such factors, combined with national and regional styles of composition and performance, contributed to the wealth of practices in solo and orchestral playing. Russian and Czech orchestras, for example, used to have a strong individual character and sound, as did, to a lesser degree, the Vienna Philharmonic, the Berlin Philharmonic and the London Symphony Orchestras. But the rise of the international conductor and the clinical exigences of the recording industry have led to the creation of a more standardised, universal orchestral sound, often lacking subtlety of instrumental timbre and sometimes bordering on the predictable and routine.

The age of recording has done a great service by preserving some of the most distinguished performances of our forebears, often given or conducted by the composers themeslves (e.g. by Rachmaninov, Elgar, Stravinsky and Bartók) or by musicians with whom they were associated, or whom they approved. Far from being old-fashioned curiosities, early recordings are significant primary source materials, illustrating in far greater detail than instrumental treatises or other printed documentation performance practices of the early twentieth century and revealing the gradual evolution of more recent performing trends. Most important, they force us 'to question unspoken assumptions about modern taste, and about the ways in which we use it to justify our interpretation of earlier performance practice'.[8] Early recordings also shed new light retrospectively on nineteenth-century performance, revealing the artistic roots of early recording artists as far back as the 1850s. They also highlight the limitations of our attempts to recreate the styles and practices of that period without the benefit of actual performances among our primary source materials.

Finally, early twentieth-century recordings and documents clearly demonstrate that any literal reconstruction of past performance practices is impossible, since musicians can never escape sufficiently the taste and judgement of their own times. Nevertheless, informed attempts at faithful reconstruction are worthwhile, for one's comprehension and appreciation of the music can gain inestimably from the effort. Essential to the cause is rediscovery of the idiosyncrasies and individuality of all the various aspects of national and regional style relevant to the composition and performance of the repertory under consideration. Such issues as the work's musical function, social context and the component parts to be addressed in the remainder of this chapter, as well as aspects of pitch, temperament and other issues discussed in Chapter 4, should also be taken into account.

Articulation

Articulation involves numerous aspects of the voice or instrument that determine how beginnings and ends of notes are executed. As a principal component (together with nuances, dynamics, tempo and other considerations) of expression and phrasing, it is as crucial to music as it is to speech. As we noted in Chapter 2, the art of rhetoric was continually emphasised, and it is this aspect that modern performers, with their all-too-standardised approach to articulation, often fail satisfactorily to emulate.

Articulation signs appeared in scores at a relatively late stage in the history of notation. They were extremely rare before the seventeenth century and, apart from ornaments, remained scarce throughout the Baroque period, leaving the performer to articulate phrases according to the conventions of the time. Couperin often used a slanting stroke or strokes to indicate those notes to be grouped closely together, while the practice of connecting notes with beams (or not, as the case may be) also provided clues to phrasing and articulation. But even in the late eighteenth century, when articulation marks of the modern, more abstract type became more common (e.g. dots, horizontal and vertical strokes, and slurs), their application was inconsistent and their meaning often ambiguous. The dot seems to have been used largely to indicate a lighter, less abrupt staccato than the stroke or wedge, as Quantz and Leopold Mozart confirm; but C. P. E. Bach regards the two signs as identical.[9] Türk emphasises the notational ambiguity of his times: strokes and dots 'have the same meaning, but some would like to indicate by the strokes that a shorter staccato be played than that indicated by the dot'.[10] But perhaps the most revealing description of staccato signs is given in Friedrich

Ex. 3.1 L. van Beethoven, Symphony No. 7 Op. 92, Allegretto

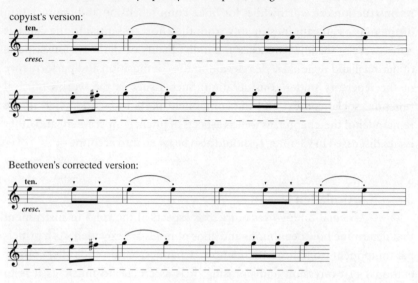

Starke's *Wiener Pianoforte-Schule* (1819–21), which describes three kinds of detached playing:

> (1) the short, sharp touch which is marked by dashes and in which each note receives a quarter of its value; (2) the semi-sharp touch, marked by dots, in which notes receive half their value; (3) portamento (*appoggiato*) which is marked by dots below or above a slur, in which each note receives three-quarters of its value.[11]

Nottebohm verifies that Beethoven distinguished between the dash and the dot from *c.* 1800, citing as evidence Beethoven's proof corrections for the slow movement of his Seventh Symphony (Ex. 3.1).

The final choice of articulation, including the interpretation of signs, depended substantially on the particular idiom and character of the work, as well as the individual taste of the performer and the qualities of the performing venue. Mattheson, for example, links detached notes with lively Allegros and slurred notes with tender Adagios.[12] Quantz, C. P. E. Bach and most eighteenth-century theorists seem to have cultivated three broad categories of articulation, with staccato and legato (indicated by a slur or *ten.*) serving as the two extremes and a semi-detached 'ordinary' manner of playing in the

Ex. 3.2 J. Hotteterre's principal tongue strokes (*Principes*, Eng. trans., p. 60)

middleground.[13] However, an increasing reverence for a more legato style, brought to full fruition in the nineteenth century, is evident in the works of theorists such as Marpurg and Türk.[14]

The resources of articulation naturally varied with (and sometimes within) the different families of instruments and their playing techniques. Techniques of articulation in most wind instruments include various tonguing patterns, which involved the release of pent-up air, the tongue being suddenly relaxed from its closed position against the upper palate or teeth. Observing that flute tonguing produces a much gentler effect than recorder tonguing, and that oboe tonguing is pronounced 'a lot more strongly',[15] Hotteterre articulated most unslurred note-patterns through the alternation of two tongue-strokes, 'tu' and 'ru', always beginning with 'tu' to emphasise the opening note. Such alternation of sharp ('tu') and softer ('ru') accent often resulted in an implied inequality and certainly helped the performer to communicate the 'good' and 'bad' notes of the bar, as in Ex. 3.2.[16]

Quantz recommends a wider armoury of tonguing consonants than would be encountered in a modern treatise. For the articulation of unslurred notes, he has: 'ti', 'di', 'ri' and 'd'll'.[17] The appropriate tonguing for any note was dependent largely upon the speed and character of the movement and the position of that note in the hierarchy of the bar. 'Ti' was the basic single-tonguing suitable for 'short, equal, lively and quick notes', but successions of such notes involved 'ti' and 'ri', 'ti' invariably being used for the first note or two of a phrase and 'ri' placed on the 'good' notes of paired tonguings (Ex. 3.3). 'Di' could be substituted for 'ti' for a gentler effect or for more sustained passages, and a double-tonguing, 'did'll'(Ex. 3.4), facilitated very fast passagework. Similar forms of double-tonguing persisted through the eighteenth century with Mahaut, Granom (as 'too-tle'),

Ex. 3.3 J. Quantz's single tonguings, *Versuch*, Eng. trans., p. 77

ti   ti   ri   ti   ri   ti   ri   ti

Ex. 3.4 J. Quantz's double tonguings, *Versuch*, Eng. trans., p. 80

did 'll   di   did 'll   di   did 'll   di   did 'll   di

Tromlitz (as 'ta-d'll), and Gunn (as, variously 'diddle', 'teddy' or 'tiddy');[18] indeed, it is a sobering thought that the 'modern' alternation of tongue and throat, 'te-che' or 'de-ghe', is descended from sixteenth-century practice.[19]

The choice of tonguing consonant was left to the player's taste and technical proficiency. When notes were slurred, only the first note of the group was tongued; much early eighteenth-century French music includes slurred note-pairings to be performed connected but slightly unequally in a manner known as 'lourer', emphasising the first of each pair. Longer slurs generally implied an equal execution of the notes they embraced, those of more than four notes often indicating that the phrase should be articulated in one breath; failing this, Quantz recommends that breath should be taken wherever possible on tied notes, between disjunct notes of continuous semiquavers or at other equivalent moments.

Mersenne equates woodwind tonguing with words in singing.[20] Singers' principal articulation resources were the consonants and the glottal or smooth beginning and ending of vowel sounds. They observed the relationship between the stresses of the words and the metrical stresses of the music, differentiating between strong and weak syllables and notes through both dynamics and note-lengths. 'Good' and 'bad' notes were commonly related to a strengthening and weakening of the voice.[21] John Butt presumes that the metrical hierarchy also influenced the performance of melismas when there was no change of syllable;[22] however, despite the increasing emphasis on legato vocal performance in the eighteenth century, most seventeenth- and eighteenth-century sources recommend detached rather than legato execution of passages or divisions. Agricola confirms that the vowels on which 'marked divisions' are made should be repeated gently with as many reper-cussions as there are notes (as in tonguing for wind instruments and bowing for strings); like Hiller, he recommends emphasising the first of a group of three or four 'running notes'.[23] Smooth passages involved articulation of only the vowel of the first note.[24] Tosi's sparing use of 'gliding' (slurred) pas-sages, limited only to a few notes, either ascending, or particularly in descending, and Marpurg's comment that each note should be sustained through to the next with no intervening silence, echoed by Hiller and others, confirm the more cantabile aims of late eighteenth-century musicians.[25]

For bowed stringed instruments, management of the bow provided the main articulation resource, but pizzicato remained a possible alternative and fingering principles were naturally closely interlinked with articulation and phrasing. The natural stroke of most pre-Tourte bows was of an articu-lated, non-legato character (especially in the upper third). Leopold Mozart (1756) writes of 'a small, even if barely audible, softness'[26] at the beginning and end of each stroke, a reference to the typical delayed attack (through only gradual take-up of hair) of pre-Tourte bows, their lightness at the tip and their balance point (closer to the hand). Unlike modern staccato, the eighteenth-century staccato stroke involved a 'breath' or articulation between notes somewhat greater than the articulation of the normal separ-ate stroke and it was often conveyed by lifting the bow from the string after each stroke, especially in slow tempos. In fast movements the bow necessar-ily remained on the string in the upper half, producing an effect similar to the modern spiccato. Articulation silences often afforded players the oppor-tunity to effect shifts of the left hand, notably on repeated notes (Ex. 3.5a), by the phrase in sequences (Ex. 3.5b), or after a lifted bow-stroke (Ex. 3.5c). True legato bowing with most pre-Tourte bows was achieved only by slur-ring, due emphasis being given to the first note of a slur. The capacity of the slur was enlarged substantially in the late eighteenth century, particularly in the last decade or so after the advent of the Tourte bow, and slurred bowings were increasingly exploited as a means of emulating the qualities of the human voice, especially in slow movements.

Keyboard articulation depended not only on the player but also to a great extent on the nature and quality of the instrument. While François Couperin writes about the harpsichord (1716), C. P. E. Bach (1753) clearly favours the clavichord for its expressive and sustaining qualities, and

Ex. 3.5 Appropriate opportunities for shifting on the violin (L. Mozart, *Versuch*, ch. 8)

Marpurg (1755) and Türk (1789) state their preference for the pianoforte, an instrument considered by Czerny (1839) to have been pre-eminent amongst keyboard instruments from the early nineteenth century. Broadly speaking, the principal difference between eighteenth- and nineteenth-century keyboard articulation was in the kind used for ordinary playing. Theorists concur that in ordinary playing the finger must always be lifted before the next note is sounded, but they disagree as to precisely when it should be lifted. Türk refuted C. P. E. Bach's theory that notes which are neither staccato nor legato nor sostenuto should be held for half their notated value, claiming that this nullified the difference between staccato and ordinary touch and resulted in a disjointed performance. His recommendations confirm the gradual change to a more legato 'ordinary' manner of performance: 'When playing notes in the ordinary manner, that is neither staccato nor legato, the finger should be lifted shortly before the written value of the note requires it. Consequently the notes in example (a) (Ex. 3.6) should be rendered approximately as in examples (b) and (c). Where single notes are supposed to be held for their full value they have to be marked *ten.* or *tenuto*.'[27] Clementi, with the improved mechanism of English pianos, took the legato trend further by promoting a cantabile ordinary manner modelled on the voice. He claims: 'The best general rule is to keep down the keys of the instrument the full length of every note'; he further adds, 'When the composer leaves the staccato and legato to the performer's taste, the best

Ex. 3.6 'Ordinary touch' as illustrated in D. G. Türk's *Clavierschule*

rule is to adhere chiefly to the legato, reserving the staccato to give spirit occasionally to certain passages, and to set off the higher beauty of the legato.'[28] Czerny's later claim that 'the legato style is the rule, and the staccato the exception' provides final confirmation of the ordinary legato style's evolution.[29]

The development of the sustaining pedal also entered the legato equation for the piano.[30] Early examples, involving stops or knee levers (as opposed to pedals) to raise the dampers from the strings, proved relatively inflexible, resulting in their sparing use. John Broadwood's introduction of a foot pedal led to increased use of the sustaining device, yet Hummel could still write in 1828 that a truly great artist had 'no occasion for pedals to work upon his audience by expression and power', even though the 'damper' and 'piano' pedals were capable of 'agreeable effects'. As late as 1830 the virtuoso pianist and teacher Christian Kalkbrenner was urging the Germans to take the sustaining pedal seriously in order to achieve the singing style of the English school.[31]

Melodic inflection

Inflection involves shaping the melodic line through phrasing, articulation, dynamic and rhythmic control, or other aspects (e.g. vibrato), thereby giving full meaning to the music. Some aspects of this process are prescribed or pre-planned (e.g. dynamic or articulation markings in varying degrees of detail according to period), some is intuitive; and it has always been the performer's responsibility to introduce those subtle, largely unnotatable dynamic inflections, whatever the musical style or period.

The relative sparseness of dynamic markings in Baroque music, the dominance of two basic markings in surviving sources (*piano* and *forte*) and the rare use of *crescendo* and *diminuendo* prescriptions have led some musicians incorrectly to introduce the principle of terraced dynamics into their performances, contrasting large sections of music played uniformly softly and

loudly.[32] Although echo effects were common in Baroque music, such interpretations ignore the fact that dynamic markings traditionally served as a
framework for the structural design of a piece or movement, with either
dynamic unity or dynamic contrast between sections (although not necessarily in the extreme 'terraced' manner) as a prevailing feature.[33] Among
other misleading annotations is a *p* followed closely by *f*, which may, dependent upon the music's character, indicate a *crescendo* (and hence *f* followed
closely by *p* a *diminuendo*) rather than any sharp dynamic contrast.
Furthermore, some indications held different meanings for different composers or theorists – Walther, for example, took *pp* to mean *più piano*, not
pianissimo. Once more, informed decisions based on considerations of style,
good taste and musicianship should prevail.

Stylish interpretation requires supplementing the notation, however
sparse or dense, with subtle gradations to enhance the melodic line and, in
singing, the expression of the words. For example, it was natural to: play the
dissonance of the appoggiatura more loudly than its resolution; add the
messa di voce, or swell, as an expressive ornament on long notes;[34] *crescendo*
a little to high notes, and *diminuendo* from them; and follow the contours of
the music through subtle shadings. Quantz gives some idea of the extent of
the performer's task, providing an ornamented adagio as an example of a
slow movement with copious additional annotated nuances.[35] Leopold
Mozart also provides numerous individual examples where subtle nuancing
would normally inflect a performance, whether or not notated;[36] for 'Not
only must one observe exactly all that has been marked and prescribed and
not play it otherwise than as written; but one must throw oneself into the
affect to be expressed and apply and execute in a certain good style all the
ties, slides, accentuation of the notes, the *forte* and *piano*; in a word, whatever belongs to tasteful performance of a piece; which can only be learnt
from sound judgement and long experience.'[37]

While the Italians and their adherents during the Baroque generally welcomed dynamic contrasts, the French traditionally considered such variation
to be excessive and even offensive. Such contrasts are confirmed in published
compositions, especially towards the mid-eighteenth century, when a steady
increase in the notation of dynamic gradations can be observed.[38] Regional
variations in the exploitation of dynamics became less distinctive over time,
and careful prescription of dynamic detail, involving a wider range of signs

and including crescendos and diminuendos, gradually became an important component of musical composition, especially from c. 1750. Nevertheless, performers continued to add instinctively to the expressive effect. Some of the theories behind the application of nuances were put into practice in late eighteenth-century string playing through the cultivation of the four divisions of the bow, nuanced bowings (<; >; < >; < > < >) categorised by Leopold Mozart and widely imitated.[39] Later theorists commonly likened nuances in music to *chiaroscuro* and the play of light in painting, Baillot especially emphasising the performer's role in making good any omission of annotated nuances and ensuring an appropriate sense of proportion in their use.[40]

Vibrato, sometimes indicated by the symbol ⋁⋀ but generally freely added by the performer, also contributed to melodic colouring.[41] It was normally employed selectively as an expressive ornament until the late nineteenth century, despite Geminiani's exceptional recommendation of what is essentially a continuous vibrato in the approved modern fashion. For technical reasons, it was generally applied fairly discreetly on most instruments during the Baroque and Classical periods, although players appear to have used a range of oscillation speeds to striking effect. In the nineteenth century vibrato practice varied according to the instrument employed; with the violin family, for example, it assumed a wider, more intense character as the century progressed, until it was eventually adopted as an almost continuous tonal colouring (albeit with some expressive variation of speed).

Accentuation

Accentuation forms another part of the performer's expressive armoury and contributes (together with other factors such as phrasing, articulation and nuances) a shape and meaning to the music that are vital for the listener's full comprehension of the performer's (and hence the composer's) intentions. Much of this surface detail is lacking in modern performance, and period performers have sought to re-establish such detail as an important expressive resource. Thus, they convey accentuation by stress or prolongation, singers bearing the additional responsibility of conforming as precisely and expressively as possible to the natural accent of the text.

Accentuation conveyed by stress may result from starting a particular (usually prescribed) note assertively (accent) or making such an emphasis just after the start of the note (*sforzando*). Accentuation by prolongation involves both adherence to the hierarchy of the bar and emphasis of impor-tant notes within phrases (called 'agogic accents').[42]

Realising the hierarchy of the bar involved giving due emphasis to the so-called *note buone*, the notes of natural rhythmic stress – particularly the first note of each bar, but also other notes, depending on the tempo. This concept, already well developed by the end of the sixteenth century, was re-stated in many seventeenth- and eighteenth-century treatises. Quantz, for example, links good musical performance to good oratory, which requires 'distinct and true pronunciation' and appropriate vocal inflections 'to arouse or still the passions'.[43] He particularly stresses the need for rhythmic flexibility and then distinguishes between

> the *principal notes*, ordinarily called *accented* or in the Italian manner, *good* notes, and those that *pass*, which some foreigners call *bad* notes. Where it is possible, the principal notes always must be emphasised more than the passing. In consequence of this rule, the quickest notes in every piece of moderate tempo, or even in the Adagio, though they seem to have the same value, must be played a little unequally, so that the stressed notes of each figure, namely the first, third, fifth, and seventh, are held slightly longer than the passing, namely the second, fourth, sixth, and eighth, although this lengthening must not be as much as if the notes were dotted.[44]

He provides examples and mentions two exceptions – quick passages in a very fast movement, in which length and accent can be applied only to the first of every four notes; and all rapid vocal passagework, unless it is slurred.

Türk uses dynamic indications to illustrate the degree of emphasis the various time-units should receive unless annotated otherwise (Ex. 3.7). These *note buone* were accommodated in wind playing by specific tonguings and in string playing by the traditional rule of down-bow. This long-stand-ing principle, formulated by the Italians early in the seventeenth century or even before, required 'good' notes to be played with the stronger down-bow and the 'bad' notes with the weaker up-stroke.[45] In bars with an uneven number of notes, players had to adjust bowings accordingly. Especially char-acteristic of French style in the late seventeenth and early eighteenth centu-

Ex. 3.7 Degrees of accentuation, as illustrated in D. G. Türk's *Clavierschule*

f   mf   pf   mf   f mf   pf mf   f   mf pf   mf   f   mf   pf

Ex. 3.8 The 'reprise d'archet' as illustrated by Georg Muffat

Ex. 3.9 'Craquer' bowling as illustrated by Georg Muffat

ries was the *reprise d'archet*, a method of such adjustment which became a stylistic nuance, involving re-taking a down-bow (when the tempo allowed) to preserve the hierarchy of the bar (Ex. 3.8). Another method of adjustment involved taking two notes in the same up-bow as in Ex. 3.9, a bowing often termed *craquer*.[46] Muffat reported that members of Lully's orchestra 'all observe the same way of playing the principal notes in the bar: above all, those that begin the bar, those that define the cadence, and those that most clearly emphasise the dance rhythm'.[47] Although the rule of down-bow provided the foundation for eighteenth-century Italian and German bowing principles, it was treated rather less systematically in those two countries. But it has remained a guiding force in bowing to this day, despite its outright rejection by Geminiani and the greater equality of emphasis in the up- and down-strokes afforded by the Tourte bow.[48]

Apart from the first note of a phrase, syncopated notes, a note that is longer or markedly higher or lower than its predecessors, dissonant notes within the phrase (whether prepared or unprepared), and notes of verbal stress (in singing) are common instances when the agogic accent offers a flexible musicianly solution.[49] Although the length of such prolongations was a matter of taste, Türk's rule that a note should not be prolonged for more than half its written value is a significant pointer to the proportional implications of this practice. Riemann published editions of standard keyboard works, marking agogic accents with the sign ∧ and recommending their use for 'notes which form centres of gravity' with a phrase, and 'more especially, in suspensions, whereby the harmonic value is rendered clearer'.[50] The use of agogic accents was often interlinked with *tempo rubato*, Johnstone, for example, describing their use as 'quasi tempo rubato' or 'a delicate give-and-take in the proportionate lengths of the notes'.[51] Another analogy involved declamation in speech and poetry, Robert Donington rightly claiming that 'true musical accentuation frequently introduces a kind of counterpoint of rhythms between the regular accents which the metre schematically implies (so that they are subliminally present in the listener's expectations), and the far from regular accents which the performer actually makes (so that the listener distinctly hears them)'.[52] It is the performer's task to realise this subtly yet clearly in his interpretation, just as a good speaker or reciter of poetry will vary his intonation and emphasis to convey meaning. As Busoni is reported to have remarked: 'The bar-line is only for the eye. In playing, as in reading a poem, the scanning must be subordinate to the declamation; you must *speak the piano*.'[53]

Tempo

Tempo, one of the fundamental yet most variable aspects of performance, has recently been subject to re-evaluation in the light of the historical evidence. Bearing directly upon the effectiveness of most other interpretative issues, including expressive and technical considerations, it influences substantially what the listener perceives. Before Maelzel developed the metronome in 1815, numerous attempts had been made to devise a convenient way of measuring time accurately, ranging from relating tempo to the human pulse (treated as averaging 80 beats per minute)[54] or to a walking pace[55] to using various forms of pendulum (from Thomas Mace, 1676, onwards), but with no great reliability.[56] Furthermore, the use of time-words (mainly Italian and French) from the early eighteenth century onwards to give a general idea of the tempo and prevailing character of the piece or movement thus headed often led to ambiguity, as Avison observed:

> The words Andante, Presto, Allegro, etc., are differently apply'd
> in . . . different kinds of music . . . For the same terms which denote

lively and gay in the opera or concert style, may be understood in
the practice of church-music, as chearful [sic] and serene, or if the
reader pleases, less lively and gay; wherefore, the Allegro etc. in this
kind of composition should always be performed somewhat slower
than is usual in concertos or operas.[57]

The most common Italian time-words of the Baroque were, in their most
usual order from slow to fast: adagio; largo; andante; allegro; vivace; and
presto.[58] However, inconsistencies in the description and inter-relationship
of some time-words have caused confusion, J. G. Walther, Sébastian de
Brossard and Leopold Mozart, for example, being among those who considered largo slower than adagio.[59] Nevertheless, the most usual order achieved
its currency because when most Baroque composers qualified these time-
words, they made the adagio even slower (molto adagio, adagio assai, and
adagissimo) and the largo a little less slow (larghetto, largo ma non tanto);
similarly, presto when qualified became faster, and vivace slower.

The few time-words included in early Baroque music were more clearly
confined to tempo and less indicative of mood than later became the case,
confusion arising, for example, from Handel's seemingly contradictory
time-words Andante allegro, which head the first movement of his Organ
Concerto Op. 4 No. 6. These time-words may indicate either a fast-moving
andante or a slowish allegro, or, more probably, a lively, cheerful andante
('allegro' translates as 'merry'). That such confusion is not confined to
Handel's music[60] places the onus on the performer to infer an appropriate
tempo from the music itself – C. P. E. Bach suggests taking its 'general mood'
and its 'fastest notes and passages' chiefly into consideration[61] – even if that
tempo appears to be contradicted by the time-word. Leopold Mozart regards
this process as 'among the highest accomplishments in the art of music . . .
Every melodic piece has at least one phrase from which one can clearly recognise the tempo the music demands. This phrase, if other considerations are
taken into account, often compels one into its own natural speed.'[62]

Like their foreign contemporaries, French composers increasingly
qualified the standard terms of tempo and, more important, mood during
the early eighteenth century. As François Couperin explains:

> All our airs for the violin, our pieces for the harpsichord, for the
> viols, etc., describe and seem to be trying to express some feeling.

> Thus, not having devised signs or characters for communicating
> our specific ideas, we try to remedy this by indicating at the begin-
> ning of our pieces, by some such words as *Tendrement, Vivement,*
> etc., as far as possible the idea we want to convey.

Rousseau adds: 'Each of these words indicates an explicit modification in the tempo of a different metre.'[63]

As dance steps can be performed correctly only within narrow margins of speed, it follows that fairly precise tempos of specific dances should be dedu-cible from practical dance reconstruction, using contemporary dance trea-tises as sources. However, such a recourse has severe limitations, as dance steps and figures (and with them, the tempos) varied widely at different times and places – compare, for example, the quick seventeenth-century English saraband with the moderate Italian and the slow French sarabande – and 'stylised' dances often underwent considerable transformation in the instrumental domain. The allemandes in Corelli's Op. 2 Trio Sonatas, for example, are variously headed presto, allegro, largo and adagio and the sarabandes of his Sonate da Camera Opp. 2 and 4 (1685 and 1694) carry equally diverse markings.[64] Bach, Handel and many other composers tended to give only a title to the movement, leaving performers to decide on its speed and character.

Late eighteenth- and early nineteenth-century composers used a variety of simple (mainly) Italian terms to indicate tempo, most treatises providing clear descriptions of each time-word's particular characteristics. The com-monest terms in classical scores are andante and allegro, both of which are often qualified with clear tempo implications. However, confusion seems to have existed over the meaning of andantino, some theorists (e.g. Galeazzi and Cartier) believing the term to signify a slower speed than andante, and some (e.g. Türk, Clementi and Hummel) the opposite.[65] Furthermore, many eighteenth-century treatises record that metre played a role in deter-mining tempo, time signatures with smaller denominators normally imply-ing faster performance than those with larger ones.[66] Sensitivity to the crucial role played by considerations of tempo seems to have increased in the late eighteenth century, Kirnberger claiming that only the composer could establish the most appropriate tempo, that time-words were inadequate and that composers should indicate tempo by stating the ideal duration of the movement in question.[67] The perceived need to define tempo more explicitly led to more extensive use of qualifying clauses, particularly by Beethoven (for example, the Andante con moto assai vivace quasi Allegretto ma non troppo in his Mass in C major). Later, Beethoven even headed some movements with dual-purpose Italian/German terms, the Italian indicating tempo and the German the relevant character. (The first movement of his Piano Sonata Op. 101 is marked *Allegretto ma non troppo, Etwas lebhaft und mit der innigsten Empfindung*).

The invention of the metronome eased many problems of tempo determination, but raised other issues, as metronome marks are not necessarily suitable to all conditions and circumstances. The metronome indications for specific works by Mozart remembered by some of his younger contemporaries appear to have limited value;[68] and while Beethoven attached great significance to his metronome markings, some have given cause for doubt – many are substantially faster than the fastest tempi taken nowadays for the same works – and his substitute markings for those he lost were often quite different, causing him intense irritation when the originals were found.[69] Brahms, like Mendelssohn before him, concluded that 'the metronome is of no value. As far at least as my experience goes, everybody has, sooner or later, withdrawn his metronome marks. Those which can be found in my works – good friends have talked me into putting them there, for I myself have never believed that my blood and a mechanical instrument go well together. The so-called "elastic tempo" is moreover not a new invention. "Con discrezione" should be added to that as to many other things.'[70] At best, metronome markings serve as useful guides to a tempo which will realise the character of the music. However, even in the twentieth century, early recordings indicate that metronome and other detailed tempo instructions were sometimes contradicted in composers' own performances of their works.[71]

Brahms was perfectly correct in claiming that there was nothing new about 'elastic tempo'. Such flexibility was a vital element in Baroque and Classical performance practices, even in the 'new music' of the Italian monodists at the turn of the sixteenth and seventeenth centuries and in Baroque recitative (in which the meaning of the text guided the ebb and flow of the performance), allowing some freedom of expressive effect within the outlines of the pulse. François Couperin, for example, notes some confusion between 'time, or measure, with what is called cadence or movement. Measure defines the number and time value of beats; cadence is properly the spirit, the soul which must be added to it.'[72] Furthermore, Quantz advocates a style of performance which 'should be easy and flowing', irrespective of the difficulties involved.[73] Over a century later, Wagner claims that 'in classical music written in the later style modification of tempo is a *sine qua non*',[74] and his particular concept of tempo flexibility influenced Hans von Bülow, Mahler and numerous other early twentieth-century musicians. Elgar stated that his works should be performed 'elastically and mystically' and not 'squarely and . . . like a wooden box',[75] and early recordings confirm that his flexibility of tempo went far beyond the copious annotations in his scores. More recent performing trends have witnessed a narrowing in the range and a tighter control of such flexibility.

The chief means of achieving freedom for expressive melodic effect (as opposed to overall tempo) was tempo rubato (literally 'stolen time'), an expression first coined by Tosi (1723) for a technique introduced centuries earlier during the Middle Ages and Renaissance.[76] Interlinked with principles of accentuation and often regarded as a species of ornament, it seems to have been applied eventually to four different expressive techniques, the most common involving a natural flexibility of the prescribed rhythm within a constant tempo, after which the ensemble between melody and accompaniment was restored.[77] The term also extended in certain cases to the modification of dynamics and/or the displacement of natural accents (resulting, for example, in unaccented 'strong' beats of the bar);[78] the expansion of the bar(s) to incorporate more notes than the time-signature theoretically allows, and a flexible yet rhythmically controlled performance of these passages;[79] or flexibility of tempo by introducing arbitrary, unwritten accelerandos or ritardandos.[80]

Czerny's systematic appreciation of the expressive potential of rubato provides perhaps the most informative survey of its range and perceived value;[81] he refers to it as 'perhaps the most important means of Expression'. Like many theorists, he recognises the importance of playing every piece 'from beginning to end, without the least deviation or uncertainty, in the time prescribed by the author, and first fixed upon by the player. But', he continues, without injury to this maxim there occurs almost in every line some notes or passages, where a small and often almost imperceptible relaxation or acceleration of the movement is necessary, to embellish the expression and increase the interest. To introduce these occasional deviations from the strict keeping of the time in a tasteful and intelligible manner, is the great art of a good player; and is only to be acquired by highly cultivated taste, much attentive practice, and by listening to great Artists on all instruments, particularly to distinguished singers.

He lists eleven situations for retarding. Many have structural significance, such as a melodic reprise or a transition to a different rhythmic movement; but introduction of the term 'espressivo' also invites a ritardando and terms such as *rallentando, ritenuto, smorzando* and *calando* 'are only distinguishable from each other by the more or less degree of *ritardando*'. Czerny adds: 'Each single passage expresses some definite passion or emotion; or at least it will admit of some such feeling being infused into it, by the style in which it may be played.' Some 'slight holding back in the time (*calando, smorzando* etc.) may generally be introduced to advantage' when the music suggests such feelings as 'wavering hesitation, tender complaining, tranquil assent, whispering a secret, sighing, and grief'. Some quickening of the time, on the other hand, will reinforce feelings of 'sudden cheerfulness, impatience, unwilling reproach, pride and ill temper'.

Charles Rosen isolates one further kind of rubato typical of the Classical style, resulting from requiring performers to extend 'the limits of harmony' and create artistic effect through harmonic disorder.[82] The second movement of Haydn's String Quartet Op. 54 No. 2 is a prime example, the arabesque of the first violin part (bb. 19ff.) comprising a written-out rubato which delays the expected melodic notes and results in dissonance through enforced harmonic overlapping. As Baillot observes, 'Often a beautiful disorder is an artistic effect';[83] such 'beautiful disorder' became increasingly significant in the performances of Chopin, Liszt and their contemporaries and reached its culmination by the turn of the century, when 'pianists and conductors especially – but, indeed, all performers in general – felt they had a right, if not a duty, to apply all manner of rhythmic flexibilities, and even to alter the composer's score on occasion, in order to achieve their own personal concept of expression'.[84] It is still important today, even if performances tend to be more regular and 'ironed-out' than nearly a century ago.

Rhythmic alteration

Tempo rubato, accentuation and other expressive practices naturally require remarkable flexibility of interpretation, involving slight modifications in the prescribed rhythms; but three particular Baroque conventions involved more radical alterations to notated rhythms, and their implementation has caused much controversy and confusion. These relate to the exaggeration of already dotted rhythms, known as 'overdotting', the practice of assimilating clashing rhythms and the French tradition of inequality (*notes inégales*).

Overdotting

Thurston Dart's claim that the execution of most dotted rhythms in music from the seventeenth to the late nineteenth centuries should be exaggerated sparked a protracted debate between scholars, particularly between Frederick Neumann and David Fuller.[85] Most of the evidence for this general practice of overdotting emanates from mid eighteenth-century German theorists and is relevant largely to German and Italian music. Agricola declares that 'Short notes after a dot, either semiquavers or demisemiquavers, or in ¢, quavers . . . are always played very short and at the very end of their value', while C. P. E. Bach states: 'Short notes which follow dotted ones are always shorter in execution than their notated length.' Leopold Mozart writes: 'Dotted notes must be held somewhat longer, but the time taken up by the extended value must be . . . stolen from the note standing after the dot'; he notates the manner of execution 'by setting down two dots followed by a shortened note'.[86] Similar advice was given to the execution of the short notes in 'Lombard rhythm'.

Overdotting was most commonly applied in the 'French overture', a genre cultivated not only by Frenchmen but also by many German composers, notably Bach and Handel. Additional to its sharply dotted manner of execution were its characteristic *tirades*, fast ascending or descending scale passages connecting two principal melody notes, which contributed to its energetic and majestic qualities. These were generally played as rapidly and

Ex. 3.10 Modification of duplets and dotted figures to accommodate triplets, as illustrated by C. P. E. Bach, *Versuch*, III, 27

as late as possible and with each note separately articulated, depending, of course, on the prevalent tempo and affect.[87] When two parts have simultaneous dotted figures of different note-values (e.g. two dotted-quaver–semiquaver figures against one dotted-crotchet–quaver), it was usual to overdot the latter to synchronise its quaver with the other part's final semiquaver.

Rhythmic synchronisation

The synchronisation of clashing binary and ternary rhythms in Baroque music is generally appropriate when duplets are set against triplets and dotted figures are set against triplets or sextuplets. Evidence for the practice is sparse and open to differing interpretation, but most eighteenth-century theorists who mention it require duplets and dotted figures to be modified to accommodate triplets when both appear simultaneously, as in Ex. 3.10. However, Agricola's claim that J. S. Bach taught his pupils to play such rhythms as notated, 'otherwise the difference between duple metre . . . and 3/8, 6/8, 9/8 and 12/8 would be eliminated' should be contemplated, along with the possibility that, in some instances, the triplets might be modified to synchronise with the duplets.[88] Where the two rhythms appear successively, each case must be assessed individually and a tasteful, musicianly solution sought. The third movement of J. S. Bach's Violin Sonata BWV 1017 includes dotted figures, triplets and evenly notated duplets (Ex. 3.11); it is likely that the duplets were synchronised with the triplets and the semiquavers played exactly as notated.

The execution of common Baroque notated rhythms such as 𝄴 ♩♪♪♪ | ♩ or 𝄴 ♪| ♪♪♪ ♩ also requires careful consideration, many performers opting for shortening the 'upbeat' note immediately following the rest and matching its rhythm with the short note in the subsequent dotted figure thus: 𝄴 ♩♪♪♪ | ♩ or 𝄴 ♪| ♪♪♪ ♩. While this is often the most appropriate and practical solution – as, for example, in 'Surely He hath Borne our Griefs' from Handel's *Messiah* – to advance any definitive ruling for such cases

Ex. 3.11 J. S. Bach, Violin Sonata in C minor BWV 1017, iii, bb. 13–16

would be to eliminate the possibility, preferable in our view, of preserving the notated quaver upbeat in, say, 'Behold the Lamb of God' from the same work.

Notes inégales

Much ink has been spilt over the French convention of *notes inégales*, which is still the subject of debate despite the excellent work of, in particular, David Fuller and Stephen Hefling.[89] This expressive practice is outlined in numerous French, Spanish and Italian sources of the late seventeenth and early eighteenth centuries, yet no two accounts seem in precise accord, thereby suggesting the importance of individual taste in its application.

The convention of *notes inégales* was generally applied consistently throughout a movement, but might be varied, or even abandoned entirely in accordance with the prevailing expression. Sometimes indicated by the term 'pointer' or 'inégaliser', but often not prescribed at all, it related most commonly to the alternate lengthening and shortening (or, less commonly, shortening and lengthening) of evenly written successions of conjunct notes, but it sometimes extended to notated dotted figures. The longer notes fall in the stronger accentual positions (e.g. in a group of four notes that start on the beat, the first and third are longer than the second and fourth) and are normally *half* the length of the basic metric pulse. Thus in 3/2 metre, successions of crotchets might be subject to the convention (although cases may be made for quavers, as is the case in 6/4); and in 3/8, 4/8, 6/8, 9/8, 12/8 the semiquaver is the value modified. But such a rule was not without exception, because in slow common time (¢, c and 4/4) the semiquaver (as opposed to the quaver) was normally (though not invariably) the value made unequal; and in 3/4 metre either the quaver (for fast tempos) or semiquaver (for slower pieces with semiquaver movement) was possible. 'Underlying all these rules', writes Fuller, 'was the assumption that the principal unit of melodic movement in a piece corresponded to the theoretically unequal one for that metre. Where the principal moving value was smaller, as was the case with courantes in 3/2, which moved in quavers more often than in crotchets, it was the smaller value that became unequal.'[90] The degree of inequality introduced was left to the performer according to the tempo and character of the music. The more energetic the music, the more pronounced would the inequality normally have been – a range from 'the barely perceptible to the equivalent of double dotting' has been suggested.[91] Inequality was never applied when notes were slurred or dotted; when any of the instructions *notes égales, marqué,* or *croches égales* was given; when dots or strokes were placed over notes that would otherwise be played unequally (the dots signified equality, while strokes indicated equal, staccato notes); when the notes moved by leap; or with repeated notes.

Although readers should be wary of applying this convention to pre-Classical music of all nationalities and periods, as some scholars have advocated, there are good cases for its employment in some seventeenth- and early eighteenth-century English music (e.g. by Purcell, Locke and others) and possibly even in German and Italian music in a French style.[92] However, as Fuller remarks, 'Possible local exceptions aside, we must assume that musicians outside France would not normally dot undotted passages and that composers who particularly desired the effect of *notes inégales* (or any other style of persistent dotting) would write dots', at least as initial guidance for performers.[93] Nevertheless, performers must not 'deny composers the possibility of shifting in and out of dotted rhythm if that was their intention'.

Although theorists ceased to discuss *notes inégales* towards the end of the eighteenth century, the convention persisted into the following century, as the evidence of barrel organs and other automatic instruments testifies. However, the increasing trend from the late eighteenth century onwards was for composers to notate their rhythmic requirements with greater unanimity and precision.

Ornamentation

As instructions regarding the execution of specific ornaments vary greatly, only a broad survey will be attempted here.[94] The essential ornaments, comprising primarily the appoggiatura, mordent, trill and turn, served not only as additional embellishment to a preconceived melody but essentially formed an organic part of that melody. C. P. E. Bach considers embellishments 'indispensable . . . they connect and enliven tones and impart stress and accent; they make music pleasing and awaken our close attention. Expression is heightened by them; let a piece be sad, joyful, or otherwise, and they will lend a fitting assistance. Embellishments provide opportunities for fine performance as well as much of its subject matter. They improve mediocre compositions. Without them the best melody is empty and ineffective, the clearest content clouded.'[95]

During the late seventeenth and early eighteenth centuries the use of symbols to indicate conventional ornaments increased, especially in France and North Germany. Many French composers (particularly of keyboard music) published tables of ornaments in which the signs were realised in conventional notation (e.g. D'Anglebert's *Pièces de clavecin* (1689)), demanding (but apparently not always getting) a more literal adherence to the text. François Couperin complains, in the preface to his third book of harpsichord pieces (1722): 'I am always surprised, after the pains that I have taken to indicate the ornaments appropriate to my pieces . . . to hear people who have learnt them without heeding my instructions. Such carelessness is unpardonable, all the more as it is no arbitrary matter to put in such ornaments as one wishes. Therefore I declare that my pieces must be performed just as I have written them and that they will never make much of an impression on people of genuine taste unless all my markings are observed to the letter.'

Obligatory ornaments such as the cadential trill, demanded by convention and context, were not always notated, especially in most non-keyboard music,[96] and the general sign (+ or ×) was employed to indicate the possible incidence of some embellishment, the exact detail of which was undefined and left to the performer, according to mood, tempo and genre. Signs with more specific intentions were also employed, many with implied interpretative formulae relating to expression, nuance, emphasis and rhythmic subtleties. Unreliable calligraphy, ambiguous indications,[97] casual performance, inconsistent terminology employed by theorists and a variety of different regional and personal styles combine to paint a confusing picture, from which a definitive interpretation of the *minutiae* of ornaments, often so subtle and flexible in rhythm and pitch that they defy expression in ordinary musical notation, is largely impracticable.

During the second half of the eighteenth century the three main channels of ornamental theory and practice – the French, German and Italian – gradually merged into some measure of general agreement.[98] The French school's complex system of symbols was adopted with increasing thoroughness and consistency in some German schools. This was mainly the work of Quantz, Marpurg, Agricola and especially C. P. E. Bach, who, amidst the emerging homophonic *style galant*, modified and extended French practices into a more international language of ornaments governed by the *Affektenlehre*. This language was more harmonic than melodic, hence the quest for 'das vermischte Geschmack', a combination of the best qualities of Italian, French and German types of ornamentation.[99] Without cataloguing signs and contexts for every ornamental figure available to the performer, C. P. E. Bach's *Versuch* became a model for numerous subsequent treatises on the subject, even though his *theoretical* inflexibility of ornamentation practice contradicts the nature and function of ornament itself. Most of his contemporary compatriots were more flexible in approach and some national schools, particularly the Italian, still left ornamentation largely to the spontaneous invention of the performer.

By the end of the eighteenth century, the extraordinary variety of interpretations of ornaments and the increasing idiosyncrasy of many composers' styles resulted in a developing trend for ornaments to be indicated as precisely as possible (e.g. by showing the exact value of appoggiaturas). A minimum of signs was used and all complex ornaments were written out as fully as possible (either in normal-sized notes as an integral part of the rhythmic scheme, in small notes extra-rhythmically, or in a compromise between the two), in such a way that their interpretation, apart from a certain rhythmic freedom, could not be doubted.[100] Wagner, for example, used the symbol for the turn in his early works, but wrote out that ornament in various forms in his later music.

A great deal of selection and taste needs to be exercised in the 'replication' of earlier approaches to ornamentation, and period performers should consider some or all of the following questions when seeking to interpret a particular ornament in a manner commensurate with the music: On what note should the ornament begin? Should it start before, on or after the beat? How fast should any repercussion be? What are the harmonic implications and how long should the dissonance (if any) last? How flexibly should the ornament be executed? Should nuances be added? Is the introduction of accidentals necessary? How should the ornament be terminated? Answers to these questions will inevitably vary according to the style, character and nationality of the music, the context and the type of ornament, and the views of those theorists whose treatises are deemed most relevant to its interpretation; but it is imperative that answers are sought and carefully considered in appropriate contexts if an informed performance is to evolve.

Extempore embellishment

Extempore embellishment was practised in varying degrees and in different forms, according largely to date, venue, individual preferences and national styles.[101] Extempore embellishment of a melody involved the performer in the free and usually spontaneous addition of melodic figures that were too variable to be indicated satisfactorily by signs – 'arbitrary' (*willkührlich*) ornaments, as Quantz calls them – as well as some of the conventional stereotyped ornaments such as trills, appoggiaturas and mordents (Quantz's 'essential' (*wesentlich*) ornaments). Melodic embellishment was confined in theory (though apparently not always in practice)[102] to solo contexts or passages of ensemble music in which a solo texture prevails. An understanding of harmony as the basic foundation of the melody to be embellished was a pre-requisite.

Of varying national Baroque styles, the French approach, in which essential ornaments were generally specifically indicated and arbitrary ones played little part, contrasted with the Italian manner, which admitted both categories of ornament but only seldom with indication as to their application. Italian influence was predominant in the German compromise but was tempered by a more selective and expressive use of ornaments (both essential and arbitrary) in keeping with the doctrine of the affections, especially by the North German school. C. P. E. Bach deliberately refrains from detailed discussion of improvised ornamentation, arguing that its implementation is too variable to classify and that it was becoming customary in his circles to write out such embellishment in full.[103]

Increasing foreign influence both before and after the revolution prompted significant changes in the French style. The Italian style was championed by Rousseau and his followers; a French translation of Tartini's treatise on ornamentation appeared in 1771; Viotti settled in Paris; and Italian music infiltrated French publications such as Cartier's *L'art du violon* (1798), disseminating further the Italian style. Framery confirms that French musicians tended to invent ornaments rather more than previously,[104] even though French composers still consistently specified their 'essential' ornaments, thus setting limits to the play of free ornamentation. The German compromise persisted to some extent in the late eighteenth century; however, because of their selective and expressive approach towards ornamentation, German musicians had begun well before 1750 to notate precisely the interpretative details of their compositions and thus write fairly fully ornamented melodies, as exemplified in the opening movement of J. S. Bach's Solo Sonata in G minor (BWV 1001) and in many of his instrumental obbligatos. Thus, the performer's freedom to embellish was severely limited, essentially restricting such opportunities to the varied reprise, as demonstrated in C. P. E. Bach's *Sechs Sonaten . . . mit veränderten Reprisen* (Berlin, 1760).[105]

The design and content of the melodic elaborations are impossible to catalogue in detail because of the wide range of styles and approaches employed. However, guidance is at hand from certain eighteenth-century works which have survived with embellishments added – for example, the various available embellished versions of Corelli's Op. 5 violin sonatas;[106] the *Zwölf Methodische Sonaten für Violine oder Flöte und Basso Continuo* by Telemann (Hamburg, 1728 and 1732); C. P. E. Bach's *Sechs Sonaten . . .* (1760) and his *Kurze und leichte Klavierstücke mit veränderten Reprisen* (Berlin, 1766, 1768); the celebrated castrato Luigi Marchesi's fourteen different embellished versions of a theme by Cherubini[107] and Franz Benda's 32 three-movement sonatas for violin and bass (composed before 1763). These works represent a surer guide to extempore ornamental practice than most contemporary treatises.

Extempore elaborations were most prolific in slow movements, especially those written in the 'skeletal outline' manner of the Italian style; but they were by no means excluded from quick movements and they also helped to sustain musical interest in repeated sections: for example, in binary form movements in which each section is repeated; in ternary form or da capo

Ex. 3.12 F. Benda, Violin Sonata No. 27, Allegretto bb. 1–2

arias in which the first 'A' section was repeated; in rondo refrains; in recapitulations of sonata-form movements; and in the concerto soloist's repetitions of tutti material. The elaborations ranged from the inclusion of merely a few trills and appoggiaturas to a complete re-working of the entire structure. Generally, however, the embellished versions comprise a balanced variety of note-values and rhythms, exploiting some patterns consistently as a means of unification. They adhere closely to the overall melodic contour of the original, its salient structural points (cadences, principal notes, phrases etc.) being emphasised through the addition of both stereotyped ornaments (such as appoggiaturas, trills, turns and mordents) and ornamental figures such as Leopold Mozart's *battement, ribattuta, groppo, tirata*, and *mezzo circulo*, passage-work of varying kinds or even simple arpeggios, especially at the approach to a cadence or modulation.[108] Other methods of elaboration included use of upper and lower auxiliary notes, simple passing notes, single note repetitions, two- or three-note *Schleifer*, and scale passages normally of no more than an octave span, the latter figures generally filling in the intervals between the notes of the given melody, especially descending leaps.

In more isolated cases, and then generally at cadences, the melodic outline may be temporarily distorted and dissolved into smaller note values faithful only to the harmonic constitution of the original. The reverse process was also exploited, involving the lengthening of note-values and condensing of melodic figuration (Ex. 3.12) in addition to a type of tempo rubato, featuring either rhythmic displacement (Ex. 3.13) or the accommodation of an irregular grouping of notes within the bar (Ex. 3.14). Tempo rubato and changes of articulation, dynamic, rhythm and phrasing also played their part in the embellishing process, Rousseau even including 'breaking the voice', 'bleating' and 'screeching' in his 'goût du chant'.[109] However, the singer's declamation should never be impaired.

Performers generally aimed to achieve a cumulative ornamental effect, a

Ex. 3.13 F. Benda, Violin Sonata No. 18, Allegro non molto, bb. 57–9

Ex. 3.14 F. Benda, Violin Sonata No. 8, Tempo di menuetto, bb. 25–8

melody normally being performed as written or very simply on its first occurrence and its variations, attendant sequences or repeated passages becoming increasingly more elaborate at each recurrence. Extempore embellishment also demonstrated the performer's virtuosity; but it also served an expressive role and, certainly towards the end of the eighteenth century, was intended to be kept within the bounds of discretion. Hiller, for example, compared graces to spices in cooking – necessary ingredients which could spoil a dish if added to excess or without due taste.[110] His views on embellishing recitatives accord with this sentiment; he recommends little or no embellishment (only occasional mordents and *Pralltriller*) in 'secco' recitative but allows more ornamental expression in the pathetic recitatives immediately preceding the expressive arias of the 'scenas'. The introduction of a brief melisma at the last cadence of a recitative was normal practice.

Despite theorists' recommendations, some performers, especially Italians, indulged in the addition of excessive and over-florid embellishment, which was in bad taste and in the final reckoning injurious to the overall musical effect. Singers such as the castrato Farinelli were often the worst offenders, encouraged by the kind of view expressed as late as 1810 by Domenico Corri: 'The singer ought to observe that the repetition of words by the composer was no doubt intended for the purpose of giving the singer an opportunity for that display of ornament, which on their first utterance even common sense forbids, and it was from this consideration, that the Da Capo in airs was first introduced, which allows the singer every latitude or ornament consistent with the rules of harmony, and the character of the composition.'[111] Tartini's *Adagio varié* published by Cartier as a supplement to his *L'art du violon* provides examples of complex embellishment, which otherwise comply fully with the general principles of melodic elaboration described above.

Such exaggerated practices, along with stylistic and social changes and the desire to reproduce the proper affect, were responsible for the marked increase in written-out embellishment. With the advent of the high Classical style, the performer's freedom of extensive improvised ornamentation was curtailed, even though we learn that Mozart and Beethoven varied their ornamental figuration in performance, especially in their slow movements.[112] Nevertheless, both Haydn and Mozart left interesting examples of 'extempore' embellishment, notably ornamented versions of arias in Haydn's *Il ritorno di Tobia* (1775) and Mozart's *Lucio Silla* (1772), as well as examples of fully written-out ornamentation which restricted the performer's freedom (e.g. Mozart's Rondo in A minor K511). Certainly by the beginning of the nineteenth century a more or less international approach towards ornamentation had emerged and composers generally endeavoured to indicate their intentions as precisely as possible, using a minimum number of signs and defining clearly any complex or unfamiliar embellishments in the few cases required by the 'complete' melodies of the time.[113] Even Italian opera composers like Rossini, realising the tasteless ornamental excesses of singers such as Luigi Marchesi, began to write out ornamentation in his operas; and although singers persisted with the addition of their own embellishments, such additions became less important as an expressive and dramatic tool.

An equivocal attitude also reigned in instrumental music, which on the one hand recognised the necessity and value of tasteful ornamentation in order to emphasise and articulate structure, and on the other attempted to control the practice, inhibiting the interpretative freedom of the performer and allowing the composer to emerge as the dominant partner. Such extempore embellishment in sonata-form recapitulations proved largely superfluous on structural grounds in the Classical style, Rosen claiming that

CHANGES IN MUSICAL STYLE

it becomes 'an actual embarrassment'. He continues: 'The idea of the reca-pitulation as a dramatic reinterpretation of the exposition attacks the prac-tice of decoration at its root: the structure itself now does the work of the improvised ornaments.'[114] Nevertheless, Ferdinand David, when leading his string quartet in the 1830s, was renowned for his addition of enterprising embellishments to the recapitulations in Haydn's quartets, and Spohr praises the manner in which the younger Eck embellished 'the poorest spots' of a quartet by Krommer with 'the most tasteful of flourishes'.[115]

Improvisation

The eighteenth and early nineteenth centuries witnessed the culmi-nation of the art of improvisation (especially at the keyboard), whether in the form of preludes, cadenzas, Eingänge, the semi-improvisational aspects of continuo realisation (even by the soloist during the orchestral ritornellos of Classical keyboard concertos)[116] or the type of independent extemporisa-tion for which Bach, Handel, Mozart and Beethoven, among others, were renowned. Particularly crucial to historical performers, however, is the appropriate and tasteful interpretation of fermatas. Their meaning could range from a straightforward prolongation, at the performer's will, of the note, chord or rest thus indicated to improvised embellishment of that note or chord in a manner appropriate to the prevalent character; they could even denote an extended cadenza.[117] Despite the availability of somewhat pro-vocative modern cadenzas for various Classical concertos and interesting examples from eminent composers of the Romantic eras,[118] it is naturally desirable that the style and content of the cadenza should not conflict with those of the work or movement.

Cadenzas, passages or sections of variable length and indefinite form, were normally extemporised by performers but were sometimes written out (e.g. by Caccini in 'Io che dal ciel cader' (1589), or by Torelli in the passages headed 'Perfidia' in some of his concerto movements,[119] or by Corelli in his various written-out *points d'orgue* above the *tasto solo* bass in some of his Op. 5 sonatas), perhaps even playing a fully integrated part in the structure of the movement (as in the harpsichord 'cadenza' in the first move-ment of Bach's Fifth Brandenburg Concerto). Derived from the vocal aria as a natural result of ornamenting cadences,[120] a cadenza was generally

introduced near the end of a composition or movement (normally a concerto or aria, but sometimes in sonatas)[121] on a pause either on the dominant of the key, or, in the case of Classical concertos, somewhat
inconclusively on the tonic six-four chord. The normal place for a cadenza in
a da capo aria was towards the end of the reprise of the da capo section, but
the end of the middle section often offered another, and sometimes the only,
possibility for the singer's improvised liberties. Tosi's recommended limit of
one cadenza per aria, however, was evidently ignored by many singers.[122]

Concerto cadenzas normally ended with a trill on the dominant chord
prior to the orchestral re-entry; in the eighteenth century, they tended to
serve as much to demonstrate the performer's musicianship and tasteful
expression as his technical prowess.[123] From Quantz's observation of the
French style that little can be added to what the composer has written,[124] it
appears that the introduction of cadenzas in eighteenth-century French
music was restricted largely to works in the Italian style. Certainly, cadenzas
were omitted from most Parisian Classical concertos and symphonies con-
certantes.

Although preceded by Tosi's rather limited survey, Quantz's account is the
first extensive discussion of cadenzas, serving as a model for Türk's and
many later studies.[125] Tartini also provides basic guidelines regarding
cadenza construction which held wide currency, especially with singers. His
recommended design involves starting with a *messa di voce, passaggii* or a
trill, continuing with metrically free, generally fast passage-work, and pro-
gressing by step or leap to a note high in the register prior to the final trill on
the supertonic.[126]

Quantz was the first writer to expand the largely ornamental early eighteenth-century concept of the cadenza, comprising normally non-thematic
elaborations of the final cadence, into a more meaningful part of the musical
design, recommending that cadenzas should be constructed from the main
motifs of the movement.[127] Although there was no uniformity of opinion
about the need for motivic pertinence in eighteenth-century cadenzas,
Mozart's keyboard cadenzas from the early 1780s normally incorporate
some thematic/motivic connection with the relevant movement. The length
of cadenzas depended to some extent on the solo instrument, Quantz claiming that 'a string player can make them as long as he likes, if he is rich enough
in inventiveness', but advising singers and wind players to make their caden-

zas last no longer than a single breath. Hiller was alone in disagreeing with this limitation for singers,[128] while wind players might be better advised to heed Quantz's view that 'Reasonable brevity . . . is more advantageous than vexing length.'[129] Robert Levin has calculated that Mozart's extant keyboard cadenzas are approximately ten per cent of the length of the relevant movement.[130]

The Classical and early Romantic eras witnessed an expansion in the scope of the cadenza. It was normally of meaningful musical substance and fulfilled an architectural function, with its climactic passage for the soloist balancing the orchestral exposition in the concerto structure, as well as the dramatic one of allowing the soloist free rein for unfettered solo display. Some cadenzas were written out by composers either for use in performance (as in Mozart's Piano Concerto K488) or as models for students to imitate, notably those by Mozart for some of his other piano concertos.[131] Mozart's cadenzas display great variety and imagination in their use of pertinent melodic material, most adopting a tripartite design (with the exception of some second and third movement examples). The first (and largest) subdivision commences either with one of the principal themes of the movement (e.g. K453, first movement) or with an energetic flourish (which may also have thematic affinities; e.g. K271, first movement) emanating from the six-four chord. This is followed by a more reflective section, often derived from the secondary group of themes, involving sequence and passing through (but rarely establishing) a variety of close keys. A descent to a sustained chord or long note in the lower register eventually serves as a point of departure for further technical display, incorporating scales, arpeggios and suchlike, prior to the brief, normally non-thematic closing transition to the final cadential trill on the dominant seventh.[132]

The early nineteenth century witnessed further developments, Beethoven's approach changing from preserving the tradition of cadenza improvisation in, for example, his Piano Concerto No. 2 and his Violin Concerto Op. 61,[133] to providing specimen cadenzas for Concertos Nos. 1, 3 and 4 (and eventually No. 2) and including a quasi-cadenza as an integral part of his Fifth Piano Concerto Op. 73 ('The Emperor'). Beethoven's extant cadenzas demonstrate a much wider harmonic, tonal and, in some cases, technical vocabulary than those of his predecessors and do not conform to the Classical model described above. Although some nineteenth-century

violinists and singers preferred to attune their cadenzas to their own technical prowess, the increasing trend during the century was for composers to
write out independent cadenzas in full in order either to guard against the
technical excesses of virtuosi or counteract the lack of invention displayed
by contemporary performers at a time when, despite the efforts of Czerny
and others, the art of improvisation was essentially on the decline.[134]

In nineteenth-century German and French opera, opportunities for
unfettered virtuoso display were rare; but improvised embellishment of fermatas remained a significant part of Italian operatic practice up to and
including the early operas of Verdi. Verdi's mature works, which include
only fully written-out cadenzas, signalled the demise of the improvised
cadenza towards the turn of the century.

Eingänge or lead-ins were indicated by fermatas and generally occurred at
imperfect cadences on the dominant or dominant seventh chord and at
perfect cadences in the dominant, mediant or submediant keys. The function of the *Eingang* was to provide a brief non-modulatory transition, generally metrical but in an improvisatory style, into a new section of a work, such
as the refrain of a rondo movement. *Eingänge* usually terminate with a
second fermata, while passages which interlink with the ensuing music
are normally termed *Übergänge*. Rules for formulating lead-ins may be
found in various treatises, notably C. P. E. Bach's *Versuch* . . . and Türk's
Clavierschule,[135] but the use of such passages is no better demonstrated than
in the finale of Mozart's Piano Sonata K333/315c or his Variations on 'Ein
Weib ist das herrlichste Ding' K613, in which an *Eingang* connecting the two
parts of the theme is also subjected to variation.

Mention of the 'vocal' appoggiatura is also pertinent to a discussion of
improvisation, as this involves additions to the written notation. It was most
commonly used in recitatives from the Baroque to the early nineteenth
century, but was also applicable in arias and ariosos. It gave expressive
emphasis to strong syllables at various cadences, whether passing or final,
whose ending is notated as two repeated notes. The intended execution,
however, involves an (often disjunct) appoggiatura and its resolution, as in
Ex. 3.15. Hansell has suggested that in such cases the appoggiatura was
doubled by an acciaccatura in the continuo keyboard accompaniment;[136] a
quick 4-3 suspension might provide a more likely and stylish alternative. As
recitatives became increasingly more elaborate during the first half of the

Ex. 3.15 Some instances of the 'vocal appoggiatura' as illustrated by G. P. Telemann, *Cantatas* (Leipzig, 1725), Preface

nineteenth century, composers tended to indicate precisely the notes to be sung. Interestingly, the appoggiatura from below, demonstrated as a possible solution by Classical theorists but comparatively rarely employed, seems to have gained more credibility in early Romantic recitative when associated with a question in the text.

Will Crutchfield raises a further issue regarding the addition of appoggiaturas, this time in the middle of melodic phrases and on top of notes that already function as appoggiaturas.[137] He claims that these appoggiaturas were most prevalent in music with German texts, 'perhaps because the language's relative paucity of feminine endings yielded fewer "natural" appoggiaturas than were present in the Italian singing that served as a model'. Crutchfield also mentions the 'divided appoggiatura', which appears to be peculiar to German sources.

Continuo accompaniment

As we noted in Chapter 2, the provision of an accompaniment from a thoroughbass is essential to most Baroque solo and ensemble performance. The practice had its origins in the sixteenth century when it was common for harpsichordists, organists and lutenists to double singers in both secular and sacred music, largely for practical reasons of ensemble, tuning and substituting for missing personnel. It came to prominence in published form in early seventeenth-century operas, secular monodies and sacred concerti by composers such as Viadana, Peri, Caccini and Cavalieri. It may be looked upon as a branch of improvisation practice, the player complying with the given bass line and harmony (normally outlined by a figured bass but sometimes inferred from the score) and supplying an extempore accompaniment to support and sometimes enhance the main melodic material.

The sources for continuo accompaniment during the seventeenth and eighteenth centuries are many and varied, comprising theoretical treatises on continuo realisation, independent keyboard tutors, surviving examples of written-out continuo parts and critical reviews of continuo performances.[138] The treatises concern themselves chiefly with the rudiments of harmony and emphasise accuracy, discretion and fluency of harmonic support in accompaniment. Few give examples of best practice or subtleties of style in realising a given bass-line,[139] and most are unhelpful in providing answers to questions regarding the appositeness of adding an accompaniment in certain repertories, especially those which lack bass figuring. David Fuller points out that it has been established only comparatively recently that Bach's motets, which lack a figured bass, were performed with harpsichord and string bass instrument in Leipzig;[140] yet 'the overtures, dances and other orchestral pieces in French opera from Lully to Rameau, long assumed to require a continuo, are now thought to have been performed without accompaniment'.[141]

The instruments used for thoroughbass accompaniment differed according to period, genre, nationality and even locality. They were only occasionally indicated by composers, so performers are often required to make decisions regarding the most suitable ones to use for the particular work, circumstances and musical forces involved. Early seventeenth-century Italian operas, for example, generally involved a lavish variety of chordal accompanying instruments such as harpsichords, organs, lutes, chitarroni, theorbos, harps, lironi, and guitars, as well as one or more melodic instruments,[142] while a chitarrone (without viol) was popular for solo songs of the period. Organ continuo was naturally pre-eminent in church performances,[143] many parts being designated as 'basso per l'organo', but the organ was also used in other contexts, notably in seventeenth-century English and German consorts and in many eighteenth-century oratorios.[144] By the eighteenth century, a harpsichord (or sometimes chamber organ) with a melodic bass instrument such as a cello, bass viol or sometimes bassoon doubling the bass-line became standard in chamber music. Some of the larger orchestras of the time even included two harpsichords,[145] one combining with a cello and often a double bass to support solo singers or instrumentalists and the other collaborating with a cello, double bass and even a bassoon to underpin the orchestral contribution.[146] In the early seventeenth century, a softly played trombone had been a possible alternative to the violone![147]

The improvisatory aspect of continuo accompaniment differs for each genre, national style, period and individual composer, as well as the venue and other circumstances of performance. Players are required to make instinctive decisions regarding taste and style; these range from questions of texture, arpeggiation, register, harmonic syntax (including the avoidance of consecutive fifths and octaves), appropriate recitative treatment and the introduction of dissonant notes or *acciaccature*,[148] to how much (if at all) to double the melody, whether to double fugal entries, how much imitation or ornamentation should be added, or whether or not to delay cadences in recitative.[149]

The various different instruments in use inevitably resulted in a variety of approaches to continuo accompaniment. These practices are investigated within the complementary series of handbooks to this volume.[150] Realisation in four parts was probably the most common type of simple keyboard accompaniment, but many theorists held more inventive aspirations, whether these involved an ornamental role, adding to rather than providing the basic harmonies and improvising melodies and imitations, or whether they were concerned with textural contrast for expressive interest, volume being varied by the number of notes played and the speed of arpeggiation.[151] Different national idioms also enter the equation,[152] the often richly decorative, flamboyant Italian approaches (e.g. in seventeenth-century sonatas for violin and basso continuo or trio sonatas) contrasting sharply, for example, with the largely circumspect early French styles. With organ accompaniment, stops were drawn discreetly, louder passages being realised more through increased texture than change of registration; and German theorists and instruments appear to have allowed greater variety of dynamic than the Italian, often employing two manuals (one louder than the other) and encouraging the use of pedals.

Approaches to recitative accompaniment also differed considerably, variants involving instruments, texture, harmony, arpeggiation and chord repetition, as well as issues of genre and many other factors which directly affected the continuo players' freedom. Approaches to the constantly changing styles and textures of unmeasured solo recitatives in early seventeenth-century opera and oratorio (on harpsichord) contrast markedly with, for example, recitatives in J. S. Bach's sacred music (involving the organ). In such recitatives, the bass notes were sometimes written in tied semibreves and minims; but, as we shall find in the Bach case study in Chapter 5, evidence suggests that the figured chords were played short and the next chord played (also short) only at the change of harmony, thereby liberating the singer and allowing the words to be more easily audible.[153] Evidence for not sustaining the notated chord durations in recitative also exists for eighteenth-century Italian opera and in the treatises of numerous theorists from Heinichen and Mattheson through to C. P. E. Bach, Petri and Türk, but it is unclear whether the bass line itself should be sustained or also played short.

Just as many keyboard treatises included instruction on the rules of harmony and thoroughbass, so various tutors for the guitar, lute, harp and cello discussed continuo playing, some cello treatises even encouraging cellists to indulge in filling out the bass line where musically appropriate and generally in the absence of a keyboard instrument. Baumgartner's *Instructions de musique, théorique et pratique, à l'usage du violoncelle* (The Hague, 1774), for example, provides general advice as to how cellists should adapt chords to suit the prevailing harmonic movement, while Baudiot's treatise focuses on the accompaniment of recitatives and Romberg's concentrates more on cultivating chamber music skills and provides an étude to demonstrate figured bass realisation.[154]

During the first half of the eighteenth century many composers began to thin out musical textures. Some dispensed altogether with keyboard accompaniment, while others omitted to provide a figured bass part for the keyboard player (e.g. in some French chamber music of the 1730s). The *tasto solo* direction became more common and German theorists such as Daube and Petri objected to the use of a basso continuo in trios and quartets.[155] On the other hand, the presence of keyboard continuo in Haydn's symphonic output is still a subject of heated debate, as are the implications of the figured bass lines or such directions as 'col basso' in Mozart's piano concertos.[156]

4   Conditions and practices

Introduction

Throughout history the role and status of musicians have undergone radical changes of emphasis. In the Baroque era employment at court or church was often for life, with changes of position only if an especially tempting offer arose elsewhere. Organists were traditionally the most rigorously trained in matters of musical theory and compositional technique, but the new class of performer involved with instrumental music and opera was also required to extemporise and embellish.[1] Opera singers and (to a lesser extent) instrumental virtuosi began to travel widely and to enjoy great esteem. Meanwhile, chamber music tended to be directed from the keyboard by the composer and was thus characterised by relatively few performance indications. Until around 1700 vocal music enjoyed an almost total supremacy; ensemble sonatas and keyboard toccatas were primarily an adjunct to worship; sinfonias were a preface to opera and oratorio.

During the Classical period ecclesiastical patronage of new music diminished, for economic as well as political reasons.[2] Court and private orchestras also gradually went into decline, though an important outlet for chamber music and smaller-scale pieces remained the private concert. Opera retained its extreme popularity even as the public concert gathered momentum and the symphony increased in size and status. After a lifetime at court, Haydn achieved great success in London in the 1790s as a freelance musician, and this was the model for many of his nineteenth-century successors. Musical priorities after 1800 moved in the direction of the symphony orchestra and music drama. A new reverence for virtuosity was nourished by the European institutions which revolutionised the teaching of music in the wake of the foundation of the Paris Conservatoire in 1795. The age of mechanisation and the railway allowed all kinds of new career possibilities for the musician, while inducing the need for standardisation in matters such as pitch, stimulating playing levels and bringing about greater integration of style and dissemination of new repertory. The rise of self-governing philharmonic societies and orchestras coincided with multifarious developments in instrument manufacture, which opened up new vistas in terms of sonority and technique. Patronage was continued by minor nobles, as symbolised by the relationship of Ludwig II of Bavaria and Richard Wagner. Meanwhile, developments in recording following Edison's tinfoil phonograph of 1877 were shortly to allow opportunities to compare and contrast different interpretations of the same piece.

How did music sound in earlier times? No amount of research into musical conditions and practices can give an unambiguous indication of the original effect. Written descriptions of concert standards within reviews are notoriously difficult to interpret. A famous example is Burney's description of the Mannheim orchestra as 'an army of generals, equally fit to plan a battle, as to fight it'; for he qualified his enthusiasm with a criticism of the wind tuning, whose sourness was reckoned by him to be a universal orchestral problem.[3] In fact, we are bound nowadays to interpret selectively some of the more wayward portrayals of musical standards if our aim is to recreate the best of what has gone before. For example, we shall probably want to ignore the celebrated account of the Lyons orchestra in 1785–6, whose problems were surely not unique. It is reported that the leader had neither intelligence nor an accurate style of performance and that there were unauthorised absences among his colleagues for reasons which we should now regard as paltry.[4] Most concerts (unlike opera) could usually count on only one rehearsal and sometimes there were none.[5] In these circumstances a composer such as Beethoven raised special challenges because he manifestly composed for ideal rather than actual situations. He was making unfamiliar technical and stylistic demands on individual orchestral musicians at a time when conditions for rehearsal and performance were unfavourable, as a result of social and political as well as musical factors.

Pitch

The establishment of historically accurate pitch levels is a complex matter, since the evidence is often elusive and imprecise. However, there can be no doubt that pitch has been unrealistically standardised in recent historical performance, with its almost exclusive focus upon a'=392 Hz (French

Baroque), a′=415 Hz (general Baroque), a′=430 Hz (Classical) and a′=435 Hz or 440 Hz (Romantic). This is no more than a convenient and over-simplified response to the evidence, even though the degree of acceptable compromise must clearly vary according to musical context. All the documentary information from the early sixteenth century onwards has pitch levels spanning an interval of no more than a fifth, a limitation presumably imposed by the basic range of the human voice.[6] But within this frame there are numerous inconsistencies which have proved controversial.

A common approach before 1800 is encapsulated in Aaron's instructions of 1523 for tuning the harpsichord. He proposed initially setting C to whatever pitch one pleased, illustrating the indefinite relationship between notation and pitch then prevalent. But other sources regretted the lack of a pitch standard, notably Praetorius (1619). In 1752 Quantz could still lament the lack of a uniform pitch, which would have enabled him to play a flute with a mere three joints, instead of a variety of *corps de rechange*.[7] He also remarked that the diversity of pitches used for tuning was most detrimental to music in general and expressed the hope that a universal standard would soon find favour. He identified Venetian pitch as the highest, but much preferred German chamber pitch as a compromise between this and its low French counterpart.[8] In 1783 Adlung complained specifically about pitch in relation to the organ; it would vary according to temperature and be imperceptibly raised by the trimming of frayed metal pipes over a number of tunings.[9]

Praetorius called his reference pitch of the organ and most other instruments chamber pitch; choir pitch, for church music, was lower by about a tone, for which few instruments were actually built.[10] Taking into account all the useful but not unambiguous evidence from Praetorius (including his drawings), Cary Karp has concluded that these levels may have been around a′=460 Hz and a′=410 Hz.[11] It seems clear that French Baroque organ music and sacred vocal music was performed at a lower pitch, perhaps below a′=390 Hz. A century after Praetorius, Brook Taylor discovered a formula to specify the pitches of musical instruments numerically, from which it can be calculated that his harpsichord was pitched a little higher than a′=390 Hz.[12] Experiments based on Taylor by Leonhard Euler (1739) and Daniel Bernoulli (1762) suggest similar pitches; commenting on these, the flautist Heinrich Lambert (1775) produced calculations suggesting that his own instrument was at a′ = 415 Hz.[13] If Lambert's pitch anticipates current

Baroque practice, there is also evidence of pitches a little below a′= 410 Hz, for example Joseph Sauveur (Paris, 1713), Christiaan Huygens (late seventeenth-century Amsterdam) and Mattheson (Hamburg, 1762) which may better reflect the general chamber pitch level in the early eighteenth century. Pascal Taskin's tuning fork c. 1780 for the Musique de la Chambre at Versailles was measured in the mid-nineteenth century at a′= 409 Hz.[14]

It has been clearly established that Bach's choir pitch was one tone higher than his chamber pitch, and that on occasion he may have used a second chamber pitch another semitone lower.[15] Indeed, Bach occasionally used the terms 'tiefer Kammerton' or 'hoher Kammerton' in his scores. At the Thomaskirche in Leipzig Bach inherited an organ which had been tuned an exact tone above Kammerton on the instructions of his predecessor Kuhnau; transposition was required and expected in ensemble with other instruments. But at Weimar he had written for a high-pitched organ and in 1720 he played another such instrument at the Jacobikirche in Hamburg, whose original pitch was subsequently measured at a′= 489.2 Hz. During Bach's lifetime the tuning fork was invented, probably by the English trumpeter John Shore in 1711. A famous early specimen pitched at a′= 422.5 Hz is reported to have been used by Handel for a 1751 performance of Messiah; the piano manufacturer J. A. Stein (whose clients included Mozart) is said to have possessed a fork at a′= 421.6 Hz. Whilst the evidence of surviving instruments suggests a gradual rise in pitch during the eighteenth century, it is probable that today's Classical pitch level of a′= 430 Hz is a little too high. Significantly, an advertisement in the Wiener Zeitung of 25 February 1789 contains a request from the woodwind maker Friedrich Lempp that prospective foreign clients should specify the required pitch, 'whether Vienna pitch, Kammerton, or even French pitch, or send him a tuning fork . . .'[16]

The tendency for pitch to climb continued in the nineteenth century, the Paris Opéra pitch being measured successively at a′= 423 Hz (1810), a′= 432 Hz (1822) and a′= 449 Hz (1855). Similar situations obtained elsewhere, for example in Dresden. In 1859 a law was passed in France stipulating as diapason normal a′= 435 Hz and this was adopted at an international conference in Vienna in 1885.[17] But by 1939 a′= 440 Hz was found to be the average level and this became the recommended international standard, though it has been consistently exceeded in various parts of the world (notably Vienna) in the quest for an ever greater degree of brilliance.

Temperament

It is customary for the scale to be tempered on keyboard instruments in such a way that most or all the concords are made somewhat impure so that few will be left inordinately so. Today's familiar equal temperament, where the octave is divided precisely into twelve semitones, found universal acceptance only in the middle of the nineteenth century. Thus the considerable complexities of different temperaments must be understood in outline by any historical performer and in detail by the keyboard specialist.[18]

The concords of triadic music – octaves, thirds and fifths – are largely incommensurate in the pure forms in which they arise within the harmonic series. Three pure major thirds fall short of a pure octave by about a fifth of a whole tone, whereas four pure minor thirds exceed an octave by half as much again. A circle of pure fifths will not cumulate in a perfect unison; furthermore, the whole tone produced by subtracting a pure minor third from a pure fourth is about 11 per cent smaller than that produced by subtracting a pure fourth from a pure fifth.

Whereas in equal temperament the fifths are only slightly reduced from pure, major thirds must be tempered (i.e. increased) seven times as much and minor thirds reduced eightfold. Mean-tone temperament avoids such heavily altered thirds (and sixths) by tempering fifths to a greater degree and allowing one 'wolf' (i.e. unpleasantly large) fifth at the cumulation of the circle of fifths. By contrast, an irregular temperament has the fifths all serviceable but tuned differently to allow frequently used thirds to be tempered less than those rarely encountered, the various keys thus acquiring a much-prized individual character.

Around 1600 various mean-tone tunings were in use, the aim being sonorous thirds and sixths without the fifths sounding too impure.[19] In mean-tone tunings diatonic semitones are larger than chromatic, for example, D♯ is lower than E♭. Each major third is divided into two equal tones. The most resonant tunings have the least tempered major and minor thirds, but these perforce have the lowest leading notes. The 'wolf' occurs between such intervals as C♯ and A♭, or G♯ and E♭. By the end of the seventeenth century one particular tuning with pure major thirds was especially popular on the organ,[20] but several others were described in detail, sometimes by means of a theoretical model dividing the octave into microtones.

Most characteristic of eighteenth-century keyboard tunings is an irregular temperament with no 'wolf' fifth and with the thirds tempered variably; their adjustment is less marked in natural keys, in which the largest semitones are thus produced. Keys with more accidentals possess more highly inflected leading notes and larger fifths. Various shadings of such tunings occurred in different parts of Europe and need to be studied for a true appreciation of composers' finer modulatory nuances. In today's historically aware climate the relatively simple but subtle tunings of Francesco Antonio Vallotti and of Andreas Werckmeister have found particular favour. A large number of writers, including J. P. Kirnberger (*Die Kunst des reinen Satzes in der Musik*, Berlin and Königsberg, 1776–9) and P. Lichtenthal (*Dizionario e bibliografia della Musica*, Milan, 1826), emphasised the importance of individual key character, which the latter used as an argument against equal temperament. The substantial literature documenting eighteenth-century awareness of different key characteristics can only be comprehended within this historical context. It is highly significant that the subject retained a fascination for later composers, such as Beethoven and Schumann.

Equal temperament was adopted by players of fretted Renaissance instruments and was subsequently endorsed for keyboard music by Frescobaldi in the late 1630s. Around 1700 a number of German theorists expressed considerable interest, including Werckmeister, Johann Georg Neidhardt and Mattheson. But there remained a preference among many musicians (including organ builders) for the subtleties of unequal tunings. In France these were generally more highly flavoured than in Germany, but in 1737 Rameau lent his support to equal temperament, having previously waxed lyrical about the effect of intervals tempered in different ways. His German counterpart was F. W. Marpurg, who around mid-century favoured the emergence of equal temperament as a uniform system which could be accepted everywhere. Some years later, Türk (2nd edn, 1802) and Hummel (1828) lent their considerable support to equal temperament, which soon completely eclipsed the old tunings.[21]

The intention underlying Bach's 'Well-tempered Clavier' remains a central issue. His title (given only to Book 1 of the '48') rules out any regular mean-tone temperament with a 'wolf' fifth. But a number of well-tempered tunings were popular in Bach's day, for example, those of Vallotti and Werckmeister, at least one by Neidhardt and the French 'tempérament ordinaire', in addition to equal temperament.[22] Neidhardt designed schemes for different sizes of venue and was the tuning theorist most respected by Bach.[23] A subtle form of irregular temperament has been shown to complement the character of the musical material assigned by Bach to each tonality, and this remains the most likely option.[24]

The unequally tempered scale finds consistent mention in non-keyboard literature. For example, Tosi (1723) made a clear distinction between major and minor semitones. Quantz (1752) differentiated E♭ as a comma higher than D♯, and to achieve this distinction added to the existing E♭ key on the flute a further key for D♯, observing that the differentiation of major and minor semitones was already second nature to singers and string players.[25] In the next century Carl Baermann, whilst admitting that no clarinet could play perfectly in tune, observed that every musician was aware that the major third of A major was distinguishable from the minor third of B♭ minor.[26] In 1905 Joachim's biographer J. A. Fuller Maitland defended his subject from the charge of faulty intonation in the latter part of his career by stating that the violinist's tuning was more just than that of a keyboard instrument tuned in equal temperament.

Vocal practices

With the rise of the public concert the supremacy of vocal music began to be challenged. Many writers advised instrumentalists to listen to the finest singers in order to understand those aspects of the art of music which could not be otherwise communicated, while at least one eighteenth-century teacher counselled all music students to learn the art of singing, whatever the quality of their voices.[27] Primary sources inevitably offer a limited idea of how singers might have actually sounded, though the early history of the gramophone teaches an important lesson that even within the last hundred years or so radical changes in tastes and practices have taken place.

As noted in Chapter 3, vocal treatises are especially useful in relation to creative areas such as ornamentation, extempore embellishment and improvisation; but there is much else of value in the writings of Caccini (1601/2), Bacilly (1668), Tosi (1723), Quantz (1752), Mancini (1774), Burney (1776–89), Hiller (1780), Corri (1810) and a host of later authors. The chronological, national and stylistic distinctions within vocal music are reflected within these sources. For example, Bacilly offers some penetrating remarks on French and Italian poetry and on the relationship of words and music, in addition to a discussion of ornamentation applicable strictly to French repertory. A couple of generations later Tosi represents a conservative Italian viewpoint, usefully distinguishing church, theatre and chamber practice. But there are some common threads; every writer emphasises the importance of perfect intonation and good breathing technique, together with clear enunciation and an understanding of the text, even in a foreign language (including Latin). The treatises uniformly assume a high level of musical education, including some knowledge of counterpoint. Tosi chillingly observes that the best time for study is with the rising of the sun and that *all* the time which can be spared from other necessary affairs should be devoted to study.

Theorists consistently documented use of the *messa di voce* (<>) on long notes and the role of rhythmic flexibility in communicating the text. Tremolo was distinguished from pitch vibrato and both were either rejected or regarded as expressive ornaments to be used sparingly. The separation of chest and head registers, blended only at the break, gave rise to the stipulations by Mattheson, Tosi and others that high notes must be softer than low. Only in the Classical period, when the chest voice was brought into the upper register, was the rule reversed. Significant for today's singers is Tosi's warning that dynamics must be appropriate for the venue, whilst Quantz advises against their undue exaggeration. An articulated style is widely reported, Tosi observing: 'the use of the slur is pretty much limited in singing and is confined within such few notes, ascending or descending, that it cannot go beyond a fourth without displeasing'. It is characteristic of Tosi that he should be especially critical of modern intonation and time-keeping, as well as the contemporary practice of imitating instrumental ornaments with the voice.

When Agricola (a pupil of J. S. Bach) published his annotated translation and commentary of Tosi in 1757, he brought the material up to date and addressed it to the style of singing at the court of Frederick the Great. He included copious scientific conjecture on the physiognomy of the human voice. Overall, his treatise, which achieved an immediate success, illustrates the tension between the Italian free creative spirit and the regimentation advocated by the Berlin school. His work combines philosophical discourse with some supremely practical advice, not least on diet.[28]

Different voice types have found particular favour at various times in musical history. The preponderance and differentiation of high voices in Baroque repertory pose special problems for today's performers. Boy trebles, whose voices broke rather later than is the case today (at between fifteen and twenty years old, according to Bacilly), played an important part in church music. The difficulty of recreating the musical status of the castrato is self-evident, especially since the individual character of the voice was originally distinguished clearly from the female soprano. Other distinctive timbres, such as the French *haute-contre* or the English countertenor, also defined the character of operatic roles. The bass tended to be regarded as inherently less expressive than higher voices, although the baritone had made considerable headway by the time of Mozart's *Don Giovanni* (1787). The size of choirs, widely variable from as few as four to as many as ninety, has proved a lively subject for discussion.[29]

The Classical period brought operatic reform, but vocal virtuosity continued to flourish. As remarked upon in Chapter 3, the repeated calls for excessive ornamentation to be curbed must be interpreted as far as possible within the musical taste of the time. Mozart's elaborations for an aria in *Lucio Silla* have already been mentioned; his ornamentation of J. C. Bach's 'Cara la dolce fiamma' from *Adriano in Siria* also offers much that is useful to both singers and instrumentalists. But increasingly, the complexity of German accompaniments rendered this type of vocal freedom less appropriate. Following a trend already signposted by Agricola, J. F. Schubert's *Neue Singe-schule* (Leipzig, 1804) warns that 'Compositions by Mozart, Haydn, Cherubini and Winter will bear fewer embellishments than those of Salieri, Cimarosa, Martin and Paisiello.'

During the nineteenth century the need for greater vocal power influenced technique, not least in the matter of vibrato, which began to be specified by composers as an expressive device and was to grow in continuity and strength. Changes in musical form and style gradually extinguished improvisatory practices, exemplified in Wagner's more prescriptive approach. But elsewhere, a pragmatic attitude to opera was not afraid to adapt it to local custom. For instance, recitatives were often composed to replace the spoken dialogue of *Fidelio*, *Der Freischütz* and *Die Zauberflöte*.[30] This was symptomatic of an approach which freely sanctioned the insertion, omission and transposition of arias, as dictated by circumstance. However, by the latter part of Verdi's career even the Italians were interpreting musical texts more literally, though in a style radically different from the increasingly international approach which appertains today.

Venues and programmes

By 1700 venues whose grand architecture was politically inspired contrasted with small spaces whose character was motivated by artistic considerations. Musicians today are often confronted with large halls lacking an appropriate acoustic, especially when performing intimate repertory such as solo motet, harpsichord suite or unaccompanied violin piece. Even theatres were smaller than might be imagined, resembling today's modest cinemas in their dimensions. Here, the proximity of performer and audience encouraged a subtle, articulate delivery, by comparison with the larger-scale Romantic approach. As has frequently been observed, an individual composition often had less identity than a single event; fluidity of numbers and personnel could characterise successive performances of individual operas.[31]

After 1800 the importance of music-making in the home was increasingly centred around the piano. Much of Schubert's output is directed towards this domestic environment, and most chamber and symphonic music in the nineteenth century routinely appeared in piano duet format. At the opposite end of the spectrum the grand civic halls which were built to house the new philharmonic societies bear witness to the large-scale music making they represented. Among the boldest of theatrical experiments was Wagner's positioning of the orchestra underneath the stage at Bayreuth, a development which (however successful) seems not to have been influential elsewhere.

In recent years original concert programmes have been increasingly subject to scrutiny, though rarely have they been recreated in the concert hall.[32] Variety and novelty were important, comprising a mixture of solo, chamber, orchestral and vocal music; the solo recital is a comparatively recent development. Surviving concert programmes testify to the mixture of instrumental and vocal music and to the custom of including movements of longer musical works within an extensive evening's entertainment. For example, on 25 November 1781 the Leipzig Gewandhaus Orchestra's inaugural concert comprised a symphony by Joseph Schmitt, a hymn by Reichardt,

Berger's Violin Concerto, a quartet of authorship now unknown, a symphony by J. C. Bach, an aria by Sacchini and a symphony by E. W. Wolff.[33] The first concert of London's Royal Philharmonic Society on 13 March 1813 consisted of Cherubini's overture *Anacréon*, a string quartet by Mozart, a vocal quartet and chorus by Sacchini, a wind serenade by Mozart, symphonies by Beethoven and Haydn, a chorus from Mozart's *Idomeneo*, a Boccherini quintet, Jommelli's celebrated chaconne and a march by Haydn. Such programmes were an entirely different type of social and musical event from today's more formal affair. As already noted, instrumental music eventually reigned supreme within the concert hall and was no longer the servant of opera or oratorio; but words flourished in other associated forms, such as the programme note, an invention of the nineteenth century.

Orchestral constitution and placement

In the first half of the eighteenth century orchestral size and make-up depended as much on circumstance as on the demands of the work to be performed.[34] Available players and size of hall were important factors, and so a surviving score might not necessarily indicate how a work was originally performed. Quantz's recommendations range from an orchestra with 4 violins to one with 12; there must have been many occasions when equivalent instruments were freely substituted, according to what was available. Handel's orchestra at the Haymarket Theatre on his arrival in 1710 comprised (at full strength) 1 trumpet, 2 oboes, 4 bassoons, 6 first and 5 second violins, 2 violas, 6 cellos, 1 double bass and 2 harpsichords. The score of *Rinaldo*, first performed in February 1711, has 4 trumpets and drums in the famous march and elsewhere a flageolet, 2 recorders and a violetta. Donald Burrows has surmised that extra players were hired for the march and the rest of the requirements were fulfilled by 'double-handed' members of the orchestra.[35] Among his later evidence are lists of performing musicians from 1714 and 1727, when George I and II respectively attended festivities at the Guildhall on the first Lord Mayor's Day of their reigns. It seems likely that Handel's orchestra remained fairly consistent between 1727 and his Foundling Hospital orchestra of 1754, whose strings were arranged in the proportion 14–6–3–2. A redistribution in the balance of the lower string parts involved a reduction in cellos and an increase from 1 to 2 double basses. There was a gradual increase in viola players, reflecting their height-ened role in the accompaniment of four-part oratorio choruses. Bach's aspirations for 'a well-appointed church music', stated in his famous memo-randum of 23 August 1730 to the Leipzig Council, amounted to a mere 18–20 players; it seems clear that he lacked even what resources he deemed necessary.[36]

Archival and musical evidence is sometimes apparently contradictory. For example, in the later eighteenth century viola parts are sometimes present even when no players are known to have been available and must often have been played by violinists. The occasional monster occasion is illustrated in Mozart's letter of 11 April 1781, rejoicing in a performance of a symphony (perhaps K338) using 40 violins, 28 lower strings, doubled wind and 6 bassoons. Exceptional festive occasions are exemplified by the cele-brated Handel Commemoration of 1784 already mentioned in Chapter 1, where the concert in Westminster Abbey featured a chorus and orchestra of over 500.[37] Large-scale performances of works by Handel and other com-posers were also heard elsewhere in Europe.

The decline in the use of keyboard continuo was patchy and cannot be reliably deduced from archival sources, though there are important shreds of documentary evidence. In 1802 Koch wrote that 'one still uses the harpsi-chord in the majority of large orchestras, partly for the support of the singers in the recitative, partly (and also chiefly) for the filling out of their harmony by means of the thorough-bass'.[38] The division of concertino and ripieno was still important, allowing the chance for soloistic, soft, chromatic and contrapuntal passages to be played only by a small group of fine players. This could improve quality, maintain dynamic contrasts and allow for an element of personal interpretation. The archival evidence mentioned in Chapter 2 cannot be interpreted too dogmatically; an orchestra needs to be studied over a period of time in order to determine what it had as its normal working strength. Furthermore, the presence of a certain number of musi-cians on a payroll does not necessarily mean that all of them customarily played on each occasion.

Many musicians regarded orchestral layout as of the utmost importance. C. P. E. Bach wrote of his father to Forkel on 13 January 1775:

> As the result of frequent large-scale performances of music in
> churches, at court, and often in the open air, in strange and incon-

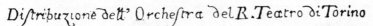

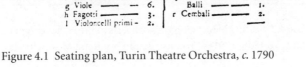

Figure 4.1 Seating plan, Turin Theatre Orchestra, c. 1790

venient places, he learned the placing of the orchestra, without any systematic study of acoustics. He knew how to make good use of this experience, together with his native understanding of building design so far as it concerns sound . . .[39]

Pictorial evidence survives for a variety of orchestral placement, and there is further commentary in the theoretical works of Quantz, Junker, Petri, Reichardt, Galeazzi and Koch,[40] as well as other instruction books, dictionaries, autobiographies, letters and more general musical literature. Quantz insisted that it was the leader's responsibility to distribute, place and arrange the instrumentalists in an ensemble.

Gradually the Baroque arrangement of ripieno and concertino harpsichords with associated continuo instruments gave way c. 1780 to the use of a single keyboard. Galeazzi's arrangement from Turin distributed winds and strings across the orchestra and was preferable with excellent players who could be counted upon to play in time (Fig. 4.1). He makes it clear that after three opera performances directed by the composer, the leader had full control of the entire company.[41] He considered the proper balance and pro-

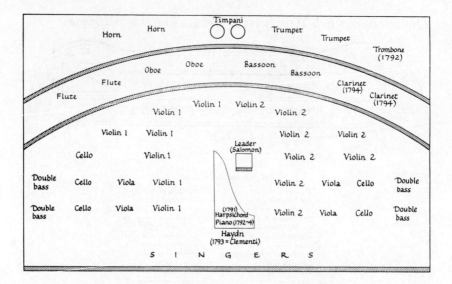

Figure 4.2 Seating plan, Salomon's concerts at the Hanover Square Rooms, London, 1791–4 (reconstruction by Simon McVeigh)

portions of the different instruments within the orchestra and the optimum placement of the players as principal objectives towards which a concert-master should strive. In French opera a wooden baton was used by a time-beater who stood at the edge of the stage with his back to both audience and orchestra; he could also act as prompter.[42]

Concert orchestras often stood to perform. First and second violins faced each other, with principal cello and bass either side of the harpsichord. On his arrival Haydn introduced an amphitheatre arrangement in London and this has been reconstructed from surviving evidence (Fig. 4.2).[43] But in general there were no standardised placements, each hall, repertory and orchestra having its own requirements. There was a measure of agreement that the visual as well as acoustical should be taken into account, that the harpsichordist and concert-master were placed centrally and that as the century progressed first and second violins were increasingly divided; weak and principal melody instruments were to be placed well forward. Until the final years of the eighteenth century, the continuo group was seen as a unit and grouped together. At the turn of the century Friedrich Rochlitz complained that placement of orchestras had not been changed to reflect new compositional procedures, for example with regard to bassoons or trumpet and drums.[44] Among useful illustrations in Clive Brown's article 'The orchestra in Beethoven's Vienna' is a sketch of the pit and stage of the Kärntnertortheater in 1821, as well as layouts for a performance of Handel's *Alexander's Feast* (arr. Mozart) in 1812 and for the Concert Spirituel *c.* 1825; they are all quite different from today's commonly employed placements.

Direction

Prior to the era of the interpretative conductor, orchestras were directed by the leader and/or the keyboard player. Thus the modern conductor of Haydn, Mozart and previous generations is something of an historical anachronism. Quantz favoured violin direction, whereas C. P. E. Bach argued eloquently in favour of the keyboard. It seems clear that different methods of direction were practised for different types of music. Until about 1810, orchestral works were normally directed by the principal violinist (concertmaster): when voices were included, a keyboard player usually participated in the direction; and in large-scale works involving chorus and orchestra there was often a third director whose sole purpose was to beat time. In orchestral music, violinist-directors such as Schuppanzigh drew criticism for their habits of foot-stamping to achieve ensemble.

Beethoven seems to have been one of the first musicians in Vienna to direct without an instrument, operating from a separate music-desk, without a baton. There are many accounts of his conducting from about 1805 onwards, indicating that he seems not to have given a continuous and regular beat. He was concerned instead with conveying the expression, disappearing below the music desk for *pianos* and leaping into the air at *fortes.*[45] But it seems that even in Beethoven's presence the direction often lay in other hands; his firmness and tact as a conductor remained questionable, even before the onset of his deafness. In the theatre, direction from the violin also gradually gave way to a conductor, though with the leader retaining a more prominent role than today. Divided direction was still the norm until many years after Beethoven's death and lasted an especially long time in England. The evidence of Berlioz and Spohr is of a wide variety of practice, and gradually the baton and interpretative maestro took sway.

Nineteenth-century changes

For purely orchestral concerts around 1800 an ensemble with six to eight first violins, a similar number of seconds, and the remainder in proportion was still the norm. There was then a gradual expansion of forces.[46] After mid-century the orchestra came to include additional wind timbres such as cor anglais and bass clarinet, which were reckoned by at least one writer in the 1880s to attenuate the uniformity of sound by then characteristic of most wind instruments.[47] Instruments were invented in large numbers, with an occasional success such as the saxophone among many patents doomed to instant failure. Improvements were often focused towards achieving greater power and (in the case of woodwinds) acquiring greater flexibility in remote keys. As we observed in Chapter 1, there was sometimes disquiet that instrumental character was being sacrificed. An increase in power among the winds with their wider bores and increased mechanisms was matched by developments in the strings. As orchestral size increased, so did lack of uniformity of constitution. Throughout the nineteenth century there were many different arrangements in the concert hall, church and opera, described and illustrated in some detail by Daniel Koury (1986). For example, the configuration by Georg Henschel which was approved by Brahms had double basses at the back of the orchestra on either side; it is reproduced as Fig. 5.3 (p. 141 below). Wagner's innovations at Bayreuth (Koury, figs. 83–6) arose from a creative lifetime of experimentation. In the concert hall the conductor apparently faced the public until quite late in the century, with at least some of the band behind him. At the opera the conductor tended to be at the base of the stage, which meant that the players also had to face the singers. For today's re-creations, seating needs to be flexible, reflecting the work performed and the sound-ideals of the composer, thus matching established custom in period performances of Baroque, Renaissance and medieval music.

5 Case studies in ensemble music

J. S. Bach: St Matthew Passion BWV 244

The performance of a 'Passion set to music' at Vespers on Good Friday, initiated in 1721 by Bach's predecessor Johann Kuhnau, quickly became the highlight of Leipzig's musical calendar. Divided into two parts which pivoted upon the Passion sermon, Bach's *St Matthew Passion* represents the culmination of this Lutheran tradition, designed not only to present the most important Gospel text of the year (thus substituting for the Gospel reading) but also to interpret it, incorporating rhetorical embellishments of the story and making relevant theological points to the congregation.[1] Bach's collaboration with the amateur poet Christian Friedrich Henrici (whose pseudonym was Picander) can be traced back to 1725 and their setting was probably first performed in its earliest version on 11 April 1727;[2] it was probably also given on 15 April 1729 in a version approximating to the copy made by Bach's son-in-law Johann Christoph Altnikol and was certainly performed again on 30 March 1736 and in the early 1740s.

Text and edition

When contemplating an edition on which to base an historical performance of Bach's *St Matthew Passion*, performers will do no better than consult the 'Urtext' edition based on *J. S. Bach, Neue Ausgabe sämtlicher Werke*, prepared by Alfred Dürr using preliminary work by Max Schneider.[3] This edition has also been published as a miniature study score (Bärenreiter), and the vocal score and complete orchestral parts are also readily available. Dürr's principal sources were the autograph score of the 1736 version, the only surviving autograph, and a set of parts made from that score. The 1736 version is significant for Bach's substitution of the extended chorale fantasia for chorus 'O Mensch, bewein dein Sünde gross' appropriated from his second version of the *St John Passion* for his original simple chorale ending Part I ('Jesum lass ich nicht von mir'), division of the continuo instruments into two distinct groups, and addition of the 'Swallow's nest' organ (facing the west choir gallery in St Thomas's) to the *cantus firmus* line of the choruses framing the work's first part. Although the sources for the edition include extensive variants, due to either Bach's tireless revision process or practical considerations arising from the 1740s performance, Dürr's scholarly edition solves numerous performance problems in a thoroughly practical manner, even if it still leaves some unanswered.

Direction

Evidence points to Bach playing all the possible roles in directing his performing forces during his Leipzig career – conductor, concertmaster and continuo harpsichordist; but it is most likely that he conducted performances of the *St Matthew Passion*, probably with a paper roll. He certainly would not have contemplated turning his back to the performers and directing from the organ, for his transposition of the parts in *Chorton* for the organ would have been superfluous if he himself had assumed the organ continuo role.[4]

Performing forces

Conductors need to make important decisions about using performing forces compatible with their historical aims. Mendelssohn's revival of the *St Matthew Passion* in 1829 in line with Romantic taste has already been mentioned in Chapter 1. He used the mixed chorus of the Berlin Singakademie (a 400-strong amateur choral society), the orchestra of the Philharmonischer Verein and a separate group of operatic soloists, replaced Bach's oboi d'amore with clarinets, added melodic phrasings, dynamic and expressive tempo indications and made extensive cuts in the arias.[5] More recently, Boult and Emery[6] stated a preference for a small choir (*c.* 60 maximum) and orchestra (*c.* 30 strings or less, 4 flutes, 4 oboes, 2 bassoons, a harpsichord and an organ.[7] Surprisingly, they claim that the 'obsolete' instruments – recorders, oboi d'amore, and viola da gamba – can be replaced by flutes, oboes or cors anglais, and cello with little loss of effect;

and they recommend using a maximum of 6 vocal soloists, drawing as necessary on local talent for economic purposes or even allotting some arias to sections of the chorus.

Up to eight soloists are used in modern performances: a tenor (Evangelist), 2 baritones (Jesus and Pilate (and the high priest)), 2 sopranos, a contralto, a countertenor, a tenor, and 2 further sopranos (the two handmaidens) normally extracted from the chorus. But it is difficult to emulate the choral and orchestral forces employed in Leipzig in the 1720s and 1730s, not least because there are neither statements by Bach himself nor contemporary reports that will establish such information with any certainty. As no music was permitted during Lent, all available personnel attached to the four Leipzig churches could feasibly have focused their attentions on the Good Friday Passion performance. Hans-Joachim Schulze argues that Bach always required 'a certain opulence of sound' and reckoned on several performers to each line, with civic musicians, former students and other guests supplementing the performing forces.[8] Others, notably Robert Marshall and Ton Koopman,[9] suggest a group of 12–16 singers, citing Bach's letter to the Leipzig town council (23 August 1730) – the *Entwurff einer wohlbestallten Kirchen Music* or 'short but very necessary plan for a well-appointed church music' – as indicating the minimum forces required. However, Joshua Rifkin claims that the *Entwurff* is unrepresentative of Bach's established performance practice and relates instead to the organisation of a liturgical music establishment over a whole year, incorporating each Leipzig church in its calculations and allowing for illness and other such eventualities. He has proposed and successfully demonstrated using just one voice per part,[10] sparking a verbal conflict, particularly with Marshall and Koopman.[11] Central to Rifkin's argument are the format and interrelationship of the original performing parts and the belief that each singer in the seventeenth and eighteenth centuries generally used a separate part (music copy). He cites specific examples as evidence, including surviving performing materials (10 vocal parts) from the 1725 performance of Bach's *St John Passion*, and concludes that there were no more than 8 singers singing at any time in the 1736 performance of the *St Matthew Passion* and that each of the choirs comprised four 'concertists', one singer per part.[12]

Bach's use of only male 'concertists' for his passion oratorios – boys for sopranos and possibly for altos, men for altos, tenors and bass/baritone – poses further problems. As eighteenth-century male voices 'broke' up to four years later than nowadays, Bach's male soprano concertists were about seventeen or eighteen years old, so we therefore have no true twentieth-century equivalent of Bach's mature teenage boy-altos and trebles and resultant homogeneous 'male' sound. The two important alto solos in the *St Matthew Passion* involve challenges of breath-control which could arguably be met only by men.[13]

Compatibility between orchestral and choral forces is also essential, strings in the proportion 3–3–1–1–1 for each orchestra representing a satisfactory balance with choirs of about 16 voices each while still preserving the work's grandeur. Dürr seems to have in mind at least 4 violinists per part,[14] but Rifkin, contradicting Schulze, reaffirms that one written part per singer and player was general practice, even in the affluent Dresden court.[15] The gamba also features in the string complement as an obbligato instrument (Nos. 35 and 57), replacing the original lute part in Nos. 56 and 57.[16]

The alternation of oboes and oboi d'amore, incompletely indicated in the sources, is sensibly clarified in Dürr's edition. Harnoncourt was the first to attempt to differentiate between these and the prescribed oboi da caccia for Nos. 48, 49, 59 and 60, commissioning reconstructions from Leipzig prototypes (by Johann Heinrich Eichentopf) discovered in museums in Stockholm and Copenhagen during the 1970s.[17] A special form of taille or tenor oboe in F covered in leather and bent in a semicircle, with a brass bell like a hunting horn,[18] the oboe da caccia had a unique dark timbre and dynamic flexibility. Bach employs it for especially tender moments, sometimes in combination with the transverse flute (as in Nos. 48 and 49).

Like Arnold Schering, Laurence Dreyfus recognises the organ as the principal continuo keyboard instrument for Bach's church music,[19] but he also concedes that there was *occasional* dual accompaniment by harpsichord and organ for a variety of practical (ensemble and better communication between players), circumstantial (organ out of order) and aesthetic reasons, particularly in Bach's own performances of his cantatas. The church records in Leipzig confirm the use of both organs for the 1736 performance of the *St Matthew Passion*, but Dürr points out that when the work was revived in the 1740s, a harpsichord replaced the organ supporting the second choir,[20] possibly explaining Bach's addition of a chordal gamba part to his 1736 autograph for No. 34. However, the alternation between organ and harpsichord (for recitatives) to which many have subscribed (e.g. Julius Rietz in his preface to the *Bach-Gesellschaft* edition) is supported by no scholarly evidence whatsoever.

Cello and violone naturally feature among the regular string continuo complement of both orchestras, but Bach's specification 'Violonc. e Org'. for No. 35 would appear to exclude the violone.[21] It was normal practice for a bassoon to complement each pair of orchestral oboes,[22] even though the relatively few bassoon parts among surviving Bach sources might suggest that Bach did not employ it as a regular continuo instrument.

Pitch

Determining an appropriate pitch for a modern 'period' performance of the work will necessarily hinge upon the instruments available and involve a degree of compromise. Establishing historical accuracy on such matters is fraught with problems, not least because the tuning and pitch of the organs at Leipzig's Thomaskirche will have varied considerably with temperature – and the pitch is likely to have been high, compared with modern standards, on account of the tuning methods used (involving shortening the pipes). Arthur Mendel claims that the basic *Kammerton* (chamber pitch) at which Bach's woodwinds, strings and voices in Leipzig normally performed was approximately $a' = 440$ Hz, about a tone below the *Chorton* of the main Thomaskirche organ, which he calculates approximately as $a' = c.$ 494 Hz; in his later study he rejects arguments advanced for a *Kammerton* of $a' = 421$ Hz or 415 Hz;[23] Bruce Haynes has challenged Mendel's views, using as evidence reported measurements of the pitches of surviving 'period' woodwind instruments and the pitch standards implicit in Bach's woodwind writing.[24] Haynes concludes that Bach's *Chorton* in Leipzig was one tone higher than his *Kammerton* and that Bach may occasionally (certainly in his Weimar years) have used a second *Kammerton* a further semitone lower. The most likely values of these pitches would appear to be $a' = c.$ 460 Hz, $c.$ 410 Hz and $c.$ 390 Hz respectively.[25] Given that Bach transposed the organ parts in *Chorton* down a tone for the 1736 performance to accommodate the other instruments, a pitch of $a' = c.$ 410 Hz would seem to be most consistent with historical evidence.

Placement of performing forces

The optimum placement of the performing forces will inevitably depend on the venue, but Bach's musical separation of the choirs and orchestras is really only meaningful if they are also separated spatially. Harnoncourt has interpreted the evidence of the sacristan Rost to conclude that the two choirs, each with its orchestra, were positioned opposite each other at the east and west ends of the Thomaskirche in the 1736 performance; such evidence is worth emulating if circumstances permit.

Vocal style and performance

As we have already observed, the reconstruction of historical singing styles has proved challenging and controversial, acquaintance with the different national styles and genres being essential, particularly the approaches to the contrasting colours of the 'chest' and 'head' registers. German and French singers, who insisted most on separation of the vocal registers, probably produced a more or less 'straight' tone, with only sparing ornamental use of a vibrato with fairly narrow oscillations.[26] Vibrato was probably suppressed entirely on dissonant notes, appoggiaturas, leading notes, chromatic notes or augmented fourths, to avoid mollifying the joint expressive effect of text and music.

Decisions also need to be taken as to whether the original literary text should be sung, even with its unfamiliar, archaic forms of words, or whether the inconsistent compromise often used nowadays should prevail. Those with historical aims should opt for Picander's original text, and thus avoid later distortions in meaning; for example in the second stanza of the chorale 'O Haupt voll Blut und Wunden', the original text, 'das grosse Weltgewichte wie bist du so bespeit', is often falsified nowadays as 'das grosse Weltgerichte . . .' Picander's original punctuation, not always faithfully reproduced because of later grammatical refinements, is also crucial to a faithful interpretation.

Recitatives

Eighteenth-century conventions regarding the performance of recitative must be assimilated and adapted according to individual taste, espe-

Ex. 5.1 J. S. Bach, *St Matthew Passion*, I, 2, bb. 1–3

cially that of 'short style' accompaniment for organist and continuo in secco recitatives. As discussed in Chapter 3, this involved continuo members playing each chord short, irrespective of its notated value, and remaining silent until the next change of harmony, thereby allowing the words to be easily distinguished (Ex.5.1).[27] Only in accompanied recitatives (involving orchestra and continuo) were the long notes intended to be played as notated. Although Jack Westrup, Friedrich-Heinrich Neumann and Peter Williams have cast doubts on whether such truncation of notated values was consistently employed,[28] Williams considers short accompaniment appropriate for the Evangelist's recitatives in the *St Matthew Passion* so that the narrative is clearly audible and contrasts dramatically with the sustained style accompanying Jesus.[29]

The surviving parts for the work present the most conclusive evidence regarding Bach's use of short accompaniment. A contemporary copy of Bach's now-lost original score represents the earliest stage of this composition, with only the one continuo line, as in the earlier *St John Passion*, and with the secco recitatives notated in long notes. The autograph score of Bach's revised 1736 version divides the continuo into two distinct parts, one for each orchestra, and retains, despite some minimally revised recitatives, the regular 'long' notation for the secco movements. However, the continuo parts for those recitatives, prepared by Bach himself and helpfully reproduced in Dürr's edition, were notated in crotchets in short accompaniment style.

Short accompaniment also involves organists in deciding how to realise the chords in the right hand for harmonic changes in which the bass note remains unchanged. Williams suggests that these figures were merely 'a guide to the director-accompanist, like the figures Corelli put above notes expressly marked tasto solo',[30] and thus served only as cues to the vocal part. Others believe that greater expressive flexibility (with regard to note-lengths) is implied and that the notated harmonies should be reflected in the organist's right hand, taste being the final arbiter.

Good taste was also crucial in the telescoping of cadences, which entailed disregarding the literal notation and pre-empting the singer in order to hurry towards a dramatic cadence;[31] but there are few (if any) instances where such telescoping is either necessary or appropriate in this Passion. However, it would be expedient for organists to respect the eighteenth-century convention of using only a stopped diapason for the accompaniment of the recitatives and the arias set for chamber music, with no change of register for expressive effect.

If much of the above appears to amount to a recipe for inflexibility, the truth was far from the case. The 'concertists' will certainly have interpreted with some freedom the metric notation, in order to follow the sense and dramatic flow of the words. As Johann Walther explains: '[Although] one writes down the vocal part in a correct measure, one has . . . the freedom to alter the value of the notes, making them longer or shorter . . . in order to express the affect.'[32] This would certainly be the case with the Evangelist, who should recount the Passion story largely as a neutral, but respond accordingly, together with the relevant continuo players, when the declamation becomes more animated.

Another convention misrepresented by musical notation for recitatives was the 'vocal' appoggiatura, common in respect of two cadential formulae. Those cadences which involve the vocal line falling by a fourth, prepared before the beat, which the appoggiatura takes and postpones the notated main note by one half, are largely accommodated in Bach's notation (Ex. 5.2); but there are numerous instances where the notated vocal line falling by a third should properly be 'filled in' by an appoggiatura, unprepared, on the beat (Ex.5.3).

Ex. 5.2 J. S. Bach, *St Matthew Passion*, I, 26, bb. 34–5

Ex. 5.3 J. S. Bach, *St Matthew Passion*, I, 18, bb. 9–11

Chorales

Whether the congregation joined in the singing of the separate chorales has been hotly debated. The arguments are difficult to resolve, simply because there were precedents for congregational singing of simple chorale settings in many cities, including Hamburg. However, it is highly unlikely that Bach's congregation participated, as the chorales are probably too complex for such performance and were not even included in the printed texts of the Passion.

The pauses notated in the chorales are simply conventional signs from the chorale books, indicating the ends of the lines; they do not necessarily demand any repose, although a breath seems a natural course of action on most occasions. Although it would be perfectly legitimate to hold all pauses, it is equally so, and more satisfactory, to treat the chorales like ordinary hymns and observe pauses only where the words admit of a break. The punctuation and sense of the text will serve as the best guides for meaningful performance; thus, the commas and semi-colons in No. 40 suggest literal interpretations of the relevant pause signs; but in bars 6 and 12, where no punctuation appears and the text flows into the subsequent strain, the pauses may justifiably be ignored.

Other interpretative observations (articulation and expression)

A few important points specific to the work regarding articulation and expression should be noted briefly by way of conclusion. Bach's articulation annotations are inconsistent in the sources; in unison passages, for instance, he often assigned different slurrings to different instruments playing the same notes. It is impossible to deduce whether these different articulations were introduced accidentally, in which case they should be regularised as in Dürr's edition, or intentionally to produce a type of subtle, articulatory heterophony.[33] Harnoncourt abhors their regularisation, claiming that such diversity sounds 'all the more beautiful, varied and "speaking"', but conflicting indications may also indicate an evolutionary process or one of gradual refinement through revision, in which case it has been customary to regularise such annotations according to the composer's last thoughts.[34] John Butt has discerned some of the motivation behind these markings, demonstrating that they give special insight into how Bach understood his music.[35] However, such issues will never be settled easily, through either scholarship or performance.

Robert Marshall's detailed study of dynamic markings in the autograph scores reveals that Bach used only three indications on the *forte* side of the spectrum (*forte, poco forte* and *mezzo forte*) but many refinements on the *piano* side (*piano, sempre piano, piano piano, più piano, poco piano* and *pianissimo*).[36] Although the dynamic markings in the sources for the *St Matthew Passion* are not especially prolific and fail fully to mirror such a range, leaving much for performers to add according to early eighteenth-century taste, Bach consistently emphasises subtlety of nuance over sheer volume. The subtleties of indications such as *un poco p* (No. 27a) and the *f* and *più piano* contrasts in the final double chorus should be rigorously observed and, along with agogic accentuation, should be placed in the service of a rhetorical concept of phrasing. It is essential to observe Bach's occasional specific staccato markings (e.g. in Nos. 49 (oboi da caccia), 57 and 60 (continuo)), his direction *a battuta* (Nos. 48 and 56), indicating that the movement in question should be performed in strict time, his effective *tasto solo* alternations in No. 29 and his *tasto solo* and *piano sempre* prescriptions for No. 64.

Rational appreciation of the word-painting, key characteristics, symbolism and numerical riddles in the work also contributes to a faithful, expressive interpretation. There are many instances of effective word-painting in the vocal line, most notably the expressive melismatic writing for 'und weinete bitterlich' (No. 38b); the instruments often add to the effect, as in the string accompaniments to Jesus's recitatives and the portrayal of weeping in 'Erbarme dich' (No. 39). The work's constant oscillation between sharp and flat keys enhances the expressive affect, as does Bach's subtle choice of key-colour – it is surely no coincidence that the opening double chorus is in E minor, a key which, according to Mattheson, is 'normally very pensive, profound, grieved and sad, though in such a way that there is still hope for consolation . . .'[37]

The number symbolism incorporated in the work is often more difficult to identify. The Jews call upon the law in ten double choruses (the four choruses of the Roman soldiers naturally are not counted), which represent the ten commandments. In the chorus of the apostles, who ask 'Herr, bin ichs?' (No. 9e) the word 'Herr' (Lord) is sung eleven times, once for each apostle save Judas. Bach even encoded words according to the numerical alphabet and concealed the resulting numbers, like numbers in the text or references to biblical passages, in his music.[38]

W. A. Mozart: Serenade for 13 instruments K361

Introduction

To Mozart's contemporaries the 'thirteen-wind Serenade' (as it remains popularly known) must have been extraordinary. Until 1782 it was not even normal for a *Harmonie* (wind-band) to employ two pairs of treble instruments, and three were unprecedented. Two pairs of horns and a sixteen-foot instrument were also virtually unheard of. The normal shape of a serenade was five movements, but Mozart added a further two, making even the menuets much grander movements than usual by adding second trios to each. Furthermore, the Serenade opens with a highly unusual slow introduction and is double the size of any contemporary work of its kind.

Mozart and Harmoniemusik

Harmoniemusik played a significant part in the social fabric of musical life during the Classical period until after 1830, and Mozart's Serenade K361 is undoubtedly its most grandiose and ambitious representative. From the middle of the eighteenth century wind bands had the function of providing background music at dinners and for social events, sometimes also appearing in private and public concerts. Mozart composed various divertimenti for the Archbishop of Salzburg in the mid-1770s. After his arrival in Vienna in 1781, he soon turned again to wind ensemble writing, as indicated by a letter to his father dated 3 November of that year describing the earliest performances of his Serenade K375, given by an itinerant street band in characteristic imitation of the aristocratic ensembles. Shortly afterwards, an Imperial Harmonie was instituted, with an eminent personnel.[39] Mozart responded to this development with a revision of K375 to include oboes and with the C minor Serenade K388. K375 belongs firmly within the wind serenade tradition, whilst exhibiting some unusual features of form and content.[40] On the other hand, K388 utterly transcends the genre, both in its minor mode and in its introduction of contrapuntal elements, notably the canon in the Menuet and Trio. But the formality of mood and structure in Mozart's two octet serenades belies the fact that *Harmoniemusik* was only secondarily intended for the concert room.

The premiere of K361

Mozart's thirteen-instrument Serenade was immediately recognised as a musical phenomenon at its first known performance during a benefit concert for the clarinettist Anton Stadler at the National Court Theatre. The event was advertised in the *Wienerblättchen* of 23 March 1784: 'Herr Stadler senior, in present service of His Majesty the Emperor, will hold a musical concert for his own benefit, at which will be given, among other well chosen pieces, a great wind piece of a very special kind composed by Herr Mozart.'[41] An important review of Stadler's playing that evening was written by Johann Schink: 'My thanks to you, brave virtuoso! I have never heard the like of what you contrived with your instrument. Never should I have thought that a clarinet could be capable of imitating the human voice as it was imitated by you. Indeed, your instrument has so soft and lovely a tone that no one with a heart can resist it – and I have one, dear Virtuoso; let me thank you.'[42] Schink's remarks here recall the assertion by eighteenth-century writers such as C. P. E. Bach and Quantz that a performer's first duty was to move an audience. As we have already observed, Stadler insisted that every student should learn basic principles through singing.[43] Significantly, Schink also reports that only four of the Serenade's seven movements were performed. Perhaps Stadler deemed its unconventional length unsuitable for his concert.[44] In any event, this abridgement is one aspect of the original conditions which nowadays we are unlikely to want to emulate.

Sources and dating

As has been observed quite recently, there are few of Mozart's works which have as much confusion, misinformation, even controversy associated with them as K361.[45] These problems affect today's performers in a variety of ways. Mozart's autograph proves that the set of parts used as a basic source for more than a century and a half was thoroughly corrupt, with more than a thousand divergences from the autograph in terms of dynamics, actual notes and details of phrasing. This pirate set of parts was published by the Bureau des Arts et d'Industrie in Vienna in 1803, causing André, the Offenbach publisher to whom Mozart's widow sold the greater part of his autograph scores, to cancel his own projected edition. Because of a series of misfortunes the 1803 material became the principal source for Breitkopf & Härtel's first collected edition in 1878.[46] To make matters worse, the Breitkopf score and parts do not agree with each other. Köchel was to have been the Serenade's editor and is known to have been working from the autograph; but on his death before the project was completed, his successor Gustav Nottebohm (apparently without access to the autograph) reinstated various errors from the corrupt parts. In effect, Nottebohm's editorial liberties in terms of dynamics and phrasing derived from his personal understanding of Mozart's style. The critical commentary was written by a third party after Nottebohm's own death. Exx. 5.4 and 5.5 show some examples of misplaced detail.

Only in 1941 did Mozart's autograph become widely available for study, when it was acquired by the Library of Congress in Washington DC.[47] The manuscript was published in facsimile in 1976, together with an annotated

Ex. 5.4 W. A. Mozart, Serenade K361, i, bb. 116–27: (a) autograph

preface by Alfred Einstein, written some thirty years earlier. It seems that the title 'Gran Partitta' was inscribed early in the work's existence, but in a hand other than that of Mozart, who throughout his life never used the term 'partita'. Similarly, the date 1780 (overwritten from 1771) represents a guess as to the date of composition by Mozart's publisher André, which was later adopted by Köchel and led to the music being associated with Munich (and *Idomeneo*) rather than Vienna. It is now widely accepted that the Serenade was written for Stadler's concert in 1784. Corroborative evidence for the later date is that during 1784 the Bohemian basset horn players Anton David and Vincent Springer were resident in Vienna. During the two-year period from late 1783 Mozart composed as many as thirteen works with basset horn, including miniatures and fragments. Furthermore, in a letter of 10 February of that year he wrote to his father: 'At the present I haven't the slightest intention of producing [the opera *L'Oca del Cairo*]. I have works to

Ex. 5.4 (a) (*cont.*)

compose which at the moment are bringing in money *but will not do so later.*
The opera will always bring in some . . .' The Serenade fits this description in
that Mozart could play no part in it, and its unusual instrumentation would
greatly inhibit future performance opportunities. An incidental piece of
musical evidence for this dating is that the use of *forte* dotted rhythms
answered by a solo voice (clarinet) at the beginning of K361 finds a parallel
in two works of this period, the Piano Quintet K452 and the Violin Sonata
K454.[48]

Editions

Until recently, all sets of parts commercially available were identical
copies of the Breitkopf & Härtel edition by, amongst others, Kalmus, Broude

Ex. 5.4 W. A. Mozart, Serenade K361, i, bb. 116–27: (b) traditional version

Brothers and Musica Rara. The first recording to follow Mozart's autograph was made by Daniel Barenboim and the English Chamber Orchestra (on modern instruments) in 1978 (EMI ASD 3426). The following year saw the publication of the score in volume VII/17/2 of the *Neue Mozart-Ausgabe* edited by Neal Zaslaw and Daniel Leeson. During the long period until 1996 when the *NMA* performance material (Bärenreiter BA 5331) and Study Score (TP 312) appeared, a score and parts were issued in 1991 by Emerson Edition, prepared from the autograph by Roger Hellyer. Either set of parts can be recommended, though the editions differ in points of detail where Mozart's autograph is not unambiguous, for example in certain dynamic markings in the second movement.

Ex. 5.4 (b) (*cont.*)

Instruments

Assembling a full complement of instruments and players for K361 is a significant achievement in itself. The wide variation in instrument design throughout Europe needs to be given due consideration. During the 1780s Vienna was an important and progressive centre of wind instrument manufacture. For example, Daniel Schubart in 1784–5 singled out Viennese clarinets as among the finest, together with those from Nuremberg, Munich, Hamburg and Berlin.[49] Meanwhile the Nuremberg clarinettist Heinrich Backofen stated in his tutor *c.* 1803 that the finest basset horns were manufactured in Vienna.[50] The homogeneous but distinctive sound quality of classical Viennese clarinets arises from a number

Ex. 5.5 W. A. Mozart, Serenade K361, ii, bb. 16–19: (a) autograph

of characteristic and progressive features, including well-designed key-work and large tone-holes for the right hand, which enhanced the chalu-meau register. All classical clarinets were restricted in the number of amenable tonalities they could handle, by comparison with other wood-winds. But in a variety of ways Viennese clarinets were probably two or three decades more advanced than the English instruments which survive in large numbers.[51] A recent report on the playing response of the surviving B♭ clarinet (Geneva, Museé des Instruments anciens de Musique, 136) by Stadler's Bohemian collaborator Theodor Lotz (1748–92) confirms its special qualities:

Ex. 5.5 (a) (*cont.*)

Playing on this Lotz clarinet, complete in all its components, was certainly a gratifying experience. It probably possessed the largest 'thickest' sound of any eighteenth-century clarinet that I tested, rounded and woody throughout its entire range . . . Particularly impressive were the good intonation between the registers and the evenness of scale in the lower register. Both are significant in light of Mozart's extensive use of this register. The dynamic range and timbral quality of this Lotz clarinet are no doubt related to the very large bore size . . . [which] would certainly give credence to Shackleton's statement [in *The New Grove*] that the Bohemian

Ex. 5.5 W. A. Mozart, Serenade K361, ii, bb. 16–19: (b) traditional version

clarinet of Mozart's time was already more highly developed than elsewhere.[52]

To complement these organological developments, it has been further established that the Austro-German tradition was among the first to embrace the modern practice of playing with the reed against the lower lip, for which the evidence includes the position of the stamp on the surviving Lotz clarinet mouthpiece. There are also several surviving clarinets by Raymund Griesbacher (1751 or 52–1818), with whom the Stadlers played basset horn trios.

Ex. 5.5 (b) (*cont.*)

Recent performances on early basset horns have helped to illuminate Mozart's fascination with the instrument, since its extraordinary acoustical make-up produces a tone-quality which can truly be described as other-worldly; this derives from the retention of a bore which is scarcely wider than on the clarinet, a much shorter instrument.[53] The first types, with a sickle-shaped tube modelled on the oboe da caccia, borrowed the box or *Buch* just above its bell from instruments such as the rackett, to achieve an extension down from the clarinet's lowest note e to the tonic c. Seven-keyed instruments from *c.* 1760 by the supposed inventors A. and M. Mayrhofer are not furnished with any intervening notes. Having become established in the 1780s, the more readily constructed shape of two limbs joined at an angle by a knee is described in Koch's *Musikalisches Lexicon* (1802). This is surely the type intended for K361. Surviving specimens testify to the provision of a key for d by this time, and its addition probably constitutes the improvement of 1782 attributed to Lotz by C. F. Cramer.[54] If the basset horns normally used by David and Springer were seven-keyed instruments in G, as Cramer suggests, both players must have been newly equipped for the Serenade, perhaps with basset horns in F belonging to the Stadlers, at least one of which was technically more advanced than those generally employed.[55] Surviving evidence relating to the relatively youthful basset horn shows Mozart and Stadler at the cutting edge of instrumental developments.

The two-keyed oboe was almost universal before 1800, a modified version of the Baroque instrument. Certain notes were problematic and led to extreme sharp keys such as E and even A major being avoided.[56] Yet the oboe was more flexible in this respect than the clarinet; its solo repertory tended to be written in F or C, yet it could happily cope with the wind-band's favourite tonalities of E♭ or (as in K361) B♭. Mozart used the upper reaches of its range in the Oboe Quartet (f‴) and in K361 (e♭‴, sensationally concluding the Adagio), although the left-thumb speaker key is documented only from *c.* 1800. Koch is an important source for such later developments, noting that the speaker key aided quiet production of e″, f″, f♯″ and g″. The radical development of clarinets and basset horns in Vienna at this time might conceivably suggest a more advanced key configuration for the oboe in K361, although modern players have recently demonstrated an astonishing flexibility and facility with minimal keywork. Oboe tone is crucially linked to reed design, which varied on a national as well as an individual basis. Within this area much research has been already been undertaken.[57] In terms of tone quality, vibrato is not mentioned in tutors, although Burney was fulsome in his praise of Carlo Besozzi's *messe di voce* on long notes.[58] It is significant that Mozart, having admired J. C. Fischer in 1765, criticised him severely in a letter to his father of 4 April 1787: 'His tone is entirely nasal, and his held notes like the tremulant on the organ.'

The bassoon was probably the most diverse of all wind instruments, with local differences in the number of keys, reed design and bore size. There was a gradual increase in mechanism from the Baroque four-keyed configuration to seven keys or more by 1820. Apart from Koch (who in 1802 called it 'Instrument der Liebe'), a useful source is Ozi's *Méthode nouvelle et raisonnée pour le basson* (Paris, c. 1787), whose preface notes that he used an instrument by Bühner and Keller of Strasbourg, with a wider bore than usual and a crook which afforded a greater volume of sound. Where today's period performances sometimes ape the powerful dynamics of ensembles with modern instruments, an ambience is created in which it is patently the bassoons which find most difficulty in competing. Ozi gives illustrated directions for fashioning reeds in his later tutor of 1802–3, evidence which needs to be assimilated with care, given the sheer diversity with which the instrument was treated. As for the double bass, Mozart's father in the 1787 edition of his *Violinschule* mentions having heard concertos, trios and solos played with great beauty on a five-string instrument. This type was commonly used in Austria and Germany, with a usual tuning of FF, AA, D, F♯, A.[59]

Mozart's horn concertos and chamber music remain a locus classicus of hand-horn technique. There is broad agreement among primary sources that evenness of tone between open and stopped notes should be the stylistic aim. However, the different crooks gave a distinctive character to each tonality, with tubing from eight to eighteen feet in length. An Austrian source from 1796 suggested that vibrato could 'be produced on no other instrument with such expressiveness and vigour as on the horn' and that the horn's richness of effect existed 'because of the roundness and fullness of its tone and because of its vibrato'.[60] This raises some interesting questions about Mozart's perceptions of horn tone-quality. Like all the wind instruments, the horn's affinity with the human voice was emphasised, the same Viennese source remarking that though the actual number of available notes was poor, a knowledgeable composer could arouse remarkable sensations with it, including love's complaints, repose, melancholy, horror and awe. The virtuoso had much to overcome in the way of embouchure and pitching, but also had at his command a wonderful array of melting, floating and *calando* effects. The particular characteristics of horns associated with Vienna are distinct from the French instrument and have been described and illustrated in some detail.[61]

Towards an historical approach

Mozart's Serenade K361 has already been recorded several times on period instruments. Most performances have adopted today's standardised classical pitch of a′=430, a little sharper than the tuning fork of 1780 belonging to the piano maker Andreas Stein, already mentioned in Chapter 4. Another feature common to these recordings is the enhanced quality of ensemble blend, bringing to the fore individual subsidiary strands within the texture. Although the historical option is surely for the piece to be directed by the principal clarinet, a conductor has often been preferred, an unhistorical (and arguably unnecessary) practice partly influenced by commercial considerations.[62] Original placement of forces is impossible to determine, although it is noteworthy that at least one celebrated illustration of a *Harmonie* has the players standing to perform.[63] Another area for discussion has proved to be the identity of Mozart's 16-foot instrument, though the contrabassoon was clearly not an option, as shown by the autograph indication 'contrabasso', as well as the unequivocal account of the Serenade's instrumentation by Schink.[64] Furthermore, the bass part contains pizzicato indications.

It is notable that even today Vienna and Prague maintain their own distinctive styles of wind playing. The Prague tradition is consistently more pointed, with tone-colour as a means to musical expression rather than an end in itself. Perhaps this approach, more articulated than elsewhere in Europe, truly dates back to Mozart's time. There is here an obvious rhetorical analogy, the musical words (indicated by slurs) as well as the sentences and paragraphs made clear.[65] As we have observed elsewhere, much feeling for the Classical language can be assimilated from primary sources, which postulate an approach where character is of paramount importance. For example, Leopold Mozart famously remarked that the first note in a slur was to be stressed and the remainder to continue smoothly and increasingly quietly. Furthermore, he expected the first note in a slur to be sustained a little longer, but always with good judgement and without altering the length of the bar.[66] A particular problem is whether dots and daggers have distinct meanings in performance; within the autograph they are not always distinct or consistent. Hellyer has suggested that if there is a pattern it is that Mozart wrote daggers in normal circumstances and dots when in combination with phrase marks (as in two slurred, two tongued note groups), or when staccatos were written below a slur.[67] Ozi's bassoon tutor proposes a harder tongue stroke for the wedge and it might well be argued that it implies an emphasis which counteracts the normal hierarchy of the bar.

Daniel Türk lays considerable emphasis on harmony and the hierarchy of the bar in his wide-ranging discussion of melodic inflection. Prominent in the equation is the role of vocal music as a model. But even with these parameters in mind, Mozart's musical notation cannot be taken too literally. For example, the opening of the initial Adagio presents three bars of tutti dotted rhythms which may well invite over-dotting. Türk notes that in general dotted notes tend to be lengthened, especially in overtures and when the composition is serious or solemn.

Characterisation of each movement must be assisted by judicious choice of tempo, for which (as we have observed) there are some valuable primary sources. But was music such as the Molto allegro of the first movement played in strict time? Some of the improvisatory flexibility of early recordings may be attributed to Wagner's influence on an important circle of interpreters; but was there ever a time when today's clean, accurate approach prevailed, as has recently been asserted in relation to Mozart's symphonies?[68] Such a viewpoint is all too indicative of a late twentieth-century dogma of constraint, where our own competence tends to be measured by skill at measuring executive control at all costs, and personality (an important element in Schink's review) all too easily underplayed. Tempo flexibility has become almost a lost art; admonitions to keep strict time (by C. P. E. Bach and others) simply recognised that the ability to keep a steady beat was difficult to acquire and a mark of professionalism. Türk advised that 'a tenderly, moving passage between two lively fiery ideas . . . can be played somewhat hesitatingly . . .'[69] The reflective opening of the development (bars 91–105) and the *piano* passage in the coda (bars 223–8) might be candidates for such slight slackening of tempo.

The minuets and trios might be expected to retain a dance-like basic pulse, although their phrasing implies various shades of nuance (and the marking Allegretto at the head of the fourth movement a faster speed than the second movement). The relationship of the central Adagio to the operatic stage has been increasingly realised in recent performances, with the adoption of faster tempi and more articulated solo playing. The Romance betrays the lyrical connotations of its genre, again notated with carefully moulded phrasing. The most controversial bar in the entire movement (and the work itself) comes just before the coda. The absence or presence of bar 111 has been the subject of at least one entire conference paper.[70] This controversy arises from Mozart's use of a *da capo* indication to recapitulate the opening section and an ambiguity in the notation of his first- and second-time bars. *NMA* leaves the question open and many players have been reluctant to jettison the bar, despite Leeson's eloquent arguments.[71] It is the Variations in particular which illustrate the sheer amount of detail inherent in the notation. The melody incorporates accents indicated as *sf* or *sfp* , the former probably indicating a new dynamic. Long and emphasised melodic appoggiaturas occur in bars 5–7, the sort which (for example) are marked out for emphasis in the second of Ozi's tutors.

Overall, a reversion to historical instruments in K361 serves to highlight Mozart's acute response to timbre and his awareness of technical possibilities. One marvels at the endlessly changing textures and at Mozart's ability to fulfil each instrument's potential. For example, the pairs of horns in F and B♭ basso are treated with great ingenuity within the texture, using notes of the harmonic series. The reduction to *Harmonie* à 11, with a single pair of horns in E♭ for the Adagio and Romance, produces an effectively contrasting colour. The characteristic tone produced by cross-fingerings on two-keyed oboes, five-keyed clarinets and their deeper-voiced counterparts is complemented by the rich sonorities of the natural horn. As a result, different tonalities within the piece assume more varied hues than in a traditional reading. But although certain elements of the 1784 performance can be recreated, no rendition more than 200 years later can ever be in any sense authentic. This is clearly a work which reflected above all the personalities of the original players and it seems more than possible that a mere portion of the Serenade was performed only once during Mozart's lifetime and that he never heard any of the music in concert.

Berlioz: *Episode de la vie d'un Artiste, Symphonie Fantastique en cinq parties* Op. 14

Introduction

Berlioz's *Symphonie Fantastique* is 'one of the most vivid documents of the romantic movement'.[72] Written early in 1830, its evolution was

conditioned by three major influences: the impact of Shakespeare, and especially of the Irish actress Harriet Smithson, in a performance of *Hamlet* by
an English touring company in Paris on 11 September 1827;[73] Goethe's
Faust, in Gérard de Nerval's translation published in December 1827; and
Beethoven's Third and Fifth Symphonies, first performed in Paris (March
1828) at the Société des Concerts du Conservatoire under Habeneck's direction.[74] These influences widened Berlioz's artistic horizons from the vocal
genres of opera, cantata and *romance* to the expressive potential of instrumental music. However, Berlioz's dramatic conception of the symphony,
allied with his resourceful orchestration, stretched the genre to new limits.

The *Symphonie Fantastique* is not only a five-movement symphony
unified by a theme (*idée fixe*) that recurs, transformed in each movement,
but also an 'Episode in an Artist's Life', related in a detailed, semi-autobio-
graphical programme.[75] The *idée fixe* represents the artist's (Berlioz's)
obsession with his beloved (Harriet Smithson), and the programme, which
Berlioz revised frequently and distributed to audiences at performances,
relates his dreams and fantasies. When the score was published (1845),
Berlioz played down the importance of this programme, claiming that
knowledge of the movements' titles alone should satisfy audiences.
However, without the programme, much of the work is incomprehensible.[76]
That Berlioz finally revised the programme (1855) to represent the whole
work, and not simply the last two movements, as an opium dream emphasises the need for performers to examine fully its content and background,
including the various literary and autobiographical sources, in order faithfully to interpret Berlioz's highly original musical drama.[77] Such investigation will normally prompt them to opt for the programme printed with the
first published score, for the later version was intended primarily for use
with the symphony's sequel, *Lélio, ou Le Retour à la Vie* (Paris, 1855).

Berlioz had an uncompromising view of the performer's role, insisting on
objectivity in interpretation and faithfulness to the composer. He thoroughly despised the adaptations of Classical works by Habeneck, Castil-
Blaze and others, describing Fétis's arbitrary revisions of Beethoven as the
work of 'a professor drunk with his own vanity'.[78] He was adamant that
music should be performed according to the taste of the composer, and not
that of the conductor or the audience, and that it should be enshrined in its
own period and not 'modernised'.[79] Such a rigid 'historical' view places

extra responsibility on performers to reproduce faithfully Berlioz's intentions and explains why, after c. 1835, Berlioz himself conducted most of the performances of the work during his lifetime. The score underwent constant revision, the chronology of which is difficult to determine, from its conception until at least the end of 1832, but it seems almost certain that all the major structural revisions had been made by 1833–4, when Liszt prepared his bravura piano transcription, which in its essentials is similar to the published orchestral score of 1845.[80]

Editions

The first 'Berlioz Edition' of the *Symphonie Fantastique*, prepared by Charles Malherbe and Felix Weingartner and incorporating additional (undifferentiated) annotations by Weingartner, is somewhat flawed.[81] But Nicholas Temperley's critical edition for the *New Berlioz Edition*, available also in a smaller study score version (but without the extensive critical apparatus), is a model of scholarly music editing.[82] Based principally on the first printed full score (Paris, Maurice Schlesinger, 1845), it also takes into account the printed orchestral parts, the autograph full score (but only to rectify errors in the principal source) and other supporting evidence such as Liszt's piano transcription. Another useful study score, prepared for the Norton Critical Edition series by Edward T. Cone, is highly accessible and kinder on the pocket. Based on the later printing by Brandus and Dufour (Paris, n.d. [c. 1858]), with reference also to the manuscript (housed in the Bibliothèque Nationale) and a set of the original (1845) printed parts, it incorporates much background information for the general reader.[83] Both Cone and Temperley regularise inconsistencies and make decisions in ambiguous situations (such as differing dynamics, phrasings or articulations). They include useful summaries of alternative readings and discuss Berlioz's self-borrowings, the work's original conception in four movements (with either the third or, more likely, the second movement providing the afterthought), the various structural alterations and other changes of melodic detail or instrumentation.

Timbre, instrumentation and orchestral balance

Instrumental colour is a crucial element in Berlioz's music, which imparts the emotions aroused by the dramatic situations outlined in his programme.[84] Progression and unity are achieved through timbre,[85] and the restoration of Berlioz's detailed prescriptions concerning instrumentation and orchestral balance is therefore integral to a faithful recreation of the variety of sounds and textures of his dramatic intentions. The individual voices of period instruments, involving the juxtaposition of established instruments and new inventions,[86] offer a more vivid and sharply defined palette of colours and realise more explicitly the symphony's drama and emotional range than the more uniform, blended timbre cultivated by modern orchestras.

The French Revolution had initiated something of a trend for performances with massed choral and instrumental forces, especially in Paris, where the orchestras associated with L'Opéra or the Société des Concerts du Conservatoire were generously staffed.[87] Not surprisingly, the *Symphonie Fantastique* continued this trend and included instruments that were not standard to the concert orchestra of the time, notably the fairly new ophicleide and cornet, the E♭ clarinet and three instruments previously associated only with opera – cor anglais, harp and bells. Berlioz was a passionate idealist. In his *Grand Traité d'instrumentation*, he describes his ideal orchestral and choral forces for Parisian festival occasions (467 players and 360 singers), just as in *Les Soirées de l'orchestre* he describes an ideal city, Euphonia, where everything is arranged to the service of art and where commerce has no place. Furthermore, he suggests a total of 119 players for 'the finest concert orchestra', including 21 first violins, 20 second violins, 18 violas, 15 cellos, 10 double basses, 4 harps, 2 piccolos, 2 flutes, 2 oboes, cor anglais, 2 clarinets, basset horn or bass clarinet, 4 bassoons, 4 valve horns, 2 valve trumpets, 2 cornets with pistons or cylinders, 3 trombones (1 alto and 2 tenor or 3 tenor), bass trombone, ophicleide, 2 pairs of timpani (4 players), bass drum and a pair of cymbals.[88] An orchestra of 130 players is reported for a proposed performance of the *Symphonie Fantastique* on 16 May 1830 at the Théâtre des Nouveautés, but Temperley considers this as probably an inflated figure, for 'it would necessitate either the wholesale doubling of wind instruments, or such a large number of string players that the balance (carefully defined by Berlioz in the more detailed sources) would be entirely upset'.[89]

Berlioz's concern for internal orchestral balance in the *Symphonie Fantastique* is demonstrated by his specification of minimum numbers of stringed instruments – 'at least 15' first violins, 'at least 15' second violins, 'at least 10' violas, 'at least 11' cellos and 'at least 9' double basses.[90] Such a large and bottom-heavy string body was considered strong enough to match the wind, particularly the brass section[91] and allowed the division of violins into six parts (v, bb. 1–39) and the double basses into four parts (iv, bb. 1–10) without leaving any single line vulnerable.

Stringed instruments

It is impossible to pursue with archaeological precision the type and condition of the stringed instruments in Berlioz's orchestras, since pre-Tourte and Tourte bows and original and 'converted' instruments may have co-existed.[92] However, since Paris was in the forefront of technical and instrumental developments in the early nineteenth century, it is probable that Tourte bows were in general use by 1830[93] and that the arched 'Dragonetti' bass bow, held 'meat-saw fashion' was the type for which Berlioz wrote the rough, earthy passage in the 'Witches' Round Dance' (v, b. 241). Most violins and violas would have been without shoulder-pads and chin-rests, and cellos without end-pins (invented *c.* 1860). Berlioz acknowledged two 'kinds' of basses – those with three (tuned GG, D, A) and four strings (EE, AA, D, G) – preferring the four-string variety. Stringing was largely of plain gut or of gut covered in silver wire, offering a warmer, more transparent sonority than the strident brilliance of the modern string sound.

Berlioz's score requires at least four harps (at least two on each part) for optimum balance. The double action harp was already in general use in Paris during the early nineteenth century, but it was smaller, quieter and sweeter in tone than its modern equivalent, hence the minimum doubling requirement. Berlioz often had to substitute a piano for the harps on his travels, Mendelssohn doing the honours in Leipzig (1843).[94]

Wind instruments (general)

Developments in wind instruments also resulted in significant changes in orchestral constitution, volume and timbre. Berlioz was among the most enthusiastic champions of developments such as the introduction of keywork and valves for wind instruments to alleviate problems of intonation and tuning. His appreciation of orchestral colour resulted in his inclusion of many of the latest and more unusual wind instruments in his orchestras, giving the 'extra' woodwind (piccolo, cor anglais, bass clarinet) regular status. To be faithful to his conception of the *Symphonie Fantastique,* performers should aim to use, if possible, Parisian wind instruments made between *c.* 1825 and *c.* 1855 (or copies).

Woodwind instruments

The constitution of woodwind sections was in such a state of flux in the early nineteenth century that orchestras probably comprised a variety of instrument-types with various fittings and accessories, keys, fingering systems, types of mouthpiece, reeds and other such features. Berlioz probably wrote his *Symphonie Fantastique* for a flute of boxwood, ebony, cocuswood or ivory with up to eight keys; but he soon recognised the new security of production, for even tone and greater accuracy of intonation, of the Boehm flute (developed in Paris in 1832, but with a conical bore until 1847), and foresaw the like progress of the single and double reeds.[95] Taking into account both the French preference for the 'hardness and shrillness' of Boehm's instrument in orchestral, as opposed to chamber, contexts,[96] and Berlioz's flute writing, involving frequent doubling of the violins or sparkling above the orchestral texture in a manner which requires a more strident, penetrative tone, it is possible that performances of the work soon after the premiere were graced by the Boehm model.

Oboes with between two and thirteen keys were employed during the early nineteenth century, the most advanced being the model (*c.* 1825) by Josef Sellner of Vienna. The work of Henri Brod and the Triébert family developed the instrument in France from *c.* 1840 such that the adaptation of the Boehm system to the oboe by Boehm himself and L.-A. Buffet (patented 1844) did not find immediate favour, '[diminishing] the compass', according to the maker A. M.-R. Barret, 'and [changing] entirely the quality of tone'.[97] The softer, warmer tone of the French pre-Boehm oboe would be the option most suitable for the pastoral atmosphere of the *Scène aux champs* together with a cor anglais whose shape may have varied from the gently curved to completely straight or to a model with an obtuse angle between the joints.[98]

By 1825, the clarinets commonly available in Paris had eleven to thirteen keys; significantly, however, Iwan Müller's thirteen-keyed B♭ clarinet, which he somewhat rashly claimed could play in any key, was rejected by a panel of judges at the Paris Conservatoire (1812). It was felt that its exclusive adoption would deprive composers of the important tonal differences of the A, B♭ and C clarinets then in use – a view to which Berlioz probably would have subscribed.[99] Mouthpieces were narrower than modern varieties with both 'reed below' and particularly 'reed-up' designs employed. The Boehm-system clarinet, devised by Hyacinthe Klosé and Louis-August Buffet and patented in 1844, gained only very slow acceptance and would have played little part in performances of the work during Berlioz's lifetime.

The bassoon took two 'national' lines of development in the early nineteenth century. The French model had a narrower bore flared at a greater rate than the German model of, for example, Almenraeder and it produced a lighter, drier, yet sweeter tone. This doubtless explains the use of four bassoons as standard practice in large Parisian orchestras. As Berlioz remarks: 'The bassoon is ordinarily written for in two parts; but large orchestras being always provided with four bassoons, it can then be without inconvenience written for in four real parts; or, still better, in three – the lowest part being doubled an octave below, to strengthen the bass.'[100] Only in the last two movements of the *Symphonie Fantastique*, and then only occasionally, did Berlioz write more than two bassoon parts, the resultant ambiguity leaving the conductor to make decisions about doubling.

Brass instruments

The development of valve systems in the second decade of the nineteenth century had far-reaching consequences. The original score of the *Symphonie Fantastique* required 4 natural horns, 2 cornets, 2 natural trumpets, 3 trombones (1 alto, 2 tenor) and 2 ophicleides (in C and B♭). However, by the mid 1840s, the brass complement for the work was specified as 4 valve horns, 2 cornets, 2 valve trumpets, 3 trombones and 2 tubas (tenor and bass), thereby confirming Berlioz's approval of newly developed instruments. The changes pose problems for those pursuing historically informed performance, since each option was sanctioned by Berlioz, but at different times.

Berlioz originally wrote for natural horns; notes not in the natural series were to be stopped with the hand (*bouché*), with a consequent change in tone colour. However, the directions in his printed score demonstrate his wish to take advantage of the more brilliant tone and uniform sound of the valve horn in the fourth (bb. 62ff.) and fifth movements (bb. 29ff., *avec les cylindres tous les sons ouverts*). Particularly interesting is the way in which he continued to exploit handstopping techniques, while encouraging players to use the valves (*bouché avec les cylindres*) – see, for example, bars 9–11, 19, 370 and 372 of the finale – an effect which, if neglected, would be 'a dangerous abuse'.[101] The ideal horns in a nineteenth-century period orchestra would thus be of the valved variety, pitched in the correct keys and with 'pure funnel' mouthpieces. The bore and bell diameter would be narrower than with the modern horn, both to facilitate hand stopping and to recreate the less weighty tone and volume capacity of nineteenth-century models.[102]

Berlioz calls for a pair of natural trumpets and a pair of the new *cornets à piston* in the *Symphonie Fantastique*, making their presence strongly felt in the culmination of the first movement and the *Marche au supplice*. The two instruments are used as contrasting tone colours, but the cornets are allotted lyrical, moving parts while the trumpets play repeated-note fanfare figures appropriate to the open, brilliant sound produced by their straighter, cylindrical tubes and shallow mouthpiece with a semi-spherical cup and wide rim. By contrast, cornet players of the time used a more horn-like mouthpiece with a narrow rim and a conical cup, resulting in a rounder, more velvety tone.

Berlioz wrote an obbligato cornet part for the second movement of the symphony for a performance in Paris on 4 May 1844.[103] Temperley and Cairns agree that this part was probably written for a particular occasion and even a particular player, perhaps Joseph-Jean-Baptiste Arban. Nowhere else in the symphony does Berlioz give the cornet such a prominent role. That he had a low opinion of it as a solo instrument[104] suggests that this obbligato was written for a special one-off occasion and should not be regarded as a permanent fixture in the work. Had Berlioz been sufficiently impressed by its success, he would doubtless have secured for it a permanent place in the printed score.

Berlioz was adamant that the first trombone part is for alto trombone, doubtless largely for its particular tone quality.[105] The second trombone part should be taken by a tenor instrument, but there exists some confusion regarding the third trombone. Temperley suggests that Berlioz's use of the word 'bass' probably 'indicated the lowest trombone part',[106] because there is nothing in the music which demands a bass trombone; in fact, the pedal notes in iv b. 122 would be impossible on a real bass instrument. Although valve trombones were popular in the nineteenth century, there is no evidence to suggest their use in the *Symphonie Fantastique*. Vital to considerations of timbre, however, would be instruments with narrow bores and small bells, which produced a lighter, more mellow tone with significantly less volume and much less flexibility in the lower range than modern instruments. Berlioz makes full use of this quieter, but better defined low-range sound, using pedals at many points in the march (e.g. bb. 62ff., 70ff. and 90ff.) to underpin the brass texture. This narrow bore trombone[107] would complement well the airy cornet texture.

Berlioz originally specified the use of one ophicleide and one serpent in the autograph of the *Symphonie Fantastique*, changed this to two ophicleides in the published score, and finally approved of tubas as effective substitutes. The Moritz tuba that Berlioz knew was quieter than modern models, with a narrower bore and more focused sound. Nevertheless, it was louder and more robust than the ophicleide, which had the advantage of greater agility and (in this context) a coarser tone-quality; it was employed to particularly good effect in the finale (e.g. b. 127), where tolling bells, bassoons and ophicleide and serpent (or two ophicleides) playing the 'Dies Irae' were supposed to remind Parisian audiences of the practice, then still extant in many churches, of employing serpents to play plainsong themes in alternation with choir and organ, producing a repulsive noise.[108] As the instrumentation of this 'Dies Irae' section contributes considerably to the dramatic expression of the work, it would seem most fitting to use if possible, the ophicleide–serpent combination in period-instrument performances; otherwise two ophicleides will suffice. The replacement of these instruments by tubas nowadays has proved much less effective, especially in the 'Dies Irae' episode, turning 'a harsh parody into a Falstaffian romp'.[109]

As we noted in Chapter 4, the general quest for greater tonal brilliance resulted in a steady rise in pitch in the early nineteenth century. Some degree of uniformity was eventually created by the adoption (1858) of a *diapason normal* of a' = 435 Hz. Such a pitch standard was independently approved by Berlioz, who had previously blamed instrument-makers for the fact that horn, trumpet, and cornet players were no longer able to play various high notes securely.[110]

Percussion

The percussion section poses fewer problems. Berlioz is specific about the duties of each player, stating that in the finale the third and fourth timpanists will play the bass drum and the third and fourth timpani will be played by the second timpanist. The score also incorporates detailed annotations regarding technical matters, accentuation (iv, b. 1) and the types of sticks to be employed,[111] sponge-headed sticks being used on the timpani and bass drum in quieter passages to create subtle, dramatic effects such as thunder (iii, b. 177).[112] Historically aware performances should involve timpani heads made of calf skin, the greater thickness of which would produce a warmer, more rounded sound, but with less definition and projection than modern varieties. For the bells in the finale, it has become standard practice to use tubular bells, but the less defined sound of real bells, located off-stage, would be more suited to the movement's macabre character. Berlioz stipulated that if bells of the correct pitch were not available, six pianos should be employed, playing the bell part (v, b. 102) in double octaves.

Distribution of the orchestra

The location for the work's premiere, the hall of the Paris Conservatoire, or a hall of similar shape and dimensions would provide the ideal venue for a historical reconstruction of the *Symphonie Fantastique*,[113] using the seating plan at the Société des Concerts (*c.* 1828) of the conductor François-Antoine Habeneck, as given by Elwart (Fig. 5.1).[114] As in Habeneck's plan, Berlioz believed that the ideal arrangement of an orchestra is in a semicircle, with the back rows raised on platforms. Ignoring the singers, the most significant features of Habeneck's arrangement are as follows: the violin sections were located at the front of the stage, facing each

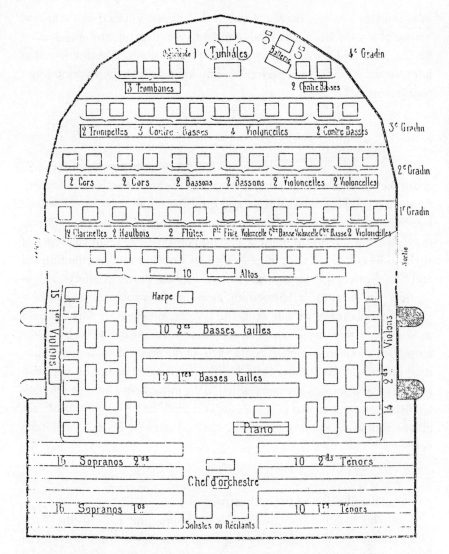

Figure 5.1 Seating plan at the Société des Concerts, Paris, *c.* 1828

other with the violas in the middle; the harp(s) were well forward, presumably for reasons of optimum balance; the cellos and basses, intermingled somewhat, adopted a quasi-triangular formation, mostly stage left, across all four tiers; the woodwind section occupied the first and second tiers on the right of the stage; the horns took up a position on the second tier where they

```
REFERENCE
15 First violins, marked    I           Tr  Tr  Tr  D  B  B
15 Second ditto      ..    2          T  T  B  B  B  V  V  V  V  B  B
10 Violas      ..    ..    A          H  H  H  H  F  F  F  F  V  V  V  V
These are on the floor or level      C  C  O  O  Fl  Fl  V  B  V  B  V  V
of the stage. The remainder
are on four straight rows,          _____
raised one above the other,
viz.:                                    A  A  A  A  A  A  A  A  A  A
12 Violoncellos, marked    V             —  —                  2  2
9 Double basses      ..    B             —  —                  2  2
2 Clarinets    ..    ..    C             —  —       Chorus     2  2
2 Oboes      ..    ..    O               —  —  —   20 Basses   2  2  2
2 Flutes      ..    ..    Fl             —  —  —               2  2  2
4 Horns      ..    ..    H               —  —  —               2  2  2
4 Bassoons    ..    ..    F
2 Trumpets    ..    ..    T                        Conductor
3 Trombones      ..    Tr
1 Drums      ..    ..    D         32 1st and 2nd Trebles          20 Tenors
```

Figure 5.2   Seating plan at the Société des Concerts, Paris, 1840

could function with either the brass (behind them on tiers three and four) or the woodwinds; the percussion was located at the rear on the fourth tier. The similarity of a later seating plan for the Société des Concerts, published in 1840 (Fig. 5.2), suggests that Habeneck's views on orchestral deployment remained relatively unchanged for some years.

Having travelled widely and conducted performances in various venues, Berlioz developed firm ideas about the most effective placement of performing forces. He wrote at length about orchestral placement[115] and his scores incorporate numerous such directions; he was especially fond of off-stage music, as, for example, in the episode with the oboe 'derrière la scène' in the *Scène aux Champs*. Acknowledging that the optimum plan depends on factors such as the shape and interior of the venue, the number of performers and even the style of the works performed, he recommends a general orchestral plan for concerts based upon an amphitheatre of at least five and, if possible, eight semicircular rows. His placement of the violins and violas is similar to Habeneck's scheme, but the flutes, oboes, clarinets, horns, and bassoons are positioned behind the first violins, a double rank of cellos and basses behind the second violins, and the trumpets, cornets, trombones and ophicleides/tubas behind the violas. The harps are placed in the foreground, near the conductor, while the rest of the cellos and basses take up positions behind the woodwind, and the timpani and other percussion are placed behind, or even in the middle of, the brass. It seems a more symmetrical layout than that commonly used by modern orchestras, with left and right sides fairly equally balanced.

Notation

Berlioz's published scores are mindful of the particular needs of the conductor, with descriptive time-words, metronome markings, detailed expressive indications – those for the *idée fixe* alone are remarkable (i, bb. 72–111) – as well as sound advice on countless details of performance (e.g. hns, *pavillons en l'air*, v, b. 29). He often indicates with the words 'solo' or 'soli', for example, those parts which should be given prominence and he takes pains to explain certain effects in footnotes – the sign \ (ii, bb. 43 and 51), for example, indicates 'that one must glide [literally 'drag the sound'] from one note to the next'. Uncharacteristically, no such explanation is provided in the finale (bb. 8–9 and 18–19), where the flutes and oboes are given the direction \ over the interval of an octave. Temperley suggests that 'some sort of rapid scale must be played' at this juncture,[116] but this seems too measured a solution, especially when it is perfectly possible for the *effect* of a portamento or 'glide' to be conveyed, even if over a much shorter interval than that notated. That no such indication appears when the phrase is echoed by the third horn (ii, bb. 11, 20–1) is explained by the fact that the effect, produced by slowly covering the bell, is impossible on a horn already being played hand-stopped.

Despite Berlioz's fairly precise annotations, some of his notational usage requires further elucidation. His adoption of the slur shows the greatest individuality; he uses it not only to indicate *legato* (in microcosm) and phrasing (on a slightly larger scale) but also to show the point of emphasis within a phrase. He achieves this by writing slurs within slurs and by slur elision, a somewhat Schenkerian usage which, rather cleverly, shows direction and musical inertia.[117] Macdonald has also advanced cogent arguments to support his view that Berlioz's accent mark > almost always means a short but real diminuendo. However, although his conclusion has some validity, one such sign under a timpani stroke (e.g. iv, bb. 1, 3, 5, etc. and 66–7, 74 etc.) suggests that it may be too sweeping. Edward Cone concedes that, in many cases, the printed score makes no distinction between an accent and a diminuendo, but he claims that the autograph and parts do differentiate between the two markings and ventures to reproduce such differences in his score.[118]

Tempo considerations

Berlioz supplied metronome marks for all but one (the *Symphonie Funèbre et Triomphale*) of his major works. These scarcely appear in the autographs but were added for publication, as with the *Symphonie Fantastique*,[119] the prescriptions for which are as follows: 1. largo ($\quarternote=56$) – allegro ($\quarternote=132$); 2. ($\quarternote=60$); 3. ($\eighthnote=84$); 4. ($\quarternote=72$); 5. larghetto ($\quarternote=63$) – allegro ($\dottedquarternote=104$). Berlioz approved of the metronome 'to establish the opening tempo and its main changes' and his copious prescriptions (e.g. for ritardandos, rallentandos, stringendos and other tempo inflections) should be heeded as closely as practicable.[120] With his uncompromising attitude to interpretative problems and rigorous time-keeping, it is not surprising that Berlioz took the strictest of stands on the question of rubato. He likened Wagner's 'free' conducting to 'dancing on a slack rope . . . *sempre tempo rubato*';[121] and he claimed that 'Chopin chafed under the restraints of time' and 'pushed rhythmic freedom much too far' – indeed, 'simply *could* not play in strict time'. However, he appreciated Ernst's ability 'of abandoning strict time, but only so that the underlying pulse may be felt all the more strongly when he returns to it'.[122]

Brahms: Symphony No. 2 in D major Op. 73

Introduction

As we observed in Chapter 4, performance practice has undergone radical developments even in the relatively short period since the late nineteenth century. Because Brahms was a contemporary of Wagner, some performances of his music were inevitably affected by the enormous changes in musical style associated with the new school. But Brahms himself was influenced by the great Classical figures from Haydn and Beethoven through to Schubert, Mendelssohn and Schumann, in addition to those Renaissance and Baroque composers cited in Chapter 1, in whom he took a practical and scholarly interest.

Brahms composed his Second Symphony between June and October 1877, though it seems likely that some drafting of ideas took place earlier. The work was premiered by the Vienna Philharmonic under Hans Richter on 30 December. On that day the writer and critic Ferdinand Pohl wrote to Brahms's publisher Simrock,

> The work is splendid and will be quickly accepted . . . Richter took great trouble over the rehearsals and will also conduct today. It's a magnificent work that Brahms is bestowing on the world, and so very accessible as well. Every movement is gold, and all four together constitute a necessary whole. Vitality and strength are bubbling up everywhere, deep feeling and charm to go with it. Such music can only be composed in the country, in the midst of nature . . . [And later that day . . .] It's over ! Model performance, warmest reception. Third movement (Allegretto), da capo, repeated calls for more. Duration of the movements: 19, 11, 5, 8 minutes. Only the Adagio, in keeping with the profound content, not applauded, but it is still the most valuable movement musically . . .[123]

Sources

Brahms normally prepared his material for the engraver and corrected proofs himself, making compositional retouchings as he went. He also continued to polish works after publication. In the Brahms Collected Edition the symphonies were edited by Hans Gál in 1926.[124] The text of the Second Symphony was based on the score originally published by Simrock (no. 8028), Brahms's personal copy in the Gesellschaft der Musikfreunde, Vienna and his autograph, at present deposited in the Pierpont Morgan Library, New York. Gál declared that the latter yielded nothing of importance in the preparation of his edition and that the original published score was free from error, aside from trivia such as missing slurs and staccato marks in divided parts and natural signs after accidentals, etc. Brahms's own score contains conductors' markings rather than textual corrections.[125] A new complete edition currently in progress seeks to correct further the texts of Brahms's lifetime publications in matters such as the duration and placement of hairpins, muddle over which stave performance signs apply to, as well as confusion of similar signs such as *rf* and *sf*, staccato and accent.[126] No sketches or drafts for the Second Symphony are extant and there are thus no revelations comparable to the pre-publication performances of the First Symphony, which had a quite different version of the slow movement from the one Brahms subsequently published.

Orchestral size and placement

Brahms's orchestral music dates from a period of changing styles. He did not write (as in the eighteenth century) for a specific place and occasion, but for the whole of greater Germany at least. Premieres of his music were given by various orchestras, including Vienna (Opp. 50, 56a, 73, 81, 90) Hamburg (Opp. 12, 13, 16), Karlsruhe (Opp. 54, 55, 68), Leipzig (Opp. 45, 77) and Hanover (Opp. 11, 15). Significantly, these orchestras varied considerably in size. The Leipzig Gewandhaus totalled between 50 and 60 players during the time of Schumann's association, rising to 72 by 1881 and 98 by 1890, still with one woodwind player per part.[127] But as late as 1864 the Düsseldorf orchestra, which Schumann had previously conducted, numbered a mere 34 players; around this time Wagner was among those who felt that permanent membership of German orchestras had not increased in line with the requirements of modern instrumentation. The critic Eduard Hanslick heard the Meiningen orchestra in 1884 under Hans von Bülow and suggested that its 48 players placed it at a disadvantage by comparison with the 90-strong Vienna Philharmonic. However, he was not unaware of the advantages of a smaller group, writing of 'the most admirable discipline' with which Bülow had transformed it into 'an instrument with which he produces nuances possible only with a discipline to which larger orchestras would not ordinarily submit'.[128] Indeed, Brahms himself favoured the more intimate blend available at Meiningen, as testified by an 1886 letter from Bülow to Richard Strauss. Brahms declined an offer to augment the strings for a performance of his Fourth Symphony on 2 April in celebration of the birthday of the orchestra's patron.[129] On a previous occasion he had already opted to premiere his First Symphony with the 49-strong Karlsruhe orchestra (strings 9–9–4–4–4). These smaller-scale ensembles give a more accurate view of Brahms's preferences than his 1878 festival performance of the Second Symphony in Hamburg with the Philharmonische Gesellschaft orchestra of 113 players (strings 25–22–16–14–10, with single woodwinds).

The eighteenth-century practice of standing in concert situations continued to prevail. In 1893 one of the oldest members of the Leipzig Gewandhaus Orchestra was quoted in an article in the *Leipziger Tageblatt* as stating: 'In the Gewandhaus we are wholly different people than in the theatre; in black dress coat and standing erect at the desk, surrounded by the finely bedecked society in the hall, a different, higher spirit dominates us.'[130] Hanslick was doubtful about this reversion to older custom at Meiningen, attributing it to Bülow's desire for discipline and concluding: 'Standing is a kind of insurance against carelessness and easetaking on the part of the players; sitting conserves their strength. The first is more military, the latter more humane.'[131]

As we have noted, orchestral seating plans were various and much discussed in print. First and second violins were consistently separated to left and right of the conductor and Brahms made use of this factor for antiphonal effects.[132] His friend Georg Henschel experimented with a variety of plans upon taking charge of the newly formed Boston Symphony in 1881. Of two possibilities he sent to Brahms, the division of the violins and the placement of cellos and basses on each wing (though separated from one another by the brass) found favour with the composer. Fig. 5.3 shows this arrangement.[133] Positioning of the double basses at the back of the orchestra was widely employed, though there is some evidence that Henschel soon abandoned the division of the cellos.[134]

Instruments and orchestral sonority

The intimacy of an orchestra of fewer than fifty runs counter to normal modern practice in this repertory. None the less, it has increasingly been acknowledged that Brahms suffers from an interpretation which applies the Wagnerian ideal of an endless, long-line melody and the heavy sound and texture appropriate for Bayreuth, though at least one leading period conductor has suggested that Brahms's music lends itself to a weight-

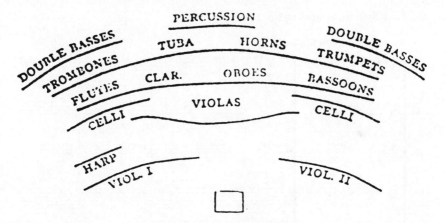

Figure 5.3 Henschel's seating plan approved by Brahms

ier sonority than he himself envisaged. In any event, his music calls for a particular tonal depth and breadth, a breathing sound capable of subtle inflection, ebb and flow. It takes much skill from each individual player to control the sound without becoming mannered in a crypto-Baroque way, or else having the wonderful subtleties of inflection and cross-rhythm ironed out. 'In terms of the sound concept we are only at the very beginning of our process of reappraisal in this repertoire, which requires much work to achieve the potentially immense rewards. The whole challenge consists in ... finding the perfect meeting-point of heart and mind, instinct and knowledge. But we should beware of instinct as a bottleable commodity. It changes with habit, usage, and redefinition of stylistic parameters.'[135]

The Classical element in Brahms's music extends to the notation of phrases, in which the language of the slur is a central element. The opening horn theme of the Second Symphony (Ex. 5.6) forms a particularly telling example; it is often played legato throughout, but Fritz Steinbach, conductor at Meiningen in 1886–1903, used to articulate it strongly, with audible gaps between slurs. According to Brahms's friend and biographer Max Kalbeck, Steinbach modelled his interpretations on those of Brahms. His pupil Walter Blume detailed Steinbach's Brahms conducting bar by bar in his unpublished typescript *Brahms in der Meininger Tradition* of 1933.[136] It is clear from a correspondence between Brahms and Joachim in 1879 that Brahms followed Classical composers in regarding the shortening of the

Ex. 5.6 J. Brahms, Symphony No. 2 Op. 73, i, bb. 1–9

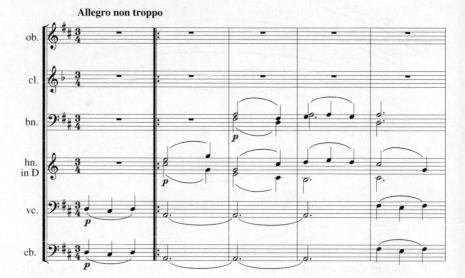

Ex. 5.7 J. Brahms, Symphony No. 2 Op. 73, iii, bb. 1–8

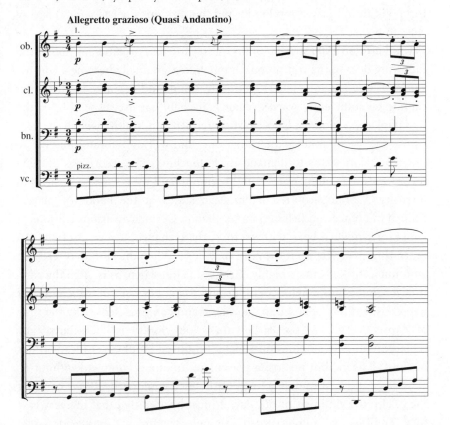

second of a pair of notes as obligatory (though during his lifetime this was no longer universally taken for granted). The *Violinschule* by Joachim and Moser draws a traditional analogy between music and rhetoric. Ex. 5.7 shows the subtle expressive detail of Brahms's phrasing in the opening eight bars of the Allegretto grazioso, including in bar 3 examples of the pairs of notes mentioned above.

Old orchestral parts belonging to the Vienna and Berlin Philharmonics indicate that many more notes used to be played in one bow-stroke than is customary today. Such spinning out of the notes, with the bow barely moving at all, was the essence of bowing technique. Nowadays it is the left hand which controls expression. The old manner produces great melodic paragraphs that sound wonderful but that are also comparatively quiet.

Harnoncourt has argued in particular that the beginning of the Adagio non troppo is always played too loudly and that Brahms's *pf* (*poco forte*) is very close to *piano*.[137]

Until around 1900 string vibrato was regarded as ornamental, and in the following decades its continuous employment gradually became a controversial issue. Joachim cited Spohr's restraint and remarked: 'the pupil cannot be sufficiently warned against its habitual use, especially in the wrong place. A violinist whose taste is refined and healthy will always recognise the steady tone as the ruling one, and will use vibrato only where the expression seems to demand it.'[138] Joachim's five recordings of 1903 incorporate some long notes with no vibrato and others where it varies in intensity. Vibrato acquired its modern status at the hands of players trained in France and Belgium rather than in Germany. Various editions of *Grove's Dictionary* bear witness to such a change, *Grove 2* (1904–10) reprinting an article from *Grove 1* (1879–89): 'When the vibrato is really an emotional thrill it can be highly effective . . . but when, as is often the case, it degenerates into a mannerism, its effect is either painful, ridiculous, or nauseous, entirely opposed to good taste and common sense.' By the time of *Grove 3* (1927–8) the earlier attack on vibrato is characteristically replaced with: 'As an emotional effect produced by physical means it has obvious dangers, but no string-player's technique is complete without its acquirement.'[139] At the same time, Carl Flesch could write, 'If we consider the celebrated violinists of our day, it must be admitted that in every case they employ an uninterrupted (though technically unobjectionable) vibrato.'[140] Though such remarks were directed primarily at soloists they broadly apply to orchestral string sound during the period. Significantly, it has been noted that the Vienna Philharmonic cultivated a particularly 'straight' string sound with little vibrato, a style it preserved until World War II.[141]

Another important area of performance practice in string playing is the use of portamento, a conspicuous slide between positions as an expressive device. Like vibrato, portamento is very difficult to introduce for purely expressive ends without self-consciousness, rather than merely to fulfil instructions. Portamenti served to shape the melody by calling attention to certain structurally important pitches. This was already a prominent feature of the technique of some violinists well before 1800 and subsequently found its way into orchestral playing, early recordings reflecting a well-established approach. Nineteenth- and early twentieth-century violin methods discuss both the mechanical execution and the artistic use of portamento, though identification of appropriate contexts in unrecorded works poses difficulties; for all the detail given (for example) by Flesch, recordings reveal no regular practice in this regard. Joachim emphasised its vocal nature: 'As a means borrowed from the human voice . . . the use and manner of executing the portamento must come naturally under the same rules which hold good in vocal art.'[142] Flesch recalled the poetic quality which could be achieved in Joachim's portamenti, while regretting their accompanying crescendos and diminuendos.[143] The dangers of over-indulgence were consistently emphasised, though the effect was clearly meant to be audible, musical taste in Brahms's day setting quite different norms from our own. In orchestral contexts the position is complicated by the more haphazard co-ordination of violin sections, by comparison with the precise ensemble expected today.[144] British concert-goers in the 1920s and 1930s were astonished by the unanimity of bowing from the visiting Berlin and Vienna Philharmonics, though at the turn of the century Joachim and Moser had argued that because each violinist had his own habits and tendencies, the beautiful illusion of a united legato was best effected by allowing a certain licence in regard to the bowing of the more delicate points.[145]

Robert Philip has observed that in early recordings it is often difficult to draw a line between convenient habit and expressive device. In orchestral playing it is sometimes unclear how many players are sliding and when different fingerings are in use simultaneously, even a deliberate expressive device becoming dissipated into a general effect. In the late 1920s (the earliest date from which there are recordings of full orchestras), there seems little or no co-ordination of portamento in British orchestras, so that the device often sounds monotonous. Although detailed conclusions about continental or American orchestral discipline should not be drawn from early British recordings, it is significant that prominent portamento was still part of the regimented string style of Berlin and Vienna around 1930. Philip's illustrated analyses of orchestral portamenti include bars 1–17 of the second movement of Brahms's Second Symphony in distinctive recordings by the Royal Albert Hall Orchestra with Landon Ronald (*c.* 1925), London Philharmonic with Beecham (1936), Berlin Philharmonic with Fiedler (*c.*

1931), Philadelphia Orchestra with Stokowski (1930) and the New York Symphony Orchestra with Damrosch (c. 1928).[146]

Brahms's orchestral palette was uniformly softer-edged than today's, resulting in a different balance of lyrical and dramatic potential. The violin had assumed most of its modern characteristics by around 1820, but apart from the silver- or copper-wound G, all the strings were generally of pure gut and there was a considerable diversity in the thickness of strings employed. The metal E gained widespread acceptance only after 1920 and gut A and D were still common for some time after that. As late as 1924 Flesch wrote that while steel is more reliable and speaks more quickly, gut has a more vivid tone colour.[147] By c. 1850 an ebony chin rest had found its modern placement to the left of the tailpiece. The introduction of the cello endpin a decade later offered that instrument a greater security, mobility and resonance.[148] Five-string basses were introduced to Meiningen by Bülow only a few years after Brahms had written a crotchet rest rather than a low D♯ in bar 13 of the first movement of the Second Symphony.

As we have already noted in relation to Berlioz, the nineteenth century was a highly complex period in terms of woodwind design. Given the divergent approaches of France and Germany, the nationality of each instrument is of paramount importance here. For example, there was widespread and continued use of variants upon the 'old system' conical flute throughout Europe and the Boehm system of 1847 was slow to be adopted in Germany, where it was actually banned from certain orchestras until 1914.[149] The introduction of the metal flute was associated with the French rather than German school, Richard Strauss remarking in 1905 that 'wooden flutes have a finer tone than metal ones (silver or gold), but the latter respond more easily'.[150] The design of Austro-German oboes was stabilised by the acceptance of Sellner's thirteen-keyed instrument, for which his treatise was revised and reprinted as late as 1901.[151] The influence of the many French designs was variable, but Strauss welcomed their flexibility and adaptability of tone, regarding some German playing as too thick, trumpet-like and over-prominent in blending with the flute. The bassoon had been reformed by Carl Almenraeder in the two decades up to his death in 1843, his eighteen-keyed chromatic model designed in collaboration with J. A. Heckel. As we noted in Chapter 3, the modern German bassoon was developed by Heckel's descendants, notably Wilhelm (1856–1909), for whose radical design the first tutor was written in 1887. Elsewhere in Europe the quite different French instrument descended from Berlioz's era was in general use, but the start of its displacement occurred at the turn of the century when Hans Richter brought two influential Viennese bassoonists to the Hallé Orchestra.

In 1891 Brahms considered that during his lifetime the art of clarinet playing had deteriorated, orchestral players in Vienna and many other places sounding fairly good, but giving no real pleasure as soloists.[152] The Meiningen clarinettist Richard Mühlfeld was a glorious exception, eventually tempting Brahms out of retirement to compose his late clarinet chamber music. Because of this connection, Mühlfeld's surviving clarinets have been the subject of particular attention; their mechanism is the Baermann system developed *c.* 1860, forerunner of the modern German clarinet which is quite distinct from the Boehm system used elsewhere today. More significantly, Mühlfeld's instruments were made of the traditional material of boxwood rather than the denser blackwoods then coming into fashion. The softer-edged sound they produce is indicative of a mellifluous woodwind choir, for which increased power was not a requirement within Meiningen's relatively small orchestra. It is noteworthy that for chamber concerts involving the use of a piano Mühlfeld sent a tuning fork ahead; his own instruments suggest that his preference was for today's modern pitch of a'=440 Hz. There is some evidence that Mühlfeld employed a strong vibrato and that on the clarinet this was unusual. In 1863 Moritz Hauptmann had claimed that a wind note with vibrato was as impossible as a vibrated harmonic.[153] This opinion was contradicted by Arrey von Dommer in 1865, who reckoned that vibrato was effective on both the flute and the oboe.[154]

Brahms's preservation of the character of the natural horn is a notable feature of his writing. An important introduction to the parameters of the early valve-horn is the tutor of 1840 by Meifred, which significantly described the difference between stopped and open notes as one of the horn's assets.[155] Valves were used as a complement to hand stopping, principally to provide missing notes, improve tuning and to make dull notes sonorous. Developments since Brahms's time, notably the introduction of the wider bored double horn, have produced more power and reliability at the expense of subtlety of colour.[156] Rotary-valved trumpets were similarly narrower in bore, producing a brighter and clearer ensemble, less massive in

tone but richer in upper harmonics. The trombones (which retained relig-
ious connotations) were more incisive than their wider-bore successors,
with a distinctive rather than a homogeneous blend. The introduction of the
tuba into Brahms's orchestra underscores the awesomeness of his chorale
passages, especially in the second movement. Pedal timpani were introduced
by Hans von Bülow to the Meiningen Orchestra, one of the first in Germany
to have them.

Tempo, flexibility and nuance

As we noted in Chapter 3, early recordings have a great deal to
impart about the relationship of notation and sound during the late nineteenth century, though Brahms's symphonies themselves were first recorded
only in the 1920s. Most difficult of all to recapture is the original approach to
Brahms's text. Significantly, his own idea of correct tempi for a particular
movement changed regularly, and he did not believe that there was only one
possibility in each case. Some broad conclusions can be drawn from Pohl's
timings for each movement at the premiere, though he must have rounded
each duration up or down to the nearest minute. Furthermore, his timings
may well have encompassed some extreme tempo modification, for example
in the coda of the first movement. There is also some evidence that in the
Allegretto grazioso Hanslick preferred Richter's tempo to Brahms's own, to
which the composer responded that 'he wanted this movement and the
opening Allegro non troppo to be 'quite peaceful, especially at the end'.[157]
But it is clear that recent performances have tended to replace Brahms's first
movement marking with an affectionate Moderato, producing a quite
different emotional effect. These readings also manifestly fail to achieve a
gripping Finale *con spirito*, whilst avoiding the opposite of a great Adagio
pathos or extreme depth of expression in the second movement.[158]

In Brahms's day tempo changes within movements were adopted as a
matter of course, whilst rubato incorporated accelerando as well as ritardando. Indeed, a willingness to allow accelerations of tempo is largely
responsible for faster recorded timings of the first movement of the Second
Symphony in pre-war performances. Adoption of fast tempi in early recordings emphasises a more volatile approach, which responds to rhetorical
detail in the music and is less constantly deliberate. Along with this comes

accentuation involving lengthening and shortening of individual notes, with dislocation of melody and accompaniment and overdotting. As we observed in Chapter 1, there has been a trend since 1900 towards greater power, firmness, clarity, control, literalness, and evenness of expression and away from informality, looseness and unpredictability. Sometimes it can be difficult to differentiate competence, style and taste, especially in terms of rhythmical precision.[159] Our own standards of good taste are rarely seen as relative, so that we tend to reconstruct those aspects of performance practice which suit our values and expectations.[160] Harnoncourt has recently argued that fashion changes so quickly that a composer's intentions can only be realised for ten years, even by an intimate circle.[161] But it is certainly true that attempts so far to recreate Brahms's own sound-world have been reluctant fully to assimilate all the available evidence.[162]

Aside from the indications of Steinbach's conducting already cited, most written information about tempo flexibility in Brahms relates to solo or chamber performance. His own playing was described by Clara Schumann's pupil Fanny Davies as free, very elastic and expansive, but balancing fundamental and surface rhythms. He listened very intently to the inner harmonies and a strictly metronomic Brahms was unthinkable. As we have already observed, Brahms remarked that modification should be applied with discretion and that his blood and a mechanical instrument did not go well together, comments that certainly need to be read in terms of the prevailing aesthetic. Countering his lingering reputation as a predominantly intellectual musician is his remark to at least one player to 'do it as you wish, but make it beautiful' and another story of his embarrassment as tears came to his eyes during a rehearsal of his Clarinet Quintet.[163] Other evidence of the composer's own approach emerges in evidence from friends and pupils, such as Georg Henschel, Richard Heuberger and Florence May.

In orchestral music a revolutionary conductor such as Bülow was imbued with Wagnerian ideals when he turned to Brahms, and one might expect a similarly free approach to tempo flexibility from Hans Richter, though Brahms found his conducting metronomic and lacking in nuance.[164] During Brahms's lifetime Nikisch was another modifier who was happy to experiment with exaggerated effects at rehearsal before achieving a fine concert balance. Weingartner was more Classical in outlook, attacking the Bülow followers as 'tempo-rubato conductors' with their 'continual alterations and dislocations of the tempo . . . in no way justified by any marks of the composer.'[165] Later were to come the opposite poles of Furtwängler's unpredictable elasticity and the excitement of his rival Toscanini within much stricter (and faster) tempi. George Szell remarked that Toscanini 'wiped out the arbitrariness of the post-romantic interpreters. He did away with the meretricious tricks and the thick incrustation of the interpretive nuances that had been piling up for decades.'[166] As in so many areas of Brahms interpretation, a huge range of options is in the broadest sense authentic, historical practice relying as much upon an appropriate attitude of mind as on strict adherence to a set of imposed rules.

6   The continuing debate

Introduction

As we have already observed, the ethos underlying historical performance has been under continual scrutiny since the 1980s. But surprisingly, no coherent opposition was ever launched during the previous two decades, when questionable technical standards were often allied to exaggerated musical mannerisms. At that time the prevailing air of supreme confidence and exclusivity among certain period players might well have provoked such a formal outburst, reflecting the verbal denunciation among players which was then common. But this never quite happened and the subsequent influence of historical music-making has been immense; as we have noted, Baroque repertory has increasingly become the province of period ensembles, whilst modern instrument groups have increasingly approached Haydn and Mozart with considerable caution. Period conductors have migrated to modern orchestras, influencing stylistic flexibility over a whole range of repertory. This sense of an evolving style has affected players and listeners alike and has arguably made all the years of experimentation worthwhile.

The social position of historical music

In a recent discussion of the role of music in society it has been plausibly argued that gains in public accessibility have been outweighed by the loss of something vital, the sense of a living culture, of people being directly engaged in music and, indeed, music of their time. A new symphony once had the appeal that a new play or film would have today. The recording world has changed all that: music has become a commodity, something to be sought and bought. The process of listening gradually became sanitised away from the touch, taste and smell of social interaction. The performer's obligation to elucidate demands immense resourcefulness and imagination in an age of sound bites, constant visual titillation and aural distraction.

Musicians are essentially rhetoricians: they have something publicly to convey, albeit in mysterious language, impossible to define.[1]

These words apply equally to many areas of historical performance as to other types of music-making, directly mirroring some pungent earlier thoughts of the prominent period conductor, Nikolaus Harnoncourt. His important collection of essays originating from the years 1954–80 was published in 1982 as *Musik als Klangrede*; it was subsequently translated into English in 1988 as *Baroque Music Today*. In particular, Harnoncourt deplores the fact that music has become a pretty adornment in our lives, whereas from the Middle Ages to the French Revolution, music was one of the foundations of our culture and the understanding of music part of a general education. People today find a car or an aeroplane more valuable than a violin, the circuitry of a computer more important than a symphony. Two hundred years ago music was a living language, which had to be continually recreated and could actually change listeners and musicians. Harnoncourt claims that music as an ornament rather than an essential part of our lives has been reduced to the merely beautiful and thereby to what can be universally appreciated.[2]

At the time of the French Revolution an attempt was made to simplify music and confine it to the emotional sphere, as evidenced by the syllabus of the newly formed Paris Conservatoire, which in turn influenced other European academies. The old relationship of master and apprentice was abandoned and everything that had to do with utterance – which requires understanding – was eliminated. To this day conservatoires drill performance techniques rather than teaching music as a language. Harnoncourt claims that our musical life is in a disastrous state, because we do not truly understand the music we play in our many opera houses and concert halls. The most remarkable aspect of this situation is that we are completely unaware of it. We believe that there is nothing *to* understand, since music addresses itself directly to our feelings. All musicians strive for beauty and emotion; it is natural for them and forms the basis of their power of expression. They are not at all interested in acquiring the knowledge that would be necessary, precisely because the unity between music and its time has been lost; nor can such a pursuit interest them because they are unaware of any deficiencies in their knowledge. As a result, they portray only the purely aesthetic and emotional components of music, ignoring the rest of its content.[3]

Some aspects of Harnoncourt's case now seem a touch overstated and generalised in an age where certain specialist performers have researched and assimilated particular historical styles with palpable success.[4] But in terms of music-making as a whole, it is difficult not to sympathise with his sentiments, which the continuing debate about the function and value of commercial classical radio stations has recently brought into sharp focus.

Wagner was a great admirer of the new approach to performing music, which replaced verbal elements of interpretation with the pictorial. More than a century after his death, most listeners want to avoid challenge, preferring programmes of the already familiar and merely comparing minor differences in interpretation. The one positive aspect of all this is that it enables us for the first time to assume an independent position from which we can survey the entire creative achievements of the past.

As we shall find later in this chapter, those elements of the period scene which are characteristic of our own time rather than that of an earlier era have subsequently been the subject of lively debate, notably in the work of Richard Taruskin.[5]

A snapshot from 1983

In 1983 Laurence Dreyfus remarked upon the conspiracy of silence surrounding the cultural phenomenon of 'Early Music'.[6] Anticipating the principal issues which have since assumed centre stage, he argued that the 'authentic' musician acts willingly in the service of the composer, denying any form of glorifying self-expression, but attains this by following the textbook rules for 'scientific method' with a strictly empirical programme to verify historical practices. These, when all is said and done, are magically transformed into the composer's intentions.[7] Dreyfus highlights the irony that the puritan has implanted the civilised ban on the uninhibited expression of feelings directly into the art form whose purpose it was, in the first place, to sublimate it.[8] In excepting such a manifestly successful and radical performer as Gustav Leonhardt, he concludes that the real advances in early music are not in the outward signs of historicity, such as original instruments, verifiable performing forces, or text-critical editions, but in the revised operations in the minds of the players, reconstructing the musical object in the here and now.

As we observed in Chapter 1, the concept of a set of rules guaranteeing correct musical behaviour was not part of the movement as it originally evolved in the generation of Dolmetsch, nor can it be justified from historical evidence. During the years after Dreyfus's article, the importance of personality and character has come to be increasingly recognised and reasserted. Writing as one for whom early music had provided some of his most thrilling musical experiences, Nicholas Kenyon was able by 1988 to welcome a subtler, freer conception of the interaction of composer, performer and listener, inspired by the evidence but not bound by it.[9] Furthermore, one might add that although our own age tends to promote standardisation in its reconstruction of the past, it is after all what is extraordinary and special in musical history which commands our rapt attention.

Dreyfus concludes by comparing the dominant social code of early music with that of the mainstream and it is here that his article provides a true snapshot of a particular phase in the early 1980s. He asserts that early music attempts to hold musicians' envious desires in check by negating every sign of social difference. The heavy price for this is an enforced routine and a uniform mediocrity. Early music is characterised by its banishment of the conductor, the equality and versatility of its ensemble members, implicit discouragement of virtuosity, mediocre technical professional standards, identification of audience with performers (and repertory), dull and homogeneous programmes and its critical reports of instruments, composers and pieces, rather than performer and interpretation. The scene described by Dreyfus could perhaps be applied to a number of post-war Mediaeval, Renaissance and Baroque ensembles, but clearly pre-dates the era of star-directors Brüggen, Norrington, Gardiner or Pinnock, whose orchestras by comparison appear to have taken on board a varying degree of characteristics from the mainstream. Indeed, the presence of a conductor in repertory such as Mozart's piano concertos is clearly motivated by some other force than historical faithfulness, since these pieces were originally directed by the soloist.

Authenticity and Early Music

Of the contributors to Kenyon's 1988 symposium (as well as the discussion in *Early Music* of 1984 which preceded it), Richard Taruskin's forthright views attracted special attention. Central among the items on Kenyon's agenda for discussion was once again the role of expression, Taruskin arguing that strict accountability in fact reduces performance practice to a lottery, for the performer can exercise no control over the state of the evidence. Furthermore, the need to satisfy a composer's intentions (assuming that were possible) bespeaks a failure of nerve, not to say an infantile dependency.[10] This leads to Taruskin's central thesis:

> I am convinced that 'historical' performance today is not really historical; that a thin veneer of historicism clothes a performance style that is completely of our own time, and is in fact the most modern style around; and that the historical hardware has won its wide acceptance and above all its commercial viability precisely by virtue of its novelty, not its antiquity.[11]

He proceeds to give examples of the change-over from the vital to the geometrical in twentieth-century performance practice and disputes that this particular style concept had its origins in historical research or in aspirations towards historical verisimilitude, let alone respect for the composer's intentions. The ambience of emotional detachment is pertinent to twentieth-century history and the hardest to justify on historical grounds. The performer simply cannot be held to the same strict standards of accountability that we rightly demand of any scholar; such standards place arbitrary obstacles in the performer's path that can frustrate the goal of performance, which for Taruskin is to please or move the audience in the here and now. The analogy of restoring a painting will not pass muster, since what is both stripped and bared come into the category of interpretation, not the original piece.

Taruskin's anthology *Text and Act* (Oxford, 1995) shows him to be no enemy of historical performance but a convincing realist, critical of so-called 'responsible performers', who are in effect transmitters rather than interpreters. He declares himself dismayed at the extent to which it has been the textual critic's, rather than the moral philosopher's, definition of authenticity which has set the tone for the movement; an equation with freedom from error or anachronism constitutes texts rather than acts. Surely a full score, or even what we may know of a first performance, cannot constitute the work itself. As for composers' intentions, experience within the era of recordings suggests a variety of attitude to performance from one to the next. Stravinsky represents a composer who changed his mind on various interpretative matters throughout his career. In any event, the text-centred, impersonal and lightweight movement is selective, especially in relation to creative aspects of performance such as ornamentation and embellishment.

Kenyon's other contributors complete a full picture of the scene as it was in the 1980s. Will Crutchfield illustrates the huge commercial success of historical performance in his chapter, 'Fashion, conviction and performance style'; but he also notes the extent of critical and scholarly discussion and the hostility it has evoked within the mainstream. He recalls that in the late nineteenth century there did not exist different style-complexes for each period and that since then the thriving triangular relationship between composers, performers and the public has broken down. One of the unspoken qualities sought by a composer in a performer was passion and conviction, neither of which can be expressed in a treatise. Some of these issues also impinge upon Robert P. Morgan's 'Tradition, anxiety and the musical scene', which emphasises the sheer change in cultural environment since early repertories were originally performed and the fact that much music took place outside a concert environment. As Gary Tomlinson reminds us, the internal interaction of the constituent signs and gestures of a work are 'only part of the conceptual worlds in which the work took on its first meanings'.[12]

The 1990s

At the beginning of the decade Peter Le Huray proved the value of perceptive case studies in his *Authenticity in Performance* (Cambridge, 1990), examining a wide variety of Baroque and Classical repertory. In *Authenticities* (Ithaca, 1995), Peter Kivy took the philosophical argument a step further by arguing for several categories of historical authenticity, relating to a composer's original conception, restoration of sound materials, the performer's individual expression and the meaning attached to a piece by its audience. The performer's personal expression becomes a central issue, in contrast to the now customary emphasis on the precedence of the composer. For Kivy, Casals is the paragon of a personalised performer. 'Why . . . should we believe the composer's plan for performance of his work must necessarily be the best one ? Why should it be true of *all* musical works that each of them as it stands *is* such that no performance change from the composer's intentions can do aught but lower its aesthetic payoff ?'[13] In terms of colour, Kivy makes the questionable assertion that the use of modern instruments in Bach's Second Brandenburg Concerto achieves a finer balance, choosing to ignore the way in which composers exploited features of the instruments which they knew. What occurred in the minds of original audiences? He observes that the opening chorus of the *St Matthew Passion* must have had an impressive, almost overwhelming effect, much like the effect Berlioz's *Grande Messe des Morts* still has on us. He thus postulates that a Bach-size chorus will merely give sonic, rather than cultural authenticity. One might counter this by arguing that to the historically sensitive listener Bach's music can remain as compelling (and startling) as it was to its audiences and that original sonorities enable its musical qualities to be perceived more distinctly.

Kivy's final enigma is that personal expression is becoming increasingly threatened by the encroachments of historical practice, that the driving force behind the historical performance movement is the desire to collapse performance into text. Kivy's concentration on the notion of authenticity (a term now largely eschewed by practitioners) and his claim for a lack of personal involvement seems somewhat outdated; nevertheless, his close examination of the so-called wishes and intentions of composers is valuable and thought-provoking. He is justified in questioning which of a composer's performance indications are determinate and which are merely recommendatory.[14]

Many of Kivy's preoccupations and prejudices re-surfaced in Roger Scruton's *The Aesthetics of Music* (Oxford, 1997). Once again, a major premise is that music has been removed from its social context by the public concert and by the development of recording. The modern rock concert has the performers as the full and final object of attention, the living embodiment of the music's spirit, whilst the audience moves excitedly in time. In contrast, the motionless and expectant audience at a classical concert focuses on the music, not the performers; indeed, the conductor (where present) will not even be facing them. In defining what exactly comprises a piece of music, Scruton asserts that a performance is the art of translating instructions to produce certain *sounds* into an organisation of *tones*; while a composer intended certain sounds to be produced by way of a performance of his work, he also intended those sounds to be heard as music – in other words, as organised in the way that music is organised. He then takes up Kivy's (and Hindemith's) point that even if we could reproduce the vibrations made by Bach's music at Leipzig, we should not hear in them the musical life that he heard. This is because performance involves an ongoing dialogue across the generations between composer and performer, in which the dead play as great a part as the living.[15] Each performer sets the piece in a new social and musical context, and dresses it accordingly; a modern player will not necessarily be able to express his musical instincts by means of period instruments as well as would a player who knew no alternative.

But Scruton is less sympathetic than Hindemith, because he then claims that the effect of period groups is to 'cocoon the past in a wad of phoney scholarship, to elevate musicology over music, and to confine Bach and his contemporaries to an acoustic time-warp'.[16] One does not need to be quite so negative in arguing for a distinction between musical material and what is done with it. Naturally, in Bach's day music had everyday applications in dance, song, work and worship; arrangement, embellishment and improvisation were normal musical activities.

Scruton's claim that music is being ossified by scholarship and must be lived, not merely studied, is effectively countered by Margaret Bent's recent analysis of historical endeavours: 'Different repertories of early music have their own grammars and their own dialects. As with "dead" languages, these grammars are recoverable, enabling us to understand the written literature, to know quite a lot about how they were performed or pronounced, even without knowing what they really sounded like.'[17]

Whatever the nature of their achievements, most prominent historical practitioners seem to be possessed of a burning musical instinct; the results of twenty interviews with such luminaries were collected in Bernard D. Sherman's *Inside Early Music: Conversations with Performers* (Oxford, 1997). The sheer quantity of practical as well as philosophical detail makes this an essential read. Unsurprisingly, the subjects are upbeat about their work, even though Susan Hellauer of the vocal group Anonymous 4 admits that since it is impossible to know what medieval music originally sounded like, no one can ever claim that they know exactly how to perform it. But the book clearly indicates that intense interest in later nineteenth-century performance practice has been counterbalanced by a variety of fresh initiatives and discoveries within the periods before 1600. A recurrent theme throughout the interviews is the stimulus of history in firing the musical imagination, which can ultimately be as important as trying to recover every detail. Responsibilities to the past are addressed by Robert Levin, who warns against those who want to

> practise and practise . . . assuming that their instincts are powerful enough and that they would be able to do these things right. But instinct is a very tricky business. It lies at the heart on a bedrock of cultural accretion . . . The alleged sins of that prior generation [of Szell, Schnabel and Furtwängler] are as nothing compared to the lack of integrity of a musician performing in front of the public when the language has been absorbed only through instrumental lessons and the habit of listening, rather than through knowing what tension and release are and knowing how the music really functions in a palpable way.[18]

Elsewhere, William Christie argues convincingly that specialisation is a way to musical freedom, whilst Gustav Leonhardt's perceptive response has already been quoted at the beginning of Chapter 1. Covering a wide range of styles, Sherman's text is full of insights, offering a window into the thoughts of such central figures as John Eliot Gardiner, Roger Norrington and Joshua Rifkin *inter alia*.

Recently, listening practice has been an important area for discussion and debate.[19] In the 1950s both Jack Westrup and Thurston Dart had already recognised that no-one could hear earlier music with the ears of those who first heard it, our experience including consciousness of many other kinds of music.[20] Shai Burstyn has rightly observed that we encounter the vast musical treasures of the past from the one vantage point available to us – our own aesthetic experience. But this should not be mistaken as the aesthetic response of past listeners. Oral orientation is the most elusive strand to capture, since its components have left only the faintest of traces, in comparison with more concrete evidence such as notated scores. In posing the question 'Did people listen in the eighteenth century?', William Weber argues for the integrity of their response, claiming that they were inclined to exaggerate their lack of auditory staying power.[21] As Weber says, today's concert is a step apart from mundane existence and the compromises involved there. It is a shift into a highly internalised realm where we achieve purity of both intellect and feeling such as we find in few places in our lives. Religion no longer provides this. But words such as classical, serious, musical, genius and masterpiece carry a set of overtones foreign to the eighteenth century. Music was more closely linked to other social activities than is true of today's classical scene. Furthermore, contemporary paintings telescoped the activities of an evening, including music and conversation, thus giving a false impression that they always took place at the same time.

The future?

What predictions can be made for the future? Early music as a concept is surely beginning to be eroded, as period principles begin to be applied to mainstream situations. The recording industry, whatever its own future, is bound to remain an important influence; and, as proved by the continuing debates, there is likely to be a certain circumspection in relation to claims of historical propriety. Musicianship, flair and conviction will surely flourish, since in reality they form an important part of historical inspiration. Indeed, the whole challenge of period performance is in finding the perfect meeting point of heart and mind, instinct and knowledge, whilst recognising that instinct changes with habit, usage and redefinition of interpretative parameters. It may be true that the past is altered by the present as much as the present is directed by the past, but the supreme legacy of the development of historical music-making throughout the twentieth century must surely remain its contribution to the enhancement of stylistic awareness among the majority of musicians within the Western art tradition.

Notes

1 Music as history

1. J. Joachim and A. Moser, *Violinschule* (3 vols., Berlin, 1902–5), vol. III, p. 5.
2. Robert Donington in *Grove's Dictionary of Music and Musicians*, 5th edn ed. E Blom (London, 1954), cited by Margaret Campbell in S. Sadie (ed.), *The New Grove Dictionary of Music and Musicians* (20 vols., London, 1980), vol. V, p. 530, art. 'Dolmetsch, Arnold'.
3. Gustav Leonhardt in B. Sherman, *Inside Early Music* (Oxford, 1997), p. 198.
4. A view expressed by Joseph Kerman, *Musicology* (London, 1985), p. 210.
5. 'A musical score is merely an indication of potential music . . . a most clumsy and ill-devised indication. How clumsy it is may be seen from the importance of the "individual renderings" of any piece of music. If a composer could indicate what he wanted with any precision there would be no room for this; as it is, two singers or players may follow faithfully the composer's intentions as given in the written notes, and yet produce widely differing results.' So wrote R. Vaughan Williams in *Some Thoughts on Beethoven's Choral Symphony with Writings on Other Musical Subjects* (London, 1953), p. 57.
6. Arnold Dolmetsch ended his book *The Interpretation of the Music of the XVIIth and XVIIIth Centuries* (London, 1915) with the telling observation, 'We can no longer allow anyone to stand between us and the composer.'
7. H. C. Robbins Landon, *The Symphonies of Joseph Haydn* (London, 1955), p. 110. See also W. Apel (ed.), *Harvard Dictionary of Music*, 2nd edn (Cambridge, Mass., 1969), art. 'Performance practice', pp. 658–9; 'In the period after Bach the problems of performance practice largely disappear, owing to the more specific directions of composers for clearly indicating their intentions.'
8. H. M. Brown, 'Pedantry or liberation?' in N. Kenyon (ed.), *Authenticity and Early Music* (London, 1988), p. 30. For example, troubadour manuscripts were copied out long after the music was composed, the fifteenth-century Squarcialupi Codex was prepared as a historical record of Florentine musicians and by the second half of the sixteenth century a number of musicians regularly performed music at least fifty years old.

9. Charles Burney delineates his century's ahistorical attitude to musical listening in his *A General History of Music* (4 vols., London, 1776–89), vol. II, p. 380: 'So changeable is taste in Music, and so transient the favour of any particular style, that its history is like that of a ploughed field: such a year it produced wheat, such a year barley, peas, or clover: and such a year it lay fallow. But none of its productions remain, except perhaps a small part of last year's crop, and the corn and weeds that now cover its surface.'

10. W. Weber, *The Rise of Musical Classics in Eighteenth-Century England* (Oxford, 1992). See especially pp. 198–222, 'The ideology of ancient music', which focuses upon the perspectives of Hawkins and Burney.

11. N. Harnoncourt, *Baroque Music Today* (London, 1988), p. 14. Richard Taruskin in Kenyon (ed.), *Authenticity and Early Music*, p. 141 quotes Donald Jay Grout in 1957: if a composer of old music 'could by some miracle be brought back to life in the twentieth century to be quizzed about the methods of performance in his own times, his first reaction would certainly be one of astonishment at our interest in such matters. Have we no living tradition of music, that we must be seeking to revive a dead one? The question might be embarrassing. Musical archaism may be a symptom of a disintegrating civilization.'

12. Van Swieten was the dedicatee of Beethoven's First Symphony and of Forkel's biography of Bach. As a diplomat in England (1769) he encountered the still flourishing Handelian tradition.

13. Mozart also 'modernised' Handel's *Acis and Galatea*, *Alexander's Feast* and the *Ode for St Cecilia's Day*.

14. G. Grove (ed.), *A Dictionary of Music and Musicians* (4 vols., London, 1879–89), vol. I, p. 30, art. 'Additional accompaniments'.

15. Brahms's lifetime witnessed the first complete editions of Bach, Handel, Palestrina, Lassus, Schütz and Couperin, as well as Mozart, Schubert, Beethoven and Schumann. Of less scholarly efforts, Joachim was to remark that 'the modern practice . . . of "editing" recognised classical and standard works cannot be too severely condemned as a Vandalism. It has actually come about that the carefully considered intentions of the composer have been superseded by the platitudes of their so-called "editors".' See Joachim and Moser, *Violinschule*, vol. III, p. 10.

16. R. Scruton (*The Aesthetics of Music* (Oxford, 1997), p. 447) notes that the dispute over authenticity was already in full swing by 1848, when F. C. Griepenkerl and A. B. Marx fought each other through the pages of the *Allgemeine musikalische Zeitung* over editions and performance styles for the music of Bach.

17. Musgrave observes that Brahms's views on the nature of Süssmayr's additions to the Mozart *Requiem* found a place in the complete edition and that Brahms even set himself in opposition to the leading Bach scholar Philipp Spitta in disputing the authenticity of the *St Luke Passion*, which is now regarded as spurious.

18. 'The Bach festival at Eisenach', *Monthly Musical Record* 14 (1884), pp. 248–9.

19. Joachim and Moser, *Violinschule*, vol. III, p. 11.

20. H. Berlioz, *Grand Traité de l'instrumentation et d'orchestration modernes* Op. 10 (Paris, 1843; Eng. trans. London, 1855), pp. 115, 116, 141.

21. F. Gleich, *Handbuch der modernen Instrumentirung für Orchester und Militairmusikcorps* (Leipzig, 1853), p. 37.

22. Grove (ed.), *A Dictionary of Music and Musicians*, vol. II, p. 486, art. 'Oboe'.

23. *Ibid.*, vol. I, p. 151, art. 'Bassoon'.

24. C. Saint-Saëns, 'The execution of classical works: notably those of the older masters', *Musical Times* 56 (1915), pp. 474–8, reprinted in *MT* 138 (1997), pp. 31–5. This is the text of a lecture delivered on 1 June 1915 before the Salon de la Pensée Française at the San Francisco Exposition and first published in the local French newspaper, *Le Franco-Californien*.

25. See Margaret Campbell in *The New Grove*, vol. V, pp. 529–30, art. 'Dolmetsch, Arnold'. During this period, even contemporary chamber music of high quality was widely regarded as inferior to large-scale orchestral works. The German critic Theodor Helm wrote the following in the *Deutsche Zeitung* of 28 December 1892, having heard the premieres of Bruckner's Eighth Symphony and Brahms's Clarinet Quintet (which he described as masterly): 'What does even the most beautiful "chamber piece" signify – a genre that is effective only in a small space and therefore addresses itself to narrow circles – in comparison with a symphony like the latest by Bruckner, whose thrillingly all-powerful tonal language . . . is capable of inspiring thousands upon thousands who have ears to hear . . .'

26. Dolmetsch, *Interpretation*, p. 458.

27. Cited from L. Dreyfus, 'Early Music defended against its devotees: a theory of historical performance in the twentieth century', *Musical Quarterly* 49 (1983), pp. 305–6.

28. R. Kirkpatrick, 'On playing the clavichord', *Early Music* 9 (1981), p. 295.

29. Dolmetsch, *Interpretation*, p. vii.

30. D. G. Türk, *Clavierschule, oder Anweisung zum Clavierspielen* (Leipzig and Halle, 1789); Eng. trans. (Haggh), p. 337.

31. H. S. Slosberg, M. V. Ullman and I. K. Whiting (eds.), *Erwin Bodky: A Memorial Tribute* (Waltham, Mass., 1965), p. 141.

32. T. Adorno, 'Bach defended against his devotees', in *Prisms*, trans. S. and S. Weber (London, 1967), pp. 133–46: 'At times one can hardly avoid the suspicion that the sole concern of today's devotees is to see that no inauthentic dynamics, modifications of tempo, oversize choirs and orchestras creep in; they seem to wait with potential fury lest any more humane impulse become audible in the rendition.'

33. P. Hindemith, *A Composer's World* (Cambridge, Mass., 1952), pp. 167–8.

34. *Ibid.*, pp. 170–1.

35. Haskell, *The Early Music Revival: A History* (London, 1988), p. 33.

36. 'Anyone who has heard Wanda Landowska play the *Italian* Concerto on her wonderful Pleyel harpsichord finds it hard to understand how it could ever again be played on a modern piano', *Jean Sebastien Bach* (Paris, 1905); Eng. trans. E. Newman (London, 1923), p. 353.

37. 'Observations on the performance of early music', reprinted in Furtwängler's *Ton und Wort: Aufsätze und Vorträge 1918 bis 1954* (Wiesbaden, 1954).

38. Dreyfus, 'Early Music defended', p. 310.

39. D. K. Nelson, 'An interview with Pinchas Zuckerman', *Fanfare* 13 (March/April 1990), p. 38.

40. R. T. Dart, *The Interpretation of Music* (London, 1954), p. 31.

41. *Ibid.*, p. 165.

42. Munrow's colleagues included James Bowman, James Tyler and Christopher Hogwood. Leonhardt's protégés and colleagues included such influential figures as Frans Brüggen, Jaap Schröder, Nikolaus Harnoncourt, Anner Bylsma, Ton Koopman, Alan Curtis and the Kuijken brothers.

43. H. M. Brown, in *The New Grove*, vol. XIV, p. 389, art. 'Performing practice'.

44. Norrington's performance note to Beethoven Symphonies 2 and 8, EMI CDC 7 47698 2 (1987).

45. Joseph Kerman, *Musicology* (London, 1985), p. 208.

46. Sleeve-note to The Hanover Band recording of Beethoven's First Symphony and First Piano Concerto, Nimbus 5003 (1982).

47. C. Brown, 'Historical performance, metronome marks and tempo in Beethoven symphonies', *Early Music* 19 (1992), pp. 247–58.

2 The application of primary sources

1. Discussion of the significance of early recordings as source materials is included elsewhere in this volume.

2. L. Libin, in *The New Grove*, vol. IX, pp. 245–54, art., 'Instruments, collections of'. Detailed information about collections may be obtained from organisations such as the American Musical Instrument Society (USA), the Galpin

Society (Great Britain), the Gesellschaft der Freunde alter Musikinstrumente (Switzerland), the Kommission für Instrumentenkunde der Gesellschaft für Musikforschung (Germany) and the Comité International des Musées et Collections d'Instruments de Musique (France).

3. E. Selfridge-Field, in H. M. Brown and S. Sadie (eds.), *Performance Practice: Music after 1600* (London, 1989), p. 16.

4. H. M. Brown, in *The New Grove*, vol. IX, p. 17, art. 'Iconography'.

5. Especially pre-1600, when composers scarcely indicated specific groupings.

6. E. Selfridge-Field, in Brown and Sadie (eds.), *Performance Practice after 1600*, pp. 14–15.

7. *Karl von Dittersdorfs Lebensbeschreibung, seinem Sohne in die Feder diktiert* (Leipzig, 1801/R1967; Eng. trans., London, 1896/R1970); L. Spohr, *Selbstbiographie* (2 vols., Kassel and Göttingen, 1860–1; Eng. trans., 1865/R1969, 2/1878); H. Berlioz, *Mémoires* (Paris, 1870; trans. and ed. D Cairns, London, 1969, rev.3/1975); R. Wagner, *Mein Leben* (privately printed, 1869, 1875 and 1881; 1st authentic edition Munich, 1963; trans. A. Gray and ed. M. Whittall, London, 1983); C. Burney, *The Present State of Music in France and Italy* (London, 1773/R1969) and *The Present State of Music in Germany, the Netherlands, and United Provinces* (London, 1775/R1969); J. F. Reichardt, *Briefe eines aufmerksamen Reisenden die Musik betreffend*, vol. I (Frankfurt and Leipzig, 1774); vol. II (Frankfurt and Breslau, 1776).

8. For example, E. Devrient, *Meine Erinnerungen an Felix Mendelssohn Bartholdy und dessen Briefe an mich* (Leipzig, 1869; Eng. trans., 1869/R1972); H. F. Chorley, *Thirty Years' Recollections* (London, 1862/R1984); G. Roger, *Le carnet d'un ténor* (Paris, 1880).

9. J.-J. Rousseau, *Dictionnaire de musique* (Paris, 1768/R1969; trans. W. Waring, London, 1779/R1975); H. C. Koch, *Musikalisches Lexikon* (Frankfurt, 1802); J. G. Sulzer, *Allgemeine Theorie der schönen Künste* (4 vols., Leipzig, 1771–4); A. Rees (ed.), *The Cyclopaedia; or, Universal Dictionary of Arts, Sciences, and Literature* (London, 1802–20).

10. For example, *Almanach musical* (Paris, 1775–83/R1972); *Musikalischer Almanach für Deutschland*, ed. J. N. Forkel (Leipzig 1781–8/R1974).

11. See A. Cohen, *Music in the French Royal Academy of Sciences* (Princeton, 1981); L. Miller and A. Cohen, *Music in the Royal Society of London, 1680–1806* (Detroit, 1987).

12. P. Scholes (ed.), *Dr. Burney's Musical Tours in Europe* (2 vols., London, 1959), vol. II, pp. 207, 156.

13. F. Neumann, 'The use of Baroque treatises on musical performance', *Music and Letters* 48 (1967), p. 316.

14. *Ibid.*, p. 319.

15. *Ibid.*
16. *Roger North on Music,* ed. J. Wilson (London, 1959), p. 194.
17. David Boyden (*The History of Violin Playing from its Origins to 1761* (London, 1965), p. 358) states that at least thirty works devoted to amateur violin instruction were printed in England alone between 1658 and 1731, these works apparently being read also in other countries. See also D. Boyden, 'Geminiani and the first violin tutor', *Acta Musicologica* 31 (1959), pp, 161–70 and D. Boyden, 'A postscript to "Geminiani and the first violin tutor"', *Acta Musicologica* 32 (1960), pp. 40–7.
18. Caccini's *Le nuove musiche* (Florence, 1601–2/R1934) and Bénigne de Bacilly's *Remarques curieuses sur l'art de bien chanter* (Paris, 1668/R1971, 4/1681; Eng. trans., 1968) are notable exceptions for their times.
19. Peter Williams provides a useful 'handlist' of the principal seventeenth- and eighteenth-century publications devoted to thoroughbass in his *Figured Bass Accompaniment* (Edinburgh, 1970); F. T. Arnold also summarises the range of such treatises, with relevant extracts in translation, in his *The Art of Accompanying from a Thorough-Bass as Practised in the Seventeenth and Eighteenth Centuries* (London 1931/R1965).
20. L. Mozart, *Versuch einer gründlichen Violinschule* (Augsburg, 1756/R1976); Eng. trans. (London, 1948), Preface, p. 8.; Boyden, *The History*, p. 360.
21. T. Labarre, *Méthode complète pour la harpe* (Paris, 1844); F. David, *Violinschule* (Leipzig, 1864); J.-L. Duport, *Essai sur le doigté du violoncelle, et sur la conduite de l'archet* (Paris, c. 1806); J. J. Dotzauer, *Violoncellschule* Op. 165 (Mainz, 1832); F. A. Kummer, *Violoncello-Schule* Op. 60 (Leipzig, 1839); A. Piatti, *Method for the Violoncello* (London, 1878).
22. J. Sellner, *Theoretisch-praktische Oboeschule* (Vienna, 1825, rev.2/1901); H. Brod, *Méthode pour le hautbois* (Paris, c. 1835); I. Müller, *Méthode pour la nouvelle clarinette et clarinette-alto* (Paris, 1825); F. Berr, *Méthode complète de clarinette* (Paris, 1836); C. Baermann, *Vollständige Clarinett-Schule* (Offenbach, 1864–75); C. Almenraeder, *Die Kunst des Fagottblasens* (Mainz, 1843); E. Jancourt, *Grande méthode pour le basson* (Paris, 1847).
23. L. F. Dauprat, *Méthode pour cor alto et cor basse* (Paris, 1824); P.-J. E. Meifred, *Méthode de cor chromatique ou à pistons* (Paris, 1840, rev.2/1849); J. F. Gallay, *Méthode complète pour le cor* (Paris, c. 1845).
24. M. Praetorius, *Syntagma musicum*, vol. I (Wittenberg and Wolfenbüttel, 1614–15/R1959, 1968); vol. II (Wolfenbüttel, 1618, 2/1619/R1958, 1980; Eng. trans., 1962, 1986); vol. III (Wolfenbüttel, 1618, 2/1619/R1958, 1976); M. Mersenne, *Harmonie universelle* (3 vols., Paris, 1636–7/R1963); L. Zacconi, *Pratica di musica . . .* (2 parts, Venice, 1592/R1967 and 1622/R1967); A. Kircher, *Musurgia universalis* (Rome, 1650/R1970) and *Phonurgia nova* (Kempten,

1673/R1966); I. F. von Mosel, *Versuch einer Ästhetik des musikalischen Tonsatzes* (Vienna, 1813, 2/1910).

25. See Brown and Sadie (eds.), *Performance Practice after 1600*, Bibliography, pp. 507–11.

26. R. Strauss, *Instrumentationslehre* (Leipzig, 1905; Eng. trans. New York, 1948) [= Berlioz's *Grand traité*, rev. and exp.]; N. Rimsky-Korsakov, ed. M. Shteynberg [*Principles of Orchestration*] (St Petersburg, 1913; Eng. trans., 1922, 2/1964).

27. H. Berlioz, *Le chef d'orchestre* (Paris, 1856; Eng. trans., 1917); F. Weingartner, *Über das Dirigieren* (Leipzig, 1895, rev.3/1905; Eng. trans., New York, 1906).

28. Praetorius, *Syntagma Musicum*, vol. III; J. D. Heinichen, *Der General-Bass in der Composition* (Dresden, 1728), Introduction, p. 24; F. Geminiani, *The Art of Playing on the Violin* (London, 1751/R1952), Preface, p. 1.

29. D. G. Türk, *Clavierschule*, facs. ed. E. R. Jacobi (Kassel, 1962), p. 332.

30. Geminiani, *The Art of Playing*, p. 7.

31. Cicero, *De Inventione*, trans. H. M. Hubbell, Loeb Classical Library no. 386 (Cambridge, Mass., and London, 1949/R1976), and *De Oratore*, trans. E. W. Sutton and H. Rackham, Loeb Classical Library no. 348 (Cambridge, Mass., and London, 1942/R1988); Aristotle, *The 'Art' of Rhetoric*, trans. J. H. Freese, Loeb Classical Library no. 193 (Cambridge, Mass., and London, 1926/R1991); Quintilian, *Institutio Oratoria*, trans. H. E. Butler (Cambridge, Mass., and London, 1921/R1986).

32. Called *elaboratio* or *elocutio* by other writers.

33. Mattheson, *Der vollkommene Capellmeister* (Hamburg, 1739/R1954), pp. 235ff.

34. Caccini, *Le nuove musiche*, A i lettori, n.p.

35. See V. Galilei, *Dialogo della musica antica et della moderna* (Florence, 1581/R1968).

36. For relevant bibliography see G. J. Buelow, 'Music, rhetoric and the concept of the affections: a selective bibliography', *Notes* 30 (1973–4), pp. 250–9.

37. Two of the most detailed works on the subject are Kircher's *Musurgia Universalis* and Mattheson's *Der vollkommene Capellmeister*, but Bernhard, Heinichen, Scheibe and J. G. Walther also addressed it.

38. Kircher, *Musurgia Universalis*, p. 558.

39. Mersenne, *Harmonie universelle*; Kircher, *Musurgia Universalis*.

40. J. J. Quantz, *Versuch einer Anweisung die Flöte traversiere zu spielen* (Berlin, 1752, 3/1789/R1952), Eng. trans. (London, 1966), p. 125. For more about key characteristics see R. Steblin, *Key Characteristics in the Eighteenth and Early Nineteenth Centuries: A Historical Approach* (Ann Arbor, 1983).

41. Mattheson, *Der vollkommene Capellmeister*, p. 146.

42. See Heinichen, *Der General-Bass in der Composition*; G. J. Buelow, 'The "loci topici" and affect in late Baroque music: Heinichen's practical demonstration', *Music Review* 27 (1966), pp. 161–76; L. G. Ratner, *Classic Music: Expression, Form, and Style* (New York, 1980); W. J. Allanbrook, *Rhythmic Gesture in Mozart* (Chicago, 1983); V. K. Agawu, *Playing with Signs: A Semiotic Interpretation of Classic Music* (Princeton, 1991), pp. 26–50.

43. J. Burmeister, *Hypomnematum musicae* (Rostock, 1599) and its later versions *Musica autoschediastike* (Rostock, 1601) and *Musica poetica: definitionibus et divisionibus breviter delineata* (Rostock, 1606/R1955).

44. H.-H. Unger, *Die Beziehungen zwischen Musik und Rhetorik im 16.–18. Jahrhundert* (Würzburg, 1941/R1969).

45. By, for example, Unger, Brandes (*Studien zur musikalischen Figurenlehre im 16. Jahrhundert* (Berlin, 1935)) and Schmitz (*Die Bildlichkeit in der wortgebundenen Musik J. S. Bachs* (Mainz, 1950)).

46. In *The New Grove*, vol. XV, pp. 795–800, art. 'Rhetoric and music'.

47. See, for example, J. N. Forkel's observations in *Musikalischer Almanach auf das Jahr 1784*, pp. 31–2, in M. E. Bonds, *Wordless Rhetoric: Musical Form and the Metaphor of the Oration* (Cambridge, Mass., 1991) pp. 121–6; and Sulzer, *Allgemeine Geschichte der schönen Künste*, in N. K. Baker and T. Christensen (eds.), *Aesthetics and the Art of Musical Composition in the German Enlightenment; Selected Writings of Johann Georg Sulzer and Heinrich Christoph Koch* (Cambridge, 1995), pp. 55–80.

48. See J. N. Forkel, *Über die Theorie der Musik* (Göttingen, 1777), pp. 25–7.

49. See, for example, Quantz, *Versuch*, Eng. trans., pp. 124–5, 163 and 231.

50. C. P. E. Bach, *Versuch über die wahre Art das Klavier zu spielen* (2 vols., Berlin, 1753 and 1762/R1957); Eng. trans. (New York, 1949), p. 152.

51. Quantz, *Versuch*, Eng. trans., p. 119.

52. Geminiani, *The Art of Playing*, p. 8.

53. See H. Watkins Shaw, *A Textual and Historical Companion to Handel's Messiah* (London, 1965), ch. 2; D. Burrows, 'Handel's performances of *Messiah*: the evidence of the conducting score', *Music and Letters* 56 (1975), pp. 319–34; and 'The autographs and early copies of *Messiah*: some further thoughts', *Music and Letters* 66 (1985), pp. 201–19; and D. Burrows, *Messiah . . . an Urtext Edition* (London, 1987).

54. A. Mendel, 'The purposes and desirable characteristics of text-critical editions', in E. Olleson (ed.), *Modern Musical Scholarship* (Stocksfield, Boston, Henley and London, 1978), p. 23.

55. Dart, *The Interpretation*, p. 14.

56. J. Caldwell, 'Editorial procedures in 18th-century music: the needs of the

nineties', in M. Burden and I. Cholij (eds.), *A Handbook for Studies in Eighteenth-Century English Music* vol. VII (Oxford, 1996), p. 31.

57. See G. Feder and H. Unverricht, 'Urtext und Urtextausgaben', *Die Musikforschung* 12 (1959), pp. 432–54; G. Henle, 'Über die Herausgabe von Urtexten', *Musica* 8 (1954), pp. 377–84.

58. W. Emery, *Editions and Musicians* (London, 1957), p. 9.

59. *Ibid.*, p. 39.

60. For example, Del Mar's examination of the *Stichvorlagen* for Beethoven's Sixth and Eighth Symphonies revealed several significant differences of articulation and dynamic markings from accepted 'established' texts.

61. Primarily through the elegantly printed, but woefully unexplained editions published by Günter Henle Verlag, Munich, although Henle was not the only publisher to capitalise on the term to sell editions.

62. Geminiani, *The Art of Playing*, p. 6; J. Mattheson, *Die neueste Untersuchung der Singspiele, nebst beygefügter musikalischen Geschmacksprobe* (Hamburg, 1744), p. 123.

63. Mattheson, *Der vollkommene Capellmeister*, facs. edn M. Reimann (Kassel, 1969), Foreword.

64. F. Couperin, preface to the *Pièces de clavecin: troisième livre* (Paris, 1722).

65. Quantz, *Versuch*, Eng. trans., pp. 22–3.

66. Tosi, *Opinioni de' cantori antichi e moderni o sieno osservazioni sopra il canto figurato* (Bologna, 1723); Eng. trans. (Pilkington), I.29, II.1, III.15 and 19, V.15, VII.4, VIII.4–5, IX.41–2, 63, X.8, 31 and VII.22–4.

67. *Ibid.*, VI.13–15; see also F. W. Marpurg, *Anleitung zum Klavierspielen* (Berlin, 1755), p. 43.

68. Tosi, *Opinioni*, Eng. trans. (Pilkington), IX.29.

69. *Ibid.*, I.28, VIII.14, V.13.

70. *Rules for Playing in a true Taste on the Violin, German Flute, Violoncello, and Harpsichord particularly the Thorough Bass . . . Op. VIII* (London, *c.* 1748); *A Treatise of Good Taste in the Art of Musick* (London, 1749).

71. Reprinted in his *The Art of Playing*.

72. C. Burney, *A General History of Music* (4 vols., London, 1776–89), ed. F. Mercer in 2 vols. (London, 1935/R1957), vol. II, p. 992.

73. Mattheson, *Der vollkommene Capellmeister*, p. 133.

74. Marpurg, *Anleitung zum Klavierspielen*, p. 43; Quantz, *Versuch*, Eng. trans., p. 298; C. Czerny, *Complete Theoretical and Practical Pianoforte School* Op. 500, 3 vols. (London, 1839), vol. III, p. 118.

3 Changes in musical style

1. English and other national practices largely comprised a synthesis of Italian, Spanish, Dutch, German and French customs, the English most closely approximating the Italians for sheer impulsiveness, expressive freedom and richness of fantasy.

2. for example, François Raguenet, *Parallèle des Italiens et des Français en ce qui regarde la musique et les opéras* (1702), in O. Strunk, *Source Readings in Music History* (New York, 1950/R1965), pp. 473–88; Jean Laurent le Cerf de Viéville, 'From the "Comparaison de la musique italienne et de la musique française"' (1704), in Strunk, *Source Readings*, pp. 489–507.

3. Quantz, *Versuch*, Eng. trans., pp. 334–5.

4. *Ibid.*, pp. 335 and 338.

5. *Ibid.*, p. 338.

6. *Ibid.*, p. 342.

7. See P. Williams, *A New History of the Organ* (London, 1980); F. Douglass, *The Language of the Classical French Organ* (New Haven, 1969).

8. R. Philip, *Early Recordings and Musical Style* (Cambridge, 1992), p. 2.

9. Quantz, *Versuch*, Eng. trans., pp. 223, 232; L. Mozart, *Versuch*, Eng. trans., p. 45; C. P. E. Bach, *Versuch*, Eng. trans., p. 154.

10. Türk, *Clavierschule*, Eng. trans. (Haggh), p. 342.

11. F. Starke, *Wiener Pianoforte-Schule* (Vienna, 1819–21), quoted in G. Nottebohm, *Beethoveniana* (Leipzig, 1872), p. 110.

12. Mattheson, *Der vollkommene Capellmeister*, p. 151. See also F. Neumann, 'Mattheson on performance practice', in G. J. Buelow and H. J. Marx (eds.), *New Mattheson Studies* (Cambridge, 1983), pp. 257–68.

13. C. P. E. Bach, *Versuch*, Eng. trans., pp. 154–6; Quantz, *Versuch*, Eng. trans., pp. 216–20, 230–2.

14. Marpurg, *Anleitung zum Clavierspielen*; Türk, *Clavierschule*.

15. J. Hotteterre, *Principes de la flûte traversière* (Paris, 1707/R1982); Eng. trans. (London, 1968), p. 63.

16. *Ibid.*, pp. 59–65.

17. See Quantz, *Versuch*, ch. 6. 'Ti' and 'ri' are the equivalents of Hotteterre's 'tu' and 'ru'.

18. A. Mahaut, *Nieuwe manier om binnen korten tijd op de dwarsfluit te leeren speelen* (Amsterdam, 1759); L. C. A. Granom, *Plain and Easy Instructions for Playing on the German Flute* (4th edn, London, 1766); J. G. Tromlitz, *Ausführlicher und gründlicher Unterricht die Flöte zu spielen* (Leipzig, 1791); J. Gunn, *The School of the German Flute* (London, 1792).

19. See S. di Ganassi dal Fontego, *Opera intitulata Fontegara* (Venice, 1535).

20. Mersenne, *Harmonie universelle*, livre 5, p. 235.

21. See A. Schneiderheinze, 'Johann Sebastian Bach, Johann Friedrich Doles und die "Anfangsgründe zum Singen"', *Beiträge zur Bachforschung* 4 (Leipzig, 1985), pp. 60–1. Similar references are to be found in the singing treatises of Agricola (1757), Marpurg (1763) and Petri (1782).

22. J. Butt, *Bach Interpretation* (Cambridge, 1990), p. 13.

23. J. F. Agricola, *Anleitung zur Singkunst* (Berlin, 1757), pp. 124, 129; J. A. Hiller, *Anweisung zum musikalisch-richtigen Gesange* (Leipzig, 1774), p. 178.

24. Agricola, *Anleitung*, p. 126.

25. Tosi, *Opinioni*, Eng. trans. (Galliard), pp. 52–3; F. W. Marpurg, *Anleitung zur Musik überhaupt und zur Singkunst besonders* (Berlin, 1763), p. 22; Hiller, *Anweisung*, p. 74.

26. L. Mozart, *Versuch*, Eng. trans., p. 97.

27. Türk, *Clavierschule*; abridged trans. C. G. Naumberger as *Treatise on the Art of Teaching and Practising the Pianoforte* (London, 1802), p. 36.

28. M. Clementi, *Introduction to the Art of Playing on the Piano Forte* (London, 1801), p. 9.

29. Czerny, *Complete Theoretical School*, vol. I, p. 186.

30. The first published instructions regarding the use of the damper and *una corda* pedals are to be found in Louis Adam's *Méthode de piano du Conservatoire* (Paris, 1804) and the earliest printed pedal markings (for stops) are in Clementi's Op. 37 Sonatas of 1798. See D. Rowland, *A History of Pianoforte Pedalling* (Cambridge, 1993).

31. F. Kalkbrenner, *Méthode pour apprendre le pianoforte* (Paris, 1830); Eng. trans. (London, 1862), p. 10.

32. See D. Boyden, 'Dynamics in seventeenth- and eighteenth-century music', in *Essays in Honor of Archibald T. Davison by His Associates* (Cambridge, Mass., 1957), pp. 185–93.

33. Sometimes the dynamic appears in the movement heading – e.g. Handel's Concerto Grosso Op. 6 no. 2, third movement: = 'Larghetto andante, e piano' – with no dynamics placed under the notes.

34. See J. O. Robison, 'The messa di voce as an instrumental ornament in the seventeenth and eighteenth centuries', *Music Review* 43 (1982), pp. 1–14.

35. Quantz, *Versuch*, Eng. trans. pp. 169–72. Quantz's example is transcribed in simpler format in B. B. Mather and D. Lasocki, *Free Ornamentation in Woodwind Music* (New York, 1976), pp. 68–74.

36. e.g. L. Mozart, *Versuch*, Eng. trans., pp. 130, 131, 218.

37. *Ibid.*, p. 216.

38. For example, in Piani's violin sonatas (1712), Geminiani's Op. 1, Veracini's Op. 2 and in the varied and abrupt dynamic changes in much Austro-German music of the time, especially that of the Mannheim composers.

39. L. Mozart, *Versuch*, Eng. trans., pp. 97–9.

40. B. Romberg, *A Complete Theoretical and Practical School for the Violoncello* (London, 1839), p. 95; Baillot, *L'art du violon* (Paris, 1835), p. 145.

41. Greta Moens-Haenen's *Das Vibrato in der Musik des Barock* (Graz, 1988) is the most comprehensive survey of Baroque vibrato.

42. A term first coined by H. Riemann in *Musikalische Dynamik und Agogik* (Leipzig, 1884).

43. Quantz, *Versuch*, Eng. trans., p. 119.

44. *Ibid.*, p. 123. As the 'quickest notes' Quantz includes the crotchet in 3/2 metre, the quaver in 3/4 and the semiquaver in 3/8, the quaver in alla breve, and the semiquaver or demisemiquaver in 2/4 or common duple time.

45. See R. Stowell, *Violin Technique and Performance Practice in the Late Eighteenth and Early Nineteenth Centuries* (Cambridge, 1985), pp. 302–4.

46. See W. Kolneder, *Georg Muffat zur Aufführungspraxis* (Strasbourg, 1970).

47. *Ibid.*, p. 57.

48. Geminiani refers to that 'wretched rule of down bow': Geminiani, *The Art of Playing*, Ex. VIII, p. 4.

49. See, for example, Türk, *Clavierschule*, Eng. trans. (Haggh), pp. 325–7, 340–1, 327–9.

50. H. Riemann, *Musik-Lexicon* (Leipzig, 1882; Eng. trans. London, 1897), p. 13, cited in Philip, *Early Recordings*, p. 41.

51. J. A. Johnstone, *Essentials in Pianoforte Playing and Other Musical Studies* (London, 1914), p. 45.

52. R. Donington in *The New Grove*, vol. I, p. 33, art. 'Accentuation'.

53. In H. T. Finck, *Success in Music and How it is Won* (New York, 1909), p. 300.

54. Quantz, *Versuch*, Eng. trans., pp. 283–94. Quantz's system is a late version of the old fixed-tactus theory; see N. Zaslaw, 'Mozart's tempo conventions', in H. Glahn, S. Sørensen, P. Ryan (eds.), *International Musicological Society: Report of the Eleventh Congress, Copenhagen 1972* (Copenhagen, 1974), vol. II, pp. 720–33.

55. M. de St. Lambert, *Les Principes du clavecin* (Paris, 1702); Eng. trans. (Cambridge, 1984), ch. 8, p. 44.

56. See R. Harding, *The Metronome and its Precursors* (London, 1938/R1983); E. Borrel, 'Les indications métronomiques laissés par les auteurs français du 18e siècle', *Revue de Musicologie* (1928), pp. 149–53; R. Kirkpatrick, '18th-century

metronomic indications', *Papers of the American Musicological Society* (1938), pp. 30–50; R. Harris-Warrick, 'The tempo of French baroque dances: evidence from 18th-century metronome devices', *Proceedings of the 1982 Meeting of the Dance History Scholars* (Cambridge, Mass., 1982), pp. 18–27.

57. C. Avison, *An Essay on Musical Expression* (London, 1752, rev. 2/1753/R1967, 3/1775), p. 107. See also R. Harding, *Origins of Musical Time and Expression* (London, 1938), ch. 2; Quantz, *Versuch*, Eng. trans., pp. 283–94.

58. All six words were qualified as required, Vivaldi being especially prolific in the variety and detail of his descriptions. See W. Kolneder, *Performance Practices in Vivaldi* (Leipzig, 1955), trans. A. de Dadelsen (Winterthur, 1979), p. 19.

59. J. G. Walther, *Musicalisches Lexicon* (Leipzig, 1732/R1953) ; S. de Brossard, *Dictionnaire de musique* (Paris, 1703); L. Mozart, *Versuch*, Eng. trans., p. 51.

60. See R. L. Marshall, *The Compositional Process of J. S. Bach* (Princeton, 1972), p. 268, for a discussion of Bach's use of Italian terms.

61. C. P. E. Bach, *Versuch*, Eng. trans., p. 151.

62. L. Mozart, *Versuch*, Eng. trans., p.33.

63. F. Couperin, *L'art de toucher le clavecin* (2nd edn, Paris 1717), ed. A. Linde (Wiesbaden, 1933/R1961), p. 24; Rousseau, *Dictionnaire de Musique*, art. 'Battre la mesure'.

64. P. G. le Huray, *Authenticity in Performance: Eighteenth-Century Case Studies* (Cambridge, 1990), p. 38.

65. F. Galeazzi, *Elementi teorici-pratici di musica con un saggio sopra l'arte di suonare il violino analizzata, ed a dimostrabili principi ridotta* (2 vols., Rome, 1791–6), vol. I, p. 36; J.-B. Cartier, *L'art du violon* (Paris, 1798), p. 17; Türk, *Clavierschule*, Eng. trans. (Haggh), p. 106; Clementi, *Introduction to the Art*, p. 13; J. N. Hummel, *Ausführliche theoretisch-praktische Anweisung zum Pianofortespiel* (Vienna, 1828), p. 66.

66. The alteration of Mozart's alla breve markings (even in several andante and larghetto movements) in the old Breitkopf Mozart edition – notably in the overture to *Don Giovanni* and in the opening of Symphony No. 39 – affect adversely the intended accentuation and could result in the adoption of a slower tempo than the composer intended.

67. J. P. Kirnberger, in Sulzer, *Allgemeine Theorie*, vol. I, p. 157. Türk later cited Kirnberger's idea.

68. See R. Münster, 'Authentische Tempi zu den sechs letzten Sinfonien W. A. Mozarts?', *Mozart-Jahrbuch* (1962–3), pp. 185–99; see also W. Malloch, 'Carl Czerny's metronome marks for Haydn and Mozart symphonies', *Early Music* 16 (1988), pp. 72–82. For Mozart's tempos in general, see further Zaslaw,

'Mozart's tempo conventions'; J.-P. Marty, 'Mozart's tempo indications and the problems of interpretation', in R. L. Todd and P. Williams (eds.), *Perspectives on Mozart Performance* (Cambridge, 1991), pp. 55–73.

69. See P. Stadlen, 'Beethoven and the metronome', *Music and Letters* 48 (1967), pp. 330–49.

70. In G. Henschel, *Personal Recollections of Johannes Brahms* (Boston, Mass., 1907), pp. 78f.

71. See R. Philip, 'The recordings of Edward Elgar (1857–1934)', *Early Music* 12 (1984), pp. 481–9.

72. Couperin, *L'art de toucher*, Preface.

73. Quantz, *Versuch*, Eng. trans., p. 124.

74. R. Wagner, *Über das Dirigieren* (Leipzig, 1869; Eng. trans., 1887/R1976), p. 43.

75. In Philip, *Early Recordings*, p. 26.

76. Tosi, *Opinioni*. For a comprehensive survey of tempo rubato, see R. Hudson, *Stolen Time: The History of Tempo Rubato* (Oxford, 1994).

77. See, for example, Tosi, *Opinioni*, Eng. trans. (Galliard), pp. 129 and 156; C. P. E. Bach, *Versuch*, Eng. trans., pp. 150–1; L. Mozart, *Versuch*, Eng. trans., p. 224; Türk, *Clavierschule*, Eng. trans. (Haggh), pp. 363–4; L. Spohr, *Violinschule* (Vienna, 1832/R1960), pp. 199 and 202.

78. See Türk, *Clavierschule*, Eng. trans. (Haggh), pp. 364–5.

79. C. P. E. Bach, *Versuch*, Eng. trans., pp. 160–1.

80. See Koch, 'Ueber den technischen Ausdruck Tempo rubato', *Allgemeine musikalische Zeitung*, Leipzig, 1808, no. 33.

81. Czerny, *Complete Theoretical School*, vol. III, pp. 31–8.

82. C. Rosen, *The Classical Style* (London, 1971), pp. 139–40.

83. Baillot, *L'art du violon*, p. 136.

84. Hudson, *Stolen Time*, p. 300.

85. See F. Neumann, 'The dotted note and the so-called French style', *Early Music* 5 (1977), pp. 310–24 [= translation of original article of 1965]; D. Fuller, 'Dotting, the "French style" and Frederick Neumann's counter-reformation', *Early Music* 5 (1977), pp. 517–43. See also F. Neumann, *Essays in Performance Practice* (Epping, 1982); R. Donington, 'What *is* rhythmic alteration?', *Early Music* 5 (1977), pp. 543–4; J. O'Donnell, 'The French style and the overtures of Bach', *Early Music* 7 (1979), pp. 190–6 and 336–45; G. Pont, 'Rhythmic alteration and the majestic', *Studies in Music* 12 (1978), pp. 68–100; and 'French overtures at the keyboard: "How Handel rendered the playing of them"', *Musicology* 6 (1980), pp. 29–50.

86. Agricola, *Anleitung zur Singkunst*, pp. 133–4; C. P. E. Bach, *Versuch*, Eng. trans.,

pp. 157–8; L. Mozart, *Versuch*, Eng. trans., pp. 41–2. See also Quantz, *Versuch*, Eng. trans., p. 67.

87. See O'Donnell, 'The French style', pp. 190–6; D. Fuller, 'The "dotted style" in Bach, Handel and Scarlatti', in P. Williams (ed.), *Bach, Handel, Scarlatti: Tercentenary Essays* (Cambridge, 1985), pp. 99–117.

88. See M. Collins, 'The performance of triplets in the seventeenth and eighteenth centuries', *Journal of the American Musicological Society* 19 (1966), pp. 281–328.

89. See D. Fuller, in *The New Grove*, vol. XIII, pp. 420–7, art. 'Notes inégales', and its bibliography; S. Hefling, *Rhythmic Alteration in Seventeenth- and Eighteenth-century Music* (New York, 1993) and the various articles mentioned in the endnotes.

90. *The New Grove*, vol. XIII, pp. 420–7, art. 'Notes inégales'. For a useful summary of the unequal values for each metre according to selected French sources, see F. Neumann, 'The French *inégales*, Quantz, and Bach', *Journal of the American Musicological Society* 18 (1965), p. 322.

91. *The New Grove*, vol. XIII, pp. 420–7, art. 'Notes inégales'.

92. See Fuller, 'The "dotted style"'. Frederick Neumann's claim that *notes inégales* should not be used in music by non-French composers even when they wrote in a French style is convincingly countered by Robert Donington, Michael Collins and David Fuller. See Neumann, 'The dotted note'; R. Donington, 'A problem of inequality', *Musical Quarterly* 53 (1967), pp. 503–17; M. Collins, 'Notes inégales: a re-examination', *Journal of the American Musicological Society* 20 (1967), pp. 481–5; Fuller, 'Dotting, the "French style"'.

93. D. Fuller, in Brown and Sadie (eds.), *Performance Practice after 1600*, p. 136.

94. For detailed surveys of eighteenth-century ornaments, the reader is referred to F. Neumann, *Ornamentation in Baroque and Post-Baroque Music with Special Emphasis on J. S. Bach* (Princeton, 1978); and *Ornamentation and Improvisation in Mozart* (Princeton, 1986).

95. C. P. E. Bach, *Versuch*, Eng. trans., p. 79.

96. *Ibid.*, p. 82.

97. Mondonville, for example, in his *Pièces de clavecin en sonates avec accompagnement de violon* Op. 3 (1734), employs different signs for similar ornaments in the harpsichord and violin parts. But his Op. 5 shows a different, more uniform approach, the ornaments in the violin and harpsichord parts being notated identically.

98. Naturally such divisions were not as clear-cut as this implies; for Austro-German ornamental practice was itself a hybrid mixture of national customs,

some parts (e.g. Celle) being primarily French-influenced, and others (e.g. Salzburg) Italian-influenced.

99. C. P. E. Bach, *Versuch*, Eng. trans., p. 85; Quantz, *Versuch*, Eng. trans., pp. 341–2.

100. See, for example, J. P. Milchmeyer, *Die wahre Art das Pianoforte zu spielen* (Dresden, 1797), p. 37.

101. See Quantz, *Versuch*, Eng. trans., p. 113.

102. See J. Spitzer and N. Zaslaw, 'Improvised ornamentation in eighteenth-century orchestras', *Journal of the American Musicological Society* 39 (1986), pp. 524–77.

103. C. P. E. Bach, *Versuch*, Eng. trans., pp. 79–80.

104. N. Framery, P. L. Ginguené and J.-J. de Momigny (eds.), *Encyclopédie méthodique* (Paris, 1791), vol. I, p. 182, art. 'Broderies'.

105. See Scheibe's criticism of Bach's approach and Birnbaum's defence of it in H. T. David and A. Mendel (eds.), *The Bach Reader* (New York, 1945, rev.2/1966), pp. 238–48.

106. See the case study on Op. 5 No. 9 in R. Stowell, *The Early Violin and Viola* (Cambridge, forthcoming).

107. See R. Haas, *Aufführungspraxis der Musik* (Wildpark-Potsdam, 1931/R1949), pp. 225ff.

108. L. Mozart, *Versuch*, Eng. trans., pp. 209–14. See also J. E. Smiles, 'Directions for improvised ornamentation in Italian method books of the late eighteenth century', *Journal of the American Musicological Society* 31 (1978), pp. 495–509.

109. Rousseau, *Dictionnaire de musique*, art. 'Goût du chant'.

110. Hiller, *Anweisung*, ch. 8.

111. D. Corri, *The Singer's Preceptor* (London, 1810), p. 3.

112. Reported by Reinecke, as quoted in Haas, *Aufführungspraxis*, p. 259. In answer to his sister's complaint about the sketchy form of the slow movement of his Piano Concerto K451, Mozart sent her an ornamented variant, implying that he expected the soloist to add extempore embellishment. The skeletal outline of the solo part in the finale of the Piano Concerto K482 (bb. 164–72) and similar passages in K488 and 491 may also require 'filling out'.

113. See, for example, Milchmeyer, *Die wahre Art*, p. 37; Galeazzi, *Elementi*, vol. I, pp. 190–1, 199.

114. Rosen, *The Classical Style*, pp. 100–1.

115. L. Spohr, *Selbstbiographie* (2 vols., Kassel and Göttingen, 1860–1; Eng. trans. 1865/R1969), vol. I, p. 31.

116. See R. Levin, in Brown and Sadie (eds.), *Performance Practice after 1600*, pp. 287–9; F. Ferguson, 'Mozart's keyboard concertos: tutti notations and per-

formance models', *Mozart-Jahrbuch* (1984–5), pp. 32–9; Neumann, *Ornamentation and Improvisation in Mozart*, pp. 253–5; Rosen, *The Classical Style*, pp. 192–5.

117. A cadenza may also be indicated by words such as 'solo', 'tenuto' or 'ad arbitrio' and will normally be implied when two movements of a work are separated only by two chords, usually constituting a Phrygian cadence, as in Bach's Third Brandenburg Concerto.

118. E.g. Schnittke's cadenzas for Beethoven's Violin Concerto; and Brahms's cadenzas for Mozart's Piano Concertos K453 and K466.

119. See F. Giegling, *Giuseppe Torelli* (Kassel, 1949), pp. 27f.

120. *Cadenza* is Italian for 'cadence'.

121. E.g. some of Haydn's early keyboard sonatas admit a cadenza opportunity, while Mozart's Piano Sonata K333/315c and Violin Sonata K306/300l include fully written-out cadenzas.

122. Tosi, *Opinioni*, Eng. trans. (Galliard), pp. 128–9.

123. For a detailed discussion of the cadenza, see P. Whitmore, *Unpremeditated Art – The Cadenza in the Classical Keyboard Concerto* (Oxford, 1991). See also Neumann, *Ornamentation and Improvisation in Mozart*, pp. 257–63; E. and P. Badura-Skoda, *Interpreting Mozart on the Keyboard* (London, 1962), pp. 214–34.

124. Quantz, *Versuch*, Eng. trans., p. 328.

125. Tosi, *Opinioni*, Eng. trans. (Galliard), pp. 128–9; Quantz, *Versuch*, Eng. trans., pp. 179–95; Türk, *Clavierschule*, ch. 5, section 2.

126. G. Tartini, *Traité des agréments* (Paris, 1771), ed. E. Jacobi (Celle and New York, 1961), pp. 117–25.

127. Giambattista Mancini echoes such advice in his *Pensieri, e riflessioni pratiche sopra il canto figurato* (Vienna, 1774; rev., enlarged 3/1777 as *Riflessioni pratiche sul canto figurato*).

128. Will Crutchfield (in Brown and Sadie (eds.), *Performance Practice after 1600*, p. 310) also points out that such recommendations were often disregarded and that singers of the period, especially castrati, were trained to execute in a single breath passages that far exceed the capacity of most singers today.

129. Quantz, *Versuch*, Eng. trans., p. 185.

130. In Brown and Sadie (eds.), *Performance Practice after 1600*, p. 280.

131. See C. Wolff, 'Zur Chronologie der Klavierkonzert-Kadenzen Mozarts', *Mozart Jahrbuch* (1978–9), pp. 235–46.

132. Among the most successful attempts to compose stylish cadenzas for concertos by Mozart are those of Marius Flothuis (for the Piano Concertos K466, 467, 482, 491, 503, 537, the Flute Concertos K313 and 314/285c–d, the Flute and

Harp Concerto K299/297c and the Violin Concertos K211, 216, 218 and 219) and Robert Levin (for the Violin Concertos K207, 211, 216, 218 and 219). Paul Badura-Skoda's *Kadenzen, Eingänge und Auszierungen zu Klavierkonzerten von Wolfgang Amadeus Mozart* (Kassel, 1967) and the efforts of Hans Henkemans are also admirable, if less attuned to the *minutiae* of Mozart's vocabulary.

133. The Violin Concerto was later adapted for piano with a written-out cadenza for piano and solo timpani.

134. See C. Czerny, *School of Extemporaneous Performance*, Op. 200, 300, 2 vols. (Paris, c. 1816).

135. C. P. E. Bach, *Versuch*, Eng. trans., pp. 143–6; Türk, *Clavierschule*, Eng. trans. (Haggh), pp. 289–96.

136. S. Hansell, 'The cadence in 18th-century recitative', *Musical Quarterly* 54 (1968), pp. 228–48.

137. In Brown and Sadie (eds.), *Performance Practice after 1600*, p. 299.

138. The major treatises on continuo accompaniment are reviewed extensively in Arnold's *The Art of Accompaniment* and Williams's *Figured Bass Accompaniment*. Some realised accompaniments for Florentine monody are among the surviving examples; see J. W. Hill, 'Realized continuo accompaniments from Florence c. 1600', *Early Music* 11 (1983), pp. 194–208.

139. Heinichen's *Der General-Bass in der Composition* is one of the more useful and informative treatises on the subject for its time. It provides information about the German approach to continuo accompaniment, including examples of common progressions and resolutions, ways around problems of voice-leading and the preparation of dissonances as well as preserving the fundamental principles of harmonic movement. It is arguably the best single guide to the interpretation of J. S. Bach's continuo parts.

140. C. Wolff, in *The New Grove*, vol. I, p. 811, art. 'Bach, Johann Sebastian'.

141. Fuller, in Brown and Sadie (eds.), *Performance Practice after 1600*, p. 122.

142. See, for example, the orchestral complement for Monteverdi's *Orfeo* (1607) or Landi's *Il Sant'Alessio* (1634).

143. Dual accompaniment may have been more practical in certain circumstances. See L. Dreyfus, *Bach's Continuo Group: Players and Practices in his Vocal Works* (Cambridge, Mass., and London, 1987) and the case study on Bach's *St Matthew Passion* in Chapter 5 of the present volume.

144. In oratorios by Handel, for example, an organ was generally employed for the choruses and apposite arias, while a harpsichord catered for the other arias and recitatives.

145. Quantz recommended one keyboard for every six string instruments.

146. A keyboard was employed, for example, for each of the concertino and ripieno

groups in concerti grossi. Interestingly, Avison (*An Essay*) remarks that if only one keyboard is employed, it may not participate in the concertino sections.

147. See A. Agazzari, *Del sonare sopra il basso* (Siena, 1607).

148. This practice seems to have been especially characteristic of Italian accompaniment in the first half of the eighteenth century. See P. Williams, 'The harpsichord acciaccatura: theory and practice in harmony, 1650–1750', *Musical Quarterly* 54 (1968), pp. 503–23.

149. In addition to Laurence Dreyfus's volume mentioned in n. 143, continuo practices pertinent to specific repertories are surveyed in the following monographs: T. Borgir, *The Performance of the Basso Continuo in Italian Baroque Music* (Ann Arbor, 1986); N. North, *Continuo Playing on the Lute, Archlute and Theorbo* (Bloomington, 1987); and P. Rogers, *Continuo Realization in Handel's Vocal Music* (Ann Arbor, 1988).

150. More detail is provided by Peter Williams in *The New Grove*, vol. IV, pp. 691–8, art. 'Continuo §5, Playing Techniques'.

151. Quantz's views on texture and arpeggiation and his illustrative Affettuoso movement are interesting, especially in relation to the treatment of dissonance. See Quantz, *Versuch*, Eng. trans., pp. 250–65.

152. Attention also needs to be paid in characterising the different national idioms exploited by, for example, J. S. Bach.

153. See P. Williams, 'Basso continuo on the organ', *Music and Letters* 50 (1969), pp. 136–52, 230–45.

154. C. N. Baudiot, *Méthode pour le violoncelle* Op. 25 (2 vols., Paris, 1826, 1828), vol. II, pp. 190–2; Romberg, *Complete Theoretical and Practical School*, p. 134.

155. J. F. Daube, *General-Bass in drey Accorden* (Leipzig, 1756); J. S. Petri, *Anleitung zur praktischen Musik* (Lauban 1767, enlarged 2/1782).

156. See H. C. Robbins Landon, *The Symphonies of Joseph Haydn* (London, 1955), p. 118; J. Webster, 'On the absence of keyboard continuo in Haydn's symphonies', *Early Music* 18 (1990), pp. 599–608; R. Goodman, 'A note on the performances', *The Hyperion Haydn Edition*, vol. I: Symphonies 73–5 (1990), p. 5, Hyperion CDA66520; F. Ferguson, 'The classical keyboard concerto', *Early Music* 12 (1984), pp. 437–45.

4 Conditions and practices

1. For further discussion of these issues, see E. Selfridge-Field, 'Introduction' in Brown and Sadie (eds.), *Performance Practice after 1600*, p. 3. As already observed in previous chapters, notation does not tell the whole story. David

Fuller has drawn an evocative parallel with the jazz musician, who must be able to realise a chord, to improvise, to ornament, to interpret rhythm and to vary a tune on repetition, with charts or fake books no less laconic than many a Baroque score.

2. For example, Beethoven's *Missa Solemnis* was intended as a type of ceremonial entertainment for state occasions.

3. Burney, *The Present State of Music in Germany*, pp. 95–7.

4. L. Vallas, *Un siècle de musique et de théâtre à Lyon 1688–1789* (Lyons, 1932), p. 432. Neal Zaslaw ('Toward the revival of the classical orchestra', *Proceedings of the Royal Musical Association* 103 (1976–7), p. 167) notes that this was not a satire, but a sober bureaucratic report, written at the request of the sponsoring organisation's board of directors.

5. On lack of rehearsal Zaslaw cites Mozart's letter of 3 July 1778 (*The Letters of Mozart and his Family*, trans. and ed. E. Anderson (3 vols., London, 1938; 2 vols., 2/1966; 2 vols., 3/1985), vol. II of 2-vol. edn, pp. 823–8); Dittersdorf, *Lebensbeschreibung*, Eng trans., pp. 48–52; H. C. Robbins Landon, *Haydn in England 1791–1795* (London, 1976), p. 299.

6. See C. Karp, in Brown and Sadie (eds.), *Performance Practice after 1600*, p. 148.

7. Quantz, *Versuch*, Eng. trans., pp. 31, 267–8; 'About thirty years ago, however, the flute was supplied with several interchangeable middle pieces, necessitated by the fact that the pitch to which we tune is so varied that a different tuning or prevailing pitch has been introduced not only in every country, but in almost every province and city, while even at the very same place the harpsichord is tuned high at one time, low at another, by careless tuners.'

8. G. B. Doni in his *Annotazioni sopra il Compendio de' generi e de' modi della musica* (Rome, 1640) had identified pitch centres in ascending order as Naples, Rome, Florence, Lombardy and Venice.

9. J. Adlung, *Anleitung zu der musikalischen Gelahrtheit* (2nd edn, Erfurt, 1783), p. 387.

10. Praetorius reports that, exceptionally, the cornamuse was tuned to his choir pitch. This lower level was easier for singers, for whom experienced players could transpose their parts down a tone and it is still occasionally found on certain old organs and wind instruments. It must be noted that the terminology used by Praetorius differs from that used in other sources, where choir pitch is the higher. Among other levels, a third standard, a minor third lower than Praetorius's chamber pitch, was widely used for most instruments in the Low Countries. See Karp, in Brown and Sadie (eds.), *Performance Practice after 1600*, p. 155.

11. *Ibid., p.* 159. But for a different interpretation see the table 'Performing-pitch levels, 1500–1850', in *The New Grove*, vol. XIV, p. 780, art. 'Pitch'.

12. B. Taylor, 'De motu nervi tensi', *Philosophical Transactions* 28 (1714), published in J. T. Cannon and S. Dostokovsky, *The Evolution of Dynamics: Vibration Theory from 1687 to 1742* (New York, 1981).

13. L. Euler, *Tentamen novae theoriae musicae* (St Petersburg, 1739); D. Bernoulli, 'Recherches physiques, méchaniques et analytiques, sur le son & sur les tons de tuyaux d'orgues différemment construits', *Mémoires de l'Académie Royale des Sciences* [1762] (Paris, 1764), pp. 431–85; J. H. Lambert, 'Observations sur les flûtes', *Nouveaux mémoires de l'Académie Royale des Sciences et Belles-Lettres* [1775] (Berlin, 1777), pp. 13–18.

14. See *The New Grove*, vol. XIV, p. 782, art. 'Pitch'.

15. Various eighteenth-century authors (such as Kuhnau and Muffat) confirm the relationship of these pitches. See also B. Haynes, 'Johann Sebastian Bach's pitch standards: the woodwind perspective', *Journal of the American Musical Instrument Society* 11 (1985), p. 55; 'Questions of tonality in Bach's cantatas: the woodwind perspective', *Journal of the American Musical Instrument Society* 12 (1986), p. 40. Karp (in Brown and Sadie (eds.), *Performance Practice after 1600*) notes that surviving double-reeds and flutes appear to be pitched at either a' = 410–15 Hz or a'=*c*. 390 Hz, whilst cornetti are at a'=460 Hz (*Chorton*).

16. R. Maunder, 'Viennese wind-instrument makers, 1700–1800', *Galpin Society Journal* 51 (1998), p. 185.

17. By this time levels had been consciously lowered in Britain towards the French standard from the widely used 'high pitch' of a'=452 Hz (to which surviving wind instruments bear ample witness).

18. Among specialist writings on the subject, see Mark Lindley in *The New Grove*, art. 'Temperament' and in Brown and Sadie (eds.), *Performance Practice after 1600*, pp. 169–85, to whose work the paragraphs (and the examples of incommensurate concords) following on pp. 87–91 are indebted.

19. Varying shades of mean-tone were surely intended in the tuning instructions of Arnolt Schlick (1511), Pietro Aaron (1523) and G. M. Lanfranco (1533). Later writers on the subject were Gioseffo Zarlino (*Le istitutioni harmoniche* (Venice, 1558/R1965, rev. 3/1573/R1966); *Dimostrationi harmoniche* (Venice, 1571/R1966, 2/1573, rev. 1588)), Costanzo Antegnati (*L'arte organica* (Brescia, 1608/R1958)), Praetorius (*Syntagma musicum*, 1619) and Mersenne (*Harmonie universelle*, 1636).

20. This was so-called '$\frac{1}{4}$-comma' mean-tone, based on a division of the octave into 31 parts, recommended for keyboard instruments by Praetorius and described

by Mersenne as 'la manière d'accorder parfaitement les orgues ordinaires'. Other popular divisions of the octave were into 43 or 55 parts, in $\frac{1}{5}$ and $\frac{1}{6}$ comma mean-tone respectively. The degree of tempering in the principal systems is tabulated in Table 1 of the article 'Mean-tone', *The New Grove*, vol. XI, p. 875.

21. Nowadays, piano tuners routinely depart from a strict model of equal temperament, stretching octaves for melodic effect at the extremities of the instrument, and sometimes varying the beating of thirds and sixths.

22. These temperaments are tabulated in detail in *The New Grove*, vol. XX, p. 337, art. 'Well-tempered Clavier'.

23. Lindley (in Brown and Sadie (eds.), *Performance Practice after 1600*, p. 182) cites Bach's son-in-law and musical protégé J. C. Altnikol, who said with reference to the Wenzelkirche organ at Naumburg rebuilt in the 1740s by Zacharias Hildebrandt (with advice from Bach), 'In tempering he [Hildebrandt] follows Neidhardt and one can modulate quite nicely in all the keys without giving the ear anything annoying to hear, which is the most beautiful for today's taste in music.'

24. Marpurg's report (1776) that Kirnberger was instructed by his teacher Bach to tune all major thirds larger than pure rules out an unsubtle irregular temperament. Kirnberger's proposals (characterised by a pure C–E) have been deemed by some writers to reflect Bach's ideals, but Werckmeister, Neidhardt, G. A. Sorge (who seems to have known and approved of Bach's tuning) and Barthold Fritz all said that the thirds among the naturals must beat.

25. But Quantz admitted (*Versuch*, Eng. trans., pp. 31, 47) that although he had introduced the extra key as long ago as 1726, it had not yet been universally accepted.

26. C. Baermann, *Vollständige Clarinett-Schule* (2 vols., Offenbach, 1864–75), vol. I, p. 1.

27. The clarinettist Anton Stadler's 'Musick Plan', a system of musical education drawn up in 1800 for the Hungarian count Georg Festetics.

28. According to Agricola (*Anleitung*), a healthy diet of pheasant, lark, merlin, trout, etc. may be injurious to the purse. In any event, excess must be avoided; it is harmful to the voice constantly to eat those things which make the lungs slimy or caustic or those that cause gluey, viscous phlegm. The old teachers prohibited herring, but it is said that Farinelli always ate one uncooked anchovy before he sang.

29. Some examples of choir sizes are given by Ellen T. Harris in Brown and Sadie (eds.), *Performance Practice after 1600*, p. 114. See also the remarks on performing forces in the case study on Bach's *St Matthew Passion* in Chapter 5 of the present volume.

30. See W. Crutchfield in Brown and Sadie (eds.), *Performance Practice after 1600*, p. 433.

31. E. Selfridge-Field in Brown and Sadie (eds.), *Performance Practice after 1600*, pp. 7–10. She observes, for example, that at the Cöthen court during Bach's employment there (1717–23) the total number of instruments, between 13 and 15, was relatively stable, but their specific distribution in both the string and wind sections varied from year to year and from genre to genre.

32. As a rare exception, the 175th season of the Royal Philharmonic Society was celebrated by a series of concerts by The Hanover Band in April and May 1988. Even here, the programmes were abbreviated on account of their original length. See C. Brown (ed.), *Beethoven and the Philharmonic* (London, 1988).

33. See Zaslaw, 'Toward the revival', p. 169.

34. See D. Koury, *Orchestral Performance Practices of the Nineteenth Century* (Ann Arbor, 1986), Chapter 2.

35. D. Burrows, 'Handel's London theatre orchestra', *Early Music* 16 (1988), p. 349. When Pierre-Jacques Fougeroux visited Handel's orchestra in 1728, he counted 24 violins, a tally which probably included violas.

36. See H. T. David and A. Mendel (eds.), *The Bach Reader: A Life of Johann Sebastian Bach in Letters and Documents* (New York, 1945/R1966), pp. 120–4.

37. Burney, in discussing the commemoration, wrote that 'Foreigners, particularly the French, must be astonished at so numerous a band moving in such exact measure, without the assistance of a *Coryphaeus* to beat the time, either with a roll of paper, or a noisy *baton* or truncheon' (C. Burney, *An Account of the Musical Performances in Westminster Abbey and the Pantheon, May 26th, 27th, 29th; and June the 3rd and 5th, 1784. In Commemoration of Händel* (London, 1785), p. 14).

38. Koch, *Musikalisches Lexikon*, col. 587, art. 'Flügel'.

39. David and Mendel (eds.), *The Bach Reader*, p. 278.

40. Quantz, *Versuch*; C. L. Junker, *Zwanzig Componisten: eine Skizze* (Bern, 1776); *Einige der vornehmsten Pflichten eines Kapellmeisters oder Musikdirektors* (Winterthur, 1782); J. S. Petri, *Anleitung zur practischen Musik* (Lauban, 1767); J. F. Reichardt, *Über die Pflichten des Ripien-Violinisten* (Berlin and Leipzig, 1776); Galeazzi, *Elementi teorici-pratici*; Koch, *Musikalisches Lexikon*.

41. Jean-Jacques Rousseau felt that Naples was the finest orchestra as far as number and intelligence of players was concerned, but that the best distributed, with ensemble to match, was Hasse's at Dresden. See Rousseau, *Dictionnaire de Musique*, p. 354.

42. The 1773 seating plan of the Grand Théâtre de Versailles is reproduced by R.

Stowell, 'Good execution and other necessary skills: the role of the concertmaster in the late 18th century', *Early Music* 16 (1988), p. 31.

43. See S. McVeigh, *Concert Life in London from Mozart to Haydn* (Cambridge, 1993), p. 212.

44. F. Rochlitz, 'Bruchstücke aus Briefen an einen jungen Tonsetzer', *Allgemeine musikalische Zeitung* 2 (1799/1800), col. 59.

45. Ignaz von Seyfried recalled that in rehearsal, 'he was very particular about expression, the delicate nuances, the equable distribution of light and shade as well as an effective *tempo rubato*, and without betraying vexation, would discuss them with the individual players'. See A. W. Thayer, *Ludwig van Beethovens Leben*, rev. E. Forbes as *Thayer's Life of Beethoven* (Princeton, 1964), vol. I, p. 371.

46. When Beethoven conducted the Fourth Symphony in 1808, there were 13 firsts and 12 seconds, in a total complement of about 55 players. For the premieres of the Seventh and Eighth Symphonies in 1813–14 there were 18 in each violin section and doubled woodwind. Galeazzi had claimed that if the number of violins exceeded 16 (as normally would be the case in the Italian opera house), the wind needed to be doubled. Leopold Mozart's letter of 15 December 1770 gives the string proportions at the Milan opera as 14–14–6–2–6.

47. Edouard E. Blitz, *Quelques considérations sur l'art du chef d'orchestre* (Leipzig, 1887), p. 80.

5 Case studies in ensemble music

Bach: St Matthew Passion

1. See L. Dreyfus, *Bach and the Patterns of Invention* (Cambridge, Mass., 1996), p. 242.

2. See J. Butt (ed.), *The Cambridge Companion to J. S. Bach*, (Cambridge, 1997), p. xiii; also J. Rifkin, 'The chronology of Bach's St. Matthew Passion', *Musical Quarterly* 61 (1975), pp. 360–87; and E. Chafe, 'J. S. Bach's "St. Matthew Passion": aspects of planning, structure, and chronology', *Journal of the American Musicological Society* 35 (1982), pp. 49–114.

3. Published by the Johann-Sebastian-Bach-Institut Göttingen and the Bach-Archiv Leipzig, series II: Masses, Passions, and Oratorios, vol. V: *Matthäus-Passion* (BA/DVfM 5038).

4. See 'Pitch' (p. 103 below).

5. See M. Geck, *Die Wiederentdeckung der Matthäus-Passion im 19. Jahrhundert.*

Die zeitgenössischen Dokumente und ihre ideengeschichtliche Deutung (Regensburg, 1967).

6. A. C. Boult and W. Emery, *The St Matthew Passion: Its Preparation and Performance* (London, 1949), Introduction.

7. They claim: that oboe and flute parts can be taken by strings; that since bassoons simply double string basses, dispensing with them involves nothing worse than a slight loss of clarity; and that either organ or harpsichord may be substituted by a piano. Interestingly, Dürr notes (Preface to his edition) that in Bach's own performances violins substituted for the recorders in No. 19.

8. H.-J. Schulze, 'Johann Sebastian Bach's orchestra: some unanswered questions', *Early Music* 17 (1989), p. 14.

9. R. Marshall, 'Bach's chorus: a preliminary reply to Joshua Rifkin', *Musical Times* 124 (1983), pp. 19–22; T. Koopman, 'One to a part? Who then turns the pages? – more on Bach's chorus', *Early Music* 25 (1997), pp. 541–2; and 'Bach's choir, an ongoing story', *Early Music* 26 (1998), pp. 109–21.

10. J. Rifkin, 'Bach's chorus: a preliminary report', *Musical Times* 123 (1982), pp. 747–54 (revised as 'Bachs Chor – Ein vorläufiger Bericht', *Basler Jahrbuch für historische Musikpraxis* 9 (1985), pp. 141–55); 'Page turns, players and ripieno parts: more questions of scoring in Bach's vocal music', *Early Music* 25 (1997), pp. 728–34. Rifkin's view has received some support from Andrew Parrott, 'Bach's chorus: a "brief yet highly necessary" reappraisal', *Early Music* 24 (1996), pp. 551–80; 'Bach's chorus: Who cares?', *Early Music* 26 (1998), pp. 99–107.

11. See Marshall, 'Bach's chorus: a preliminary reply'; Rifkin, 'Bach's chorus: a response to Robert Marshall', *Musical Times* 124 (1983), pp. 161–2. See also J. Butt, 'Bach's vocal scoring: what can it mean?', *Early Music* 26 (1998), pp. 99–107.

12. John Butt ('Bach's vocal scoring', p. 102) cites further evidence from the autograph score for one-to-a-part scoring.

13. Nos. 39 and 60 in Dürr's edition. The numbering of all movements relates to this edition.

14. For the two movements with violin obbligatos (Nos. 39 and 42), Dürr claims that 'In Bach's performances the players on one of the two desks reinforced the violin I part when it was weakened by the demands of the solo violin.'

15. J. Rifkin, 'More and less on Bach's orchestra', *Performance Practice Review* 4 (1991), pp. 5–13.

16. Dürr's edition includes the original lute part as an appendix and follows the notation of the final separate gamba part, providing variants as *ossia*

readings for its ornamental figuration in line with its evolution through the sources.

17. N. Harnoncourt, 'The oboe da caccia', notes to *Das Kantatenwerk*, vol. VII (Teldec Records, 1973), p. 13.

18. Eichentopf was a distinguished Leipzig maker of brass instruments; models by other eighteenth-century makers generally have wooden bells.

19. A. Schering, *Johann Sebastian Bachs Leipziger Kirchenmusik* (Leipzig, 1936, 2/1954). Dreyfus's conclusions are drawn from consulting surviving organ parts among Bach's orchestral sources, which have been transposed down a tone in order to accommodate the Leipzig organs' high *Chorton* (choir pitch) with the *Kammerton* (chamber pitch, a tone lower) of the instrumental ensemble. See L. Dreyfus, *Bach's Continuo Group*, p. 11.

20. The older east-end organ in the Thomaskirche was dismantled in the early 1740s.

21. Although, as Dürr indicates, the parts include no tacet marking.

22. See J. Mattheson, *Das neu-eröffnete Orchestre* (Hamburg, 1713), p. 269; A. Dürr, *Die Kantaten von Johann Sebastian Bach* (2 vols., Kassel, 1975); K. Brandt, 'Fragen zur Fagottbesetzung in den kirchenmusikalischen Werken Johann Sebastian Bachs', *Bach-Jahrbuch* (1968), p. 66.

23. A. Mendel, 'On the pitches in use in Bach's time', *Musical Quarterly* 41 (1955), pp. 332–55 and 466–80, especially pp. 471ff.; 'Pitch in Western music since 1500, a re-examination', *Acta Musicologica* 1 (1978), pp. 1–93, especially p. 79.

24. Haynes, 'Johann Sebastian Bach's pitch standards', pp. 55–114; and 'Questions of tonality', pp. 40–67.

25. See C. Karp, in Brown and Sadie (eds.), *Performance Practice after 1600*, p. 163.

26. See Mattheson, *Der vollkommene Capellmeister*, Eng. trans., pp. 270–1; see also Moens-Haenen, *Das Vibrato*; J. Butt, *Music Education and the Art of Performance in the German Baroque* (Cambridge, 1994), pp. 70, 138, 144.

27. Among those who cite the convention were J. D. Heinichen, *Neu erfundene und gründliche Anweisung* (Hamburg, 1711); F. E. Niedt, *Musicalische Handleitung* (part III) (Hamburg, 1717); D. Kellner, *Treulicher Unterricht im General-Bass* (Hamburg, 1732). See Dreyfus, *Bach's Continuo Group*, pp. 76–88.

28. Schering, *Johann Sebastian Bachs Leipziger Kirchenmusik*, p. 111; A. Mendel, 'On the keyboard accompaniments to Bach's Leipzig church music', *Musical Quarterly* 36 (1950), pp. 339–62; J. A. Westrup, 'The continuo in the "St. Matthew Passion"', *Bach-Gedenkschrift 1950* (Zurich, 1950) pp. 103–17; F.-H. Neumann, 'Die Theorie des Rezitativs im 17. und 18. Jahrhundert' (diss., Göttingen, 1955), pp. 360–72; Williams, 'Basso continuo on the organ', p. 240.

29. For full discussion of the arguments for and against 'short accompaniment', see Dreyfus, *Bach's Continuo Group*, pp. 72–107.

30. Williams, 'Basso continuo on the organ', p. 238.

31. See R. Donington, *The Interpretation of Early Music* (London, 1963, rev. London, 1975), pp. 210–11; J. A. Westrup, 'The cadence in Baroque recitative', *Natalica Musicologica Knud Jeppesen* (Copenhagen, 1962), pp. 243–52; Hansell, 'The cadence', p. 228.

32. Walther, *Musikalisches Lexikon*, p. 515.

33. See D. Barnett, 'Non-uniform slurring in 18th-century music: accident or design?', *Haydn Yearbook* 10 (1978), pp. 179–99.

34. Harnoncourt, *Baroque Music Today*, p. 44; see G. von Dadelsen, 'Die Crux der Nebensache – Editorische und praktische Bemerkungen zu Bachs Artikulation', in Dadelsen, *Über Bach und Anderes* (Tübingen, 1983), pp. 144–58.

35. See Butt, *Bach Interpretation*.

36. R. L. Marshall, 'Tempo and dynamic indications in the Bach sources: a review of the terminology', in P. Williams (ed.), *Bach, Handel, Scarlatti: Tercentenary Essays* (Cambridge, 1985), pp. 259–76.

37. J. Mattheson (*Das neu-eröffnete Orchestre*, 1713) in Steblin, *A History of Key Characteristics*, p. 48; for further information on Bach's tonal plan see E. Chafe, 'Key structure and tonal allegory in the Passions of J. S. Bach: an Introduction', *Current Musicology* 31 (1981), pp. 39–54.

38. For further discussion regarding the significance of numerology, see R. Tatlow, *Bach and the Riddle of the Number Alphabet* (Cambridge, 1991), and T. A. Smith, 'More evidence of numeral-logical design in Bach's St. Matthew Passion', *Bach: Journal of the Riemenschneider Bach Institute* 17/iii (1986), pp. 24–9.

Mozart: Serenade K361

39. The imperial octet (*Kaiserlich-Königliche Harmonie*) of Triebensee and Wendt (oboes), the Stadlers (clarinets), Rupp and Eisen (horns), Kautner and Druben (bassoons) was described by Carl Friedrich Cramer in a footnote to a review of a Hamburg concert of 20 December 1783. See *Magazin der Musik, erster Jahrgang, zweyte Hälfte* (Hamburg, 1783), p. 1400, note 190.

40. For example, the recapitulation of the first movement introduces a new second subject, whilst in the revised version à 8, there is no exposition repeat. The central Adagio retains the tonic key of E♭.

41. This advertisement implies (but does not prove) that this performance was the premiere. The players would all have been free of court duties because it was Lent, a traditional period for servants' vacation.

42. J. F. Schink, *Litterarische Fragmente* (Graz, 1985), p. 286.

43. See E. Hess, 'Anton Stadler's "Musik Plan"', *Mozart-Jahrbuch* (1962), pp. 37–54, and P. Poulin, 'A view of eighteenth-century musical life and training: Anton Stadler's "Musick Plan"', *Music and Letters* 71 (1990), pp. 215–24.

44. Alternatively, Stadler may simply have wanted to reserve some of the music for a later occasion. D. N. Leeson and D. Whitwell, 'Concerning Mozart's Serenade in B♭ for thirteen instruments, K361 (370a)', *Mozart-Jahrbuch* (1976–7), p. 108, postulate that movements 1, 2, 5 and 7 were performed at the 1784 concert. It seems likely that on the evening of 23 March Mozart was at the house of his pupil Barbara Ployer for the premiere of his Piano Concerto K449 and so did not hear the Serenade; at any event, no description of the public reaction to Stadler's concert appears in any of Mozart's letters.

45. Leeson and Whitwell, 'Concerning Mozart's Serenade in B♭', p. 97.

46. *Gesamtausgabe der Werke Mozarts* (Leipzig, 1876–1905).

47. For a history and description of the manuscript, see Leeson and Whitwell, 'Concerning Mozart's Serenade in B♭', pp. 98–101.

48. D. Leeson, 'A revisit: Mozart's Serenade for thirteen instruments, K361 (370a), the "Gran Partitta"', *Mozart-Jahrbuch* (1997), pp. 181–223. Leeson examines the implications of the relevant watermarks for dating the Serenade and (as in his 1976/7 article) proposes a new Köchel listing of K449a.

49. D. Schubart, *Ideen zu einer Ästhetik der Tonkunst* [1784–5] (Vienna, 1806).

50. H. Backofen, *Anweisung zur Klarinette, nebst einer kurzen Abhandlung über das Bassett-Horn* (Leipzig, c. 1803/R1986)

51. English clarinets were largely intended for the amateur and military market and do not possess the depth of tone characteristic of continental instruments. On Mozart's clarinet and basset horn writing in the Serenade K361 see C. Lawson, *Mozart: Clarinet Concerto* (Cambridge, 1996), pp. 18–23. On pp. 84–90 Nicholas Shackleton's Appendix 2 lists surviving clarinets and basset horns which are relevant in design and provenance to a study of Mozart.

52. D. Ross, 'A comprehensive performance project in clarinet literature with an organological study of the development of the clarinet in the eighteenth century' (DMA thesis, University of Iowa, 1985), pp. 251–2.

53. This distinctive quality accounts for a lack of consensus among makers of Boehm-system instruments as to what design and bore-size is appropriate.

54. C. F. Cramer, *Magazin der Musik, erster Jahrgang, erste Hälfte* (Hamburg, 1782), p. 654. In addition to the basset horns in F and G used by Mozart, they were also

constructed in E, E♭ and D, according to J. G. Albrechtsberger's *Gründliche Anweisung zur Composition* (Leipzig, 1790).

55. Albrechtsberger specifically mentions an exceptional basset horn with chromatic extension developed by the Stadler brothers of Vienna. Extraordinarily, the second basset horn part of Trio 1 of the first Menuetto contains instances of a single note (low e♭) which is not present on any surviving eighteenth-century instruments.

56. See B. Haynes, 'Oboe fingering charts. 1695–1816', *Galpin Society Journal* 31 (1978), pp. 68–93.

57. For example, T. Warner, 'Two late eighteenth-century instructions for making double reeds', *Galpin Society Journal* 15 (1962), pp. 25–33.

58. Burney, *The Present State of Music in Germany*, p. 46.

59. This was the tuning cited in 1790 by Albrechtsberger, for a violone or contrabass with thick strings and frets tied at every semitone round the fingerboard.

60. J. F. Schönfeld, *Jahrbuch der Tonkunst von Wien und Prag* (1796), p. 193.

61. See, for example, H. Fitzpatrick, *The Horn & Horn-Playing and the Austro-Bohemian Tradition from 1680 to 1830* (Oxford, 1970), pp. 125–49.

62. On disc the Serenade's directors have included Frans Brüggen, Alan Hacker, Anthony Halstead, Philippe Herreweghe, Christopher Hogwood and Barthold Kuijken.

63. Wind-band of the prince of Oettingen-Wallerstein: silhouette on gold ground (1791) in Schloss Wallerstein, reproduced in *The New Grove*, vol. VIII, p. 168, art 'Harmoniemusik'.

64. This proves the inappropriateness of its popular title: the 'thirteen-wind Serenade'. It should be noted that Mozart used the contrabassoon in the *Maurerische Trauermusik* K477/479a of 1785. At its premiere that instrument was almost certainly played by Theodor Lotz, maker of Stadler's basset clarinet.

65. L. Mozart (*Versuch*, Eng. trans., p. 45) regrets that the importance of slurs was often ignored.

66. *Ibid.*, pp. 123–4, 130.

67. See preface to the Emerson edition. Hellyer observes, however, that one can find many exceptions to each principle and often a lack of consistency between parts.

68. N. Zaslaw, *Mozart's Symphonies* (Oxford, 1989), pp. 508–9: 'A neo-classical performance . . . cannot have the on-going shaping, the personal interpretation, that we treasure in performances . . . by great modern conductors, nor would it have been practical to create such performances in the single rehearsal usually allotted symphonies in the eighteenth century . . . The results are bound to be more neutral and less personal, more objective and less subjective.' Sandra

Rosenblum (*Performance Practices in Classic Piano Music* (Bloomington and Indianapolis, 1988), pp. 362ff.) argues for a single underlying tempo for each movement, with any deviation barely noticeable to the listener.

69. Türk, *Clavierschule*, Eng. trans. (Haggh), pp. 360–1.

70. D. Leeson, 'The "Gran Partitta's" mystery measure', *Mozart-Jahrbuch* (1991), pp. 220–5.

71. Hellyer sets out the problem as follows: In his autograph Mozart did not write out the Romance reprise, but included the conventional instructions to reuse the opening text. The last bar of this he wrote as a first time bar, with signs above and below the score, which he then smudged, as though he intended to alter them. This he never did, but neither did he delete them. There is no part-nering second time bar indication. Had he included one, it could only have been over the first bar of the coda, where the voice leading for those instru-ments that continue playing is faultless. Into the Allegretto, both voice leading and harmonic continuity would be nonsensical. There are plenty of examples in Mozart's music for the sudden silencing of those instruments which do not continue, as into the coda here, even those playing dissonant notes. It was common for Mozart to omit the second time bar sign if it was to lie over the first bar of a structurally new section of music. Had Mozart actually intended the deletion of the first time bar sign, his normal practice would have been to obliterate it or to scratch it out.

Berlioz: Episode de la vie d'un Artiste, Symphonie Fantastique en cinque parties Op. 14

72. H. J. Macdonald, *Berlioz Orchestral Music* (London, 1969), p. 30.

73. Berlioz and Smithson eventually married on 3 October 1833, but the vacilla-tions in their relationship persisted and they separated once and for all in October 1844.

74. Berlioz informs us that Habeneck used to direct the Conservatoire Concerts from a violin part. (See Berlioz, *Mémoires*, vol. II, pp. 236–7; Eng. trans., p. 406.) Berlioz himself directed later performances as a conductor, partly because he was concerned that others might misinterpret his music. Such concern is also probably one reason why the work was not published until 1845.

75. Berlioz urged audiences initially to consider the programme 'as the spoken text of an opera, serving to introduce the musical movements whose character and expression it motivates' (trans. E. T. Cone, Norton Critical Score; see n. 83 below), p. 21. For a discussion of the various forms of the programme see

Nicholas Temperley, 'The Symphonie Fantastique and its programme', *Musical Quarterly* 57 (1971), pp. 593–608; see also Cone, Norton Critical Score, pp. 18–35.

76. See Macdonald, *Berlioz*, p. 33.

77. Among the literary influences were De Quincey's *Confessions of an Opium Eater* in Musset's translation, Chateaubriand's *René* and Goethe's *Faust*. Autobiographical sources include Berlioz's own writings, essays, letters and memoirs, which tell us much about the genesis, composition and reception of his works.

78. In F. Dorian, *The History of Music in Performance* (New York, 1942), p. 247. See also Berlioz's 'Instruments added by modern composers to scores of old masters', from his *A Travers Chants* (Paris, 1862), in *The Art of Music and Other Essays*, trans. and ed. E. Csicsery-Ronay (Bloomington, 1994), pp. 148–9.

79. Hugh Macdonald, in *The New Grove*, vol. II, p. 601, art. 'Berlioz, Hector'.

80. Julian Rushton (*The Musical Language of Berlioz* (Cambridge, 1983), p. 12) claims that revisions were made as late as 1844 when the symphony was in proof, a habit that suited Berlioz's reluctance to publish his works until he had himself introduced them to audiences.

81. *H. Berlioz: Werke*, vol. I, ed. C. Malherbe and F. Weingartner (Leipzig, 1900). See J. Barzun, 'Errors in the "complete" edition of the scores', in *Berlioz and the Romantic Century*, 2 vols., 3rd edn (New York, 1969), vol. II, pp. 358–81.

82. *Hector Berlioz, New Edition of the Complete Works* (Kassel, 1967–), vol. XVI, ed. N. Temperley. The study score was published (Kassel, 1972) with a foreword by Hugh Macdonald.

83. *H. Berlioz: Symphonie Fantastique*, Norton Critical Score, ed. E. T. Cone (New York, 1971).

84. Throughout his *Grand Traité d'instrumentation*, Berlioz reviews the dramatic potential of the timbre of most available instruments. Berlioz's essay 'De l'imitation musicale' (*Revue et Gazette Musicale de Paris* (1 and 8 January 1837)) is his most complete and explicit statement of the aims and limitations of programme music.

85. Barzun (*Berlioz and the Romantic Century*, vol. I, p. 448) shows how timbre is used as a substitute for strict harmonic practice as the vehicle for musical progression. He also shows how unity can be found in the seemingly structureless first movement of the *Symphonie Fantastique* through the instrumental combinations used. Schumann's analysis of the work (available in translation in the Norton Critical Score) also considers ways in which Berlioz achieves tonal cogency and structural coherence. See also P. Banks, 'Coherence and diversity in the *Symphonie fantastique*', *19th-Century Music* 8 (1984), pp. 37–43.

86. Berlioz always showed a keen interest in new musical instruments, hence his championing of Adolphe Sax and his selection as a judge at the 1851 Exhibition.

87. See A. Carse, *The Orchestra from Beethoven to Berlioz* (Cambridge, 1948), pp. 56–7.

88. Berlioz, *Grand Traité d'instrumentation*, Eng. trans., p. 241. Berlioz's treatise had originally been written in sixteen instalments for the *Revue et Gazette Musicale* (21 November 1841 to 17 July 1842).

89. N. Temperley, *New Berlioz Edition*, vol. XVI, Foreword, pp. XIII–XIV.

90. With these minimum string strengths an orchestra of at least 94 players is required.

91. Berlioz's concession that the wind instruments may be doubled in the *Marche au Supplice* reflects their greater importance in this movement.

92. Broadly speaking, a 'converted' instrument would comprise: a taller, thinner and more sharply curved bridge; a narrower, longer canted neck, mortised into the top block and tilted back to achieve the required string tension and to allow the longer fingerboard to follow the angle of the strings; a longer, more substantial bass-bar; and a thicker soundpost.

93. Certainly Berlioz's bowing demands suggest this.

94. See Koury, *Orchestral Performance Practices*, p. 105.

95. A. Carse, *Musical Wind Instruments* (London, 1939/R1965), pp. 91–4 and 98–100; A. Baines, *Woodwind Instruments and their History* (London, 1957, 3/1967), pp. 316–17 and 322.

96. D. Charlton, in Brown and Sadie (eds.), *Performance Practice after 1600*, p. 410.

97. *Ibid.*, p. 411.

98. Not until *c.* 1839 did Brod produce his *cor anglais moderne*, the first completely straight model with a curved brass crook to carry the reed, but a curved upper joint persisted in France for some years.

99. Interestingly, Berlioz (*Grand Traité*, Eng. trans., p. 107) condemned the practice of certain players of transposing everything on the B♭ instrument as 'faithlessness of execution'.

100. Berlioz, *Grand Traité*, Eng. trans., p. 101.

101. *Ibid.*, p. 141.

102. Rushton (*The Musical Language*, p. 268 n. 41) observes that the bore of the horns in normal use has widened by up to 12 per cent.

103. See D. Cairns, 'Berlioz, the cornet, and the *Symphonie Fantastique*', *Berlioz Society Bulletin* 47 (July 1964), pp. 2–6.

104. Berlioz, *Grand Traité*, Eng. trans., p. 146.

105. There is only one note in the symphony that cannot be played by a tenor trombone (the E♭ in iv, b. 122).

106. Berlioz's comments in his *Grand Traité* (Eng. trans., p. 152) would seem to support such an interpretation.

107. Rushton (*The Musical Language*, p. 268 n. 41) gives *c.* 10mm.

108. See F.-J. Fétis, *Curiosités historiques de la musique* (Paris, 1830), pp. 407–8.

109. Rushton, *The Musical Language*, p. 89.

110. H. Berlioz, *A Travers Chants* (Paris, 1862); ed. L. Guichard (Paris, 1971), pp. 296–8.

111. In his *Grand Traité* (p. 262) Berlioz writes of the sound from each of the three main types of timpani sticks – those with wooden heads, those with heads covered with leather or sponge-headed sticks.

112. Interestingly, Berlioz claimed that his attempts to reproduce the rumbling of distant thunder were 'not for the puerile pleasure of imitating this majestic sound, but rather to make *silence* more perceptible, and thus to increase the impression of uneasy sadness and painful isolation' (in Norton Critical Score, ed. Cone, p. 29). Performers should take note and act accordingly.

113. The recording by John Eliot Gardiner and the Orchestre Révolutionnaire et Romantique (Philips Dig. 434 402–2) was actually undertaken in that hall.

114. A. A. E. Elwart, *Histoire de la Société des Concerts du Conservatoire Impérial de Musique* (2nd edn, Paris, 1864), p. 115.

115. Berlioz, *Grand Traité*, Eng. trans., pp. 254–5. See also D. Kern Holoman's discussion in *Berlioz* (London, 1989), pp. 354–6.

116. Temperley, *New Berlioz Edition*, vol. XVI, 'Foreword', p. XV.

117. See H. J. Macdonald, 'Two peculiarities of Berlioz's notation', *Music and Letters* 50 (1969) pp. 25–32; N. Temperley, 'Berlioz and the slur', *Music and Letters* 50 (1969), pp. 388–92.

118. Macdonald, 'Two peculiarities', pp. 32–6; Norton Critical Score, ed. Cone, p. 198.

119. H. Macdonald, 'Berlioz and the metronome', in P. Bloom (ed.), *Berlioz Studies* (Cambridge, 1992), p. 18.

120. Berlioz, *Grand Traité* (2nd edn, Paris, 1855), p. 300. Macdonald ('Berlioz and the metronome', p. 21) warns that those metronome marks which cannot be found on the metronome's fine calibrations may be suspect.

121. in Dorian, *The History of Music in Performance*, p. 247.

122. Berlioz, *Mémoires*, p. 420; Eng. trans., pp. 436–7.

Brahms: Symphony No. 2 Op. 73

123. *Briefwechsel* (16 vols., Berlin 1907–22/R1974), vol. X, p. 66.

124. Volumes I and II of *Johannes Brahms: Sämtliche Werke: Ausgabe der Gesellschaft der Musikfreunde in Wien* (Breitkopf & Härtel, Leipzig, n.d., *Revisionsbericht* dated 1926): Dover reprint, New York, 1974.

125. For example, in two places in the second movement of the Second Symphony Brahms marked for himself 'voran' (press on), erasing these for the printing. Other sources for the Symphony are the autograph, a fair copy and printer's proof of the four-hand version.

126. At the time of writing only the first of the symphonies has appeared in this new Henle edition by Robert Pascall.

127. The string complement on these occasions was respectively 12–10–8–8–6 and 20–20–13–10–10.

128. E. Hanslick, *Concerte, Componisten und virtuosen der letzten fünfzehn Jahre 1870–1885* (Berlin, 1886), p. 417; Eng. trans. (Freeport, NY, 1950), p. 273.

129. 'Hans von Bülow/Richard Strauss: Briefwechsel', *Richard Strauss Jahrbuch* 1954, pp. 7–88; separate English trans. by A. Gishford (London, 1955), p. 27.

130. E. Creuzburg, *Die Gewandhaus-Konzerte zu Leipzig, 1871–1931* (Leipzig, 1931), p. 122, in Koury, *Orchestral Performance Practices*, p. 175. The violins and violas in Leipzig did not sit to play until about ten years after the advent of Artur Nikisch as conductor, which would be about 1905.

131. Hanslick, *Concerte*, p. 417.

132. The luxuriant sound of first and second violins together was first favoured by Leopold Stokowski.

133. Reproduced from G. Henschel, *Personal Recollections of Johannes Brahms* (Boston, 1907), p. 84.

134. J. H. Mueller, *The American Symphony Orchestra: a Social History of Musical Taste* (Bloomington, 1951), p. 305. Roger Norrington's seating plan for his Brahms recordings not only follows Henschel in positioning the basses across the back of the orchestra (divided only by the timpani) but also preserves the cello section intact next to the first violins.

135. John Eliot Gardiner in Sherman, *Inside Early Music*, p. 374.

136. Blume indicates some violent changes of tempo not marked in the scores, as well as individual features such as lingering upbeats. The influence of Steinbach is specifically acknowledged in the recordings by Sir Charles Mackerras (Telarc, CD-80450).

137. Interview with Nikolaus Harnoncourt in his 1997 recordings of the symphonies (Teldec 0630–13136–2)

138. Joachim and Moser, *Violinschule*, vol. II, p. 96a.

139. Extracts from *Grove* editions are quoted by R. Philip, in Brown and Sadie (eds.), *Performance Practice after 1600*, p. 462.

140. C. Flesch, *The Art of Violin Playing*, vol. I (Berlin, 1923, trans. London, 1924), p. 40.

141. Philip, in Brown and Sadie (eds.), *Performance Practice after 1600*, p. 467.

142. Joachim and Moser, *Violinschule*, vol. II, p. 92.

143. C. Flesch, *Violin Fingering, its Theory and Practice* (Eng. trans., London, 1966 [but written pre-1944]), p. 338. He noted that this mannerism continued to be taught at the Berlin Hochschule until after 1907.

144. This is ascribed by Philip (*Early Recordings*, p. 179) to the shortage of rehearsal time and the prevalence of the deputy system, especially in Britain and France.

145. Joachim and Moser, *Violinschule*, vol. III, p. 16.

146. Philip, *Early Recordings*, pp. 179–204.

147. Flesch, *The Art of Violin Playing*, vol. I, pp. 10–11.

148. The cello endpin was not universally adopted until half a century later; it was eschewed, for example, by Joachim's cellist Robert Hausmann.

149. N. Toff, *The Development of the Modern Flute* (New York, 1979), pp. 76–7.

150. R. Strauss, *Instrumentationslehre* (Leipzig, 1905); Eng. trans. (New York, 1948), p. 227.

151. J. Sellner, *Theoretisch-praktische Oboeschule* (Vienna, 1825, rev.2/1901).

152. B. Litzmann (ed.), *Letters of Clara Schumann and Johannes Brahms 1853–1896* (London, 1927), p. 196.

153. In *Jahrbuch für musikalische Wissenschaft* 1 (1863), p. 22.

154. A. von Dommer, *H. C. Koch's Musikalisches Lexikon* (Heidelberg, 1865), p. 100. That vibrato was becoming more widespread is suggested by the instruction at the head of the intermezzo of Carl Reinecke's 'Undine' Flute Sonata Op. 167 that it should be played 'without any vibrato at all'.

155. P.-J. E. Meifred, *Méthode pour le cor chromatique ou à pistons* (Paris, 1840).

156. Richard Strauss noted that it took practice to change the bright horn in B♭ into the soft and noble timbre of the horn in F. As Charles Mackerras has remarked (in an interview accompanying his Brahms Symphony recordings) on the lengths of tubing on the Vienna horn, playing was more precarious but 'nobody cared if you cracked the odd note'.

157. B. Sherman, 'Tempo and proportions in Brahms: period evidence', *Early Music* 25 (1997), p. 475, n. 14.

158. R. Brinkmann, *Johannes Brahms: Die Zweite Symphonie: Späte Idylle* (Eng. trans., Harvard, 1995), pp. 29–32. He tabulates the timings of various recorded performances from different periods up to 1983. Timings of other recordings

(to 1992) appear in Sherman, 'Tempo and proportions', p. 467. By comparison with Richter's reported 19, 11, 5 and 8 minutes for the four movements, recent historically aware performances have taken 19.37, 8.48, 4.51 and 8.45 minutes (Norrington, 1993), 19.38, 8.50, 5.03 and 9 minutes (Mackerras, 1997) and 21.06, 9.01, 5.35 and 9.47 minutes (Harnoncourt, 1997). Bülow's own overall timing of 38 minutes without first repeat (Meiningen, 1884) closely matches that of Richter. Sherman (*ibid.*, pp. 463–4) cites written evidence on Brahms's tempi by Fanny Davies (1905), Walter Blume (1933) and Max Rudolf (born 1902, but writing in 1980), which mainly contradicts the recorded trends. He rightly points out that descriptive terms such as 'too quickly' may have had a different meaning for Davies than for us.

159. For example, Stravinsky's Paris recordings of *The Rite of Spring*, *Petrushka* and *The Firebird* may, to modern ears, sound rhythmically imprecise, compared with his later recordings; but at the time he regarded them as 'documents which can serve as a guide to all executants of my music'. See I. Stravinsky (with W. Nouvel), *Chroniques de ma vie* (Paris, 1935–6, 2/1962); Eng trans. (London and New York, 1936/R1975), pp. 150–1.

160. See the comments on musical taste in Chapter 3 and also R. Hill in B. Gilliam (ed.), *Music and Performance during the Weimar Republic* (Cambridge, 1994), pp. 39–41.

161. Interview accompanying his 1997 recordings for Teldec 0630–13136–2.

162. In the note to his recording EMI CDC 7 54875 2 Roger Norrington claims without further justification that earliest gramophone recordings are of limited help in seeking a historical viewpoint.

163. R. H. Schauffler, *The Unknown Brahms: his Life, Character and Works* (New York, 1933), p. 180.

164. W. Frisch, *Brahms: the Four Symphonies* (New York, 1996), pp. 166–9.

165. Weingartner, *Über das Dirigieren*, Eng. trans., pp. 27–9.

166. Quoted in H. Schonberg, *The Great Conductors* (London, 1968), p. 252.

6 The continuing debate

1. Gavin Henderson (Trinity College of Music, London) cited by John Eliot Gardiner in an address given at the Association of British Orchestras' conference in January 1998 and reprinted in *BBC Music Magazine* (May 1998), pp. 42–5.

2. Harnoncourt, *Baroque Music Today*, pp. 11–13 and 19–27. He also observes: 'The essential difference between the listening habits of earlier times and those of today lies in the fact that we desire to listen often to a work that we love,

whereas people of earlier times did not. People today are happy to listen again and again to works that are familiar, but would not care to listen *only* to those which are new. We are like children who want to hear the same story over and over again, because we remember beautiful parts we encountered the first time it was read to us.'

3. *Ibid.*, pp. 22–3.

4. For example, William Christie and Les Arts Florissants in the French Baroque repertory.

5. For example, R. Taruskin, 'The pastness of the present and the presence of the past', in Kenyon (ed.), *Authenticity and Early Music*, pp. 137–207.

6. Dreyfus, 'Early music defended', in which he observes that *The New Grove* does not contain an article entitled 'Early Music', or any coherent discussion of the twentieth-century revival of earlier repertories, instruments, and practices.

7. As Dreyfus points out (*ibid.*, p. 300), the critic Theodor Adorno observed that 'while no one would claim that the essence of a musical work is tantamount to the sum of historically demonstrable facts surrounding its performance, the "fans of old music" go right ahead in claiming that authenticity is guaranteed by reconstructing the relevant instruments, texts and practices. But in so doing Early Music has no room for crucial nonempirical considerations – such as emotional expression or the meaning of a work – without which, all would agree, music making is inconceivable.' As Dreyfus further remarks, Adorno (d. 1969) did not know Early Music as it blossomed in the late 1960s and 1970s 'but confronted the barbaric gropings of the 1950s and a bit beyond'.

8. *Ibid.*, p. 302.

9. N. Kenyon, 'Introduction: live issues and questions', in Kenyon (ed.), *Authenticity and Early Music*, pp. 1–18.

10. R. Taruskin, *Text and Act* (Oxford, 1995), p. 98.

11. *Ibid.*, p. 102.

12. G. Tomlinson, 'The historian, the performer, and authentic meaning in music', in Kenyon (ed.), *Authenticity and Early Music*, p. 123.

13. P. Kivy, *Authenticities* (Ithaca and London, 1995), pp. 161, 170. He argues (p. 46) that 'a performer who plays Bach, say, on a modern instrument, with phrasing and dynamics that depart from the *Urtext*, may very well be closer to the composer's wishes and intentions in those very respects . . . It is an open question, in every individual case . . . whether "mainstream" or "historically reconstructed" performance conforms more closely to authorial wishes or intentions. Nor is this a logician's trick. It is simply the result of using words in their proper senses.'

14. *Ibid.*, p. 12. In a notable return to the discussion of personal expression,

Laurence Dreyfus ('Mozart as early music: a Romantic anecdote', *Early Music* 20 (1992), pp. 297–309) emphasises this very point, regretting the passing of the individual expressive qualities inherent within the Flonzaley Quartet's 1921 recording of Mozart's D minor Quartet K421.

15. Scruton, *The Aesthetics of Music*, p. 445.
16. *Ibid.*, p. 448.
17. M. Bent, '"Authentic" listening?', *Early Music* 25 (1997), p. 567.
18. R. Levin in Sherman, *Inside Early Music*, pp. 331–2.
19. For example, in S. Burstyn, 'In quest of the period ear', *Early Music* 25 (1997), pp. 693–700.
20. J. Westrup, *An Introduction to Musical History* (London, 1955) and T. Dart, *The Interpretation of Music* (London, 1954).
21. W. Weber, 'Did people listen in the eighteenth century?', *Early Music* 25 (1997), pp. 678–91.

Select bibliography

Pre-1900

Adlung, J., *Anleitung zu der musikalischen Gelahrtheit* (Erfurt, 1758/R1953, 2/1783)

Agricola, J. F., *Anleitung zur Singkunst* (Berlin, 1757/R1966)

Avison, C., *An Essay on Musical Expression* (London, 1752, rev.2/1753/R1967, 3/1775)

Bach, C. P. E., *Versuch über die wahre Art das Clavier zu spielen* (2 vols., Berlin, 1753 and 1762/R1957; Eng. trans., New York, 1949)

Bacilly, B. de, *Remarques curieuses sur l'art de bien chanter* (Paris, 1668/R1971, 4/1681; Eng. trans., Brooklyn, 1968)

Baillot, P., *L'art du violon: nouvelle méthode* (Paris, 1835; Eng. trans., Illinois, 1991)

Baillot, P., Rode, P., and Kreutzer, R., *Méthode de violon* (Paris, 1803/R1974)

Baillot, P., Levasseur, J. H., Catel, C.-S., and Baudiot, C. N., *Méthode de violoncelle* (Paris, 1804/R1974; Eng. trans., *c.* 1850)

Baudiot, C. N., see Baillot, P.

Bériot, C. A. de, *Méthode de violon*, Op. 102 (Paris, 1858)

Berlioz, H., *Grand traité d'instrumentation et d'orchestration modernes* (Paris, 1843, rev.2/1855; Eng. trans., London, 1855)

Mémoires de Hector Berlioz (Paris, 1870), trans. and ed. D. Cairns (London, 1969)

Burney, C., *The Present State of Music in France and Italy* (London, 1773/R1969)

The Present State of Music in Germany, the Netherlands, and United Provinces (London, 1775/R1969)

Caccini, G., *Le nuove musiche* (Florence, 1601[1602]/R1934 and 1973)

Cartier, J.-B., *L'art du violon* (Paris, 1798, 2/1801, enlarged 3/*c.* 1803/R1973)

Catel, C.-S., see Baillot, P.

Clementi, M., *Introduction to the Art of Playing on the Piano Forte* (London, 1801/R1974)

Corri, D., *The Singer's Preceptor* (London, 1810)

Couperin, F., *L'art de toucher le clavecin* (Paris, 1716, enlarged 2/1717/R1969; Eng. trans., New York, 1974)

Czerny, C., *Complete Theoretical and Practical Pianoforte School*, Op. 500 (London, 1839)

Dittersdorf, K. von, *Karl von Dittersdorfs Lebensbeschreibung, seinem Sohne in die Feder diktiert* (Leipzig, 1801/R1967; Eng. trans., London, 1896/R1970)

Duport, J.-L., *Essai sur le doigté du violoncelle, et sur la conduite de l'archet* (Paris, c. 1806)

Francoeur, L. J., *Diapason général de tous les instrumens à vent* (Paris, n.d., 2/1772)

Fröhlich, F. J., *Vollständige theoretisch-praktische Musikschule* (Bonn, 1810–11)

Galeazzi, F., *Elementi teorico-pratici di musica con un saggio sopra l'arte di suonare il violino analizzata, ed a dimostrabili principi ridotta . . .* (2 vols., Rome, 1791–6)

García, M., *Traité complet de l'art du chant* (Paris, 1847/R1985; Eng. trans., 1924)

Geminiani, F., *The Art of Playing on the Violin* (London, 1751/R1952)

   A Treatise of Good Taste in the Art of Musick (London, 1749/R1969)

Gunn, J., *The School of the German Flute* (London, 1792)

Habeneck, F. A., *Méthode théorique et pratique de violon* (Paris, c. 1840)

Heinichen, J. D., *Der General-Bass in der Composition* (Dresden, 1728)

Hiller, J. A., *Anweisung zum musikalisch-richtigen Gesange* (Leipzig, 1774)

   Anweisung zum musikalisch-zierlichen Gesange (Leipzig, 1780/R1976)

Hotteterre, J., *Principes de la flûte traversière . . .* (Paris, 1707/R1982; Eng. trans., London, 1968)

Hummel, J. N., *Ausführliche theoretisch-praktische Anweisung zum Piano-forte Spiel* (Vienna, 1828/R1929)

Kastner, G., *Traité général d'instrumentation* (Paris, 1837)

   Cours d'instrumentation considéré sous les rapports poétiques et philosophiques de l'art (Paris, 1839, rev. suppl.1844)

Klosé, H. E., *Méthode pour servir à l'enseignement de la clarinette à anneaux mobiles* (Paris, 1843, enlarged 1868)

Koch, H. C., *Musikalisches Lexikon* (Frankfurt, 1802)

Kreutzer, R., see Baillot, P.

Levasseur, J. H., see Baillot, P.

Mace, T., *Musick's Monument* (London, 1676)

Mancini, G., *Pensieri, e riflessioni pratiche sopra il canto figurato* (Vienna, 1774, rev. and enlarged 3/1777; Eng. trans., 1967)

Marpurg, F. W., *Anleitung zum Klavierspielen* (Berlin, 1755–61)

   Anleitung zur Musik überhaupt und zur Singkunst besonders (Berlin, 1763)

Mattheson, J., *Der vollkommene Capellmeister* (Hamburg, 1739/R1954; Eng. trans., Ann Arbor, 1981)

Mersenne, M., *Harmonie universelle* (3 vols., Paris, 1636–7/R1963)

Milchmeyer, J. P., *Die wahre Art das Pianoforte zu spielen* (Dresden, 1797)

Mozart, L., *Versuch einer gründlichen Violinschule* (Augsburg, 1756/R1976; Eng. trans., London, 1948, 2/1951)

Ozi, E., *Nouvelle Méthode de basson adoptée par le Conservatoire* (Paris, 1803/R1973)

Praetorius, M., *Syntagma musicum* (3 vols., Wolfenbüttel, 1614–1615; 1618, 2/1619; and 1618, 2/1619; Eng. trans., 1962, 1986)

Quantz, J. J., *Versuch einer Anweisung die Flöte traversiere zu spielen* (Berlin, 1752, 3/1789/R1952; Eng. trans., London, 1966)

Reichardt, J. F., *Briefe eines aufmerksamen Reisenden die Musik betreffend*, vol. I (Frankfurt and Leipzig, 1774); vol. II (Frankfurt and Breslau, 1776)

Rode, P., see Baillot, P.

Romberg, B., *A Complete Theoretical and Practical School for the Violoncello* (London, 1839)

Rousseau, J.-J., *Dictionnaire de musique* (Paris, 1768/R1969), trans. W. Waring (London, 1779/R1975)

Saint-Lambert, M. de, *Les principes du clavecin* (Paris, 1702; Eng. trans., Cambridge, 1984)

Schubart, C. D. F., *Ideen zu einer Ästhetik der Tonkunst* (Vienna, 1806)

Schubert, J. F., *Neue-Singschule* (Leipzig, 1804)

Simpson, C., *The Division-Violist: or an Introduction to the Playing of a Ground* (London, 1659, 2/1667)

Speer, D., *Grund-richtiger . . . Unterricht der musicalischen Kunst* (Ulm, 1687)

Spohr, L., *Violinschule* (Vienna, 1832/R1960; Eng, trans., London, 1843)
     Selbstbiographie (2 vols., Kassel and Göttingen, 1860–1; Eng. trans., 1865/R1969)

Sulzer, J. G., *Allgemeine Theorie der schönen Künste* (4 vols., Leipzig, 1771–4, enlarged 2/1792–4)

Tartini, G., *Traité des agréments* (Paris, 1771; Eng. trans., Celle, 1961)

Tosi, P., *Opinioni de' cantori antichi e moderni o sieno osservazioni sopra il canto figurato* (Bologna, 1723; Eng. trans., London, 1742 and London, 1987)

Tromlitz, J. G., *Ausführlicher und gründlicher Unterricht die Flöte zu spielen* (Leipzig, 1791; Eng. trans., Cambridge, 1991)

Türk, D. G., *Clavierschule, oder Anweisung zum Clavierspielen* (Leipzig and Halle, 1789, enlarged 2/1802/R1967; Eng. trans., Lincoln, Nebraska, 1982)

Wagner, R., *Über das Dirigieren* (Leipzig 1869; Eng. trans., 1887/R1976)

Walther, J. G., *Musicalisches Lexicon* (Leipzig, 1732)

Post-1900

Aldrich, P. C., 'The "authentic" performance of baroque music', in *Essays on Music in Honor of Archibald Thompson Davison by His Associates* (Cambridge, Mass., 1957), pp. 161–71

Arnold, F. T., *The Art of Accompanying from a Thorough-Bass as Practised in the Seventeenth and Eighteenth Centuries* (London 1931/R1965)

Badura- Skoda, E. and P., *Mozart-Interpretation* (Vienna, 1957; Eng. trans., London, 1962)

Baines, A., *Woodwind Instruments and their History* (London, 1957)

Brass Instruments: their History and Development (London, 1976)

Barbour, J. M., *Tuning and Temperament* (East Lansing, Michigan, 1951, 2/1953/R1973)

Borrel, E., 'Les indications métronomiques laissés par les auteurs français du 18e siècle', *Revue de Musicologie* (1928), pp. 149–53

L'interprétation de la musique française (de Lully à la révolution) (Paris, 1934)

Boyden, D., 'Dynamics in seventeenth- and eighteenth-century music', in *Essays in Honor of Archibald T. Davison by His Associates* (Cambridge, Mass., 1957), pp. 185–93

The History of Violin Playing from its Origins to 1761 (London, 1965)

Brinkman, R., *Late Idyll: The Second Symphony of Johannes Brahms*, trans. P. Palmer (Harvard, 1995)

Brown, C., 'The orchestra in Beethoven's Vienna', *Early Music* 16 (1988), pp. 4–20

'Historical performance, metronome marks and tempo in Beethoven symphonies', *Early Music* 19 (1992), pp. 247–58

Brown, H. M., and Sadie, S. (eds.), *Performance Practice* (2 vols., London, 1989)

Buelow, G. J., *Thorough-Bass Accompaniment according to Johann David Heinichen* (Berkeley and Los Angeles, 1966)

'The "loci topici" and affect in late baroque music: Heinichen's practical demonstration', *Music Review* 27 (1966), pp. 161–76

'Music, rhetoric and the concept of the affections: a selective bibliography', *Notes* 30 (1973–4), pp. 250–9

Burrows, D., 'Handel's London theatre orchestra', *Early Music* 16 (1988), pp. 349–57

Burstyn, S., 'In quest of the period ear', *Early Music* 25 (1997), pp. 693–700

Butt, J., *Bach Interpretation: Articulation Marks in Primary Sources of J. S. Bach* (Cambridge, 1990)

Music Education and the Art of Performance in the German Baroque (Cambridge, 1994)

'Bach's vocal scoring: what can it mean?', *Early Music* 26 (1998), pp. 99–107

Carse, A., *The Orchestra from Beethoven to Berlioz* (Cambridge, 1948)

Chafe, E., 'Key structure and tonal allegory in the Passions of J. S. Bach: an introduction', *Current Musicology* 31 (1981), pp. 39–54

'J. S. Bach's "St. Matthew Passion": aspects of planning, structure and chronology',

Journal of the American Musicological Society 35 (1982), pp. 49–114

Collins, M., 'The performance of triplets in the seventeenth and eighteenth centuries', *Journal of the American Musicological Society* 19 (1966), pp. 281–328

'Notes inégales: a re-examination', *Journal of the American Musicological Society* 20 (1967), pp. 481–5

'A reconsideration of French overdotting', *Music and Letters* 50 (1969), pp. 111–23

Cook. N., *Music: A Very Short Introduction* (Oxford, 1998)

Cyr, M., *Performing Baroque Music* (Aldershot, 1992)

Dart, T., *The Interpretation of Music* (London, 1954)

Day, J., see le Huray, P. G.

Dolmetsch, A., *The Interpretation of the Music of the XVII and XVIII Centuries* (London, 1915)

Donington, R., 'A problem of inequality', *Musical Quarterly* 53 (1967), pp. 503–17

A Performer's Guide to Baroque Music (London, 1973)

'What *is* rhythmic alteration?', *Early Music* 5 (1977), pp. 543–4

Baroque Music: Style and Performance (London, 1982)

The Interpretation of Early Music (London, 1963, rev. 3/1974)

Dreyfus, L., *Bach's Continuo Group* (Cambridge, Mass., and London, 1987)

'Early music defended against its devotees: a theory of historical performance in the twentieth century', *Musical Quarterly* 49 (1983), pp. 297–322

'Mozart as early music: a Romantic anecdote', *Early Music* 20 (1992), pp. 297–309

Ferand, E. T., *Improvisation in Nine Centuries of Western Music: An Anthology with a Historical Introduction* (Cologne, 1961)

Ferguson, F., 'Mozart's keyboard concertos: tutti notations and performance models', *Mozart-Jahrbuch* (1984–5), pp. 32–9

Ferguson, H., *Keyboard Interpretation* (London, 1975)

Fuller, D., 'Dotting, the "French style" and Frederick Neumann's counter reformation', *Early Music* 5 (1977), pp. 517–43

'The "dotted style" in Bach, Handel and Scarlatti', in P. Williams (ed.), *Bach, Handel, Scarlatti: Tercentenary Essays* (Cambridge, 1985), pp. 99–117

Gilliam, B. (ed.), *Music and Performance during the Weimar Republic* (Cambridge, 1994)

Haas, R., *Aufführungspraxis der Musik* (Wildpark-Potsdam, 1931)

Hansell, S., 'The cadence in 18th-century recitative', *Musical Ouarterly* 54 (1968), pp. 228–48

Harding, R., *The Metronome and its Precursors* (London, 1938/R1983)

Origins of Musical Time and Expression (London, 1938)

Harnoncourt, N., *Baroque Music Today; Music as Speech* (London, 1988)

Harris-Warrick, R., 'The tempo of French baroque dances: evidence from 18th-century metronome devices', *Proceedings of the 1982 Meeting of the Dance History Scholars* (Cambridge, Mass., 1982), pp. 18–27

Haskell, H., *The Early Music Revival: A History* (London, 1988)

Haynes, B., 'Johann Sebastian Bach's pitch standards: the woodwind perspective', *Journal of the American Musical Instrument Society* 11 (1985), pp. 55–114

'Questions of tonality in Bach's cantatas: the woodwind perspective', *Journal of the American Musical Instrument Society* 12 (1986), pp. 40–67

Hefling, S., *Rhythmic Alteration in Seventeenth- and Eighteenth-century Music* (New York, 1993)

Hindemith, P., *A Composer's World* (Cambridge, Mass., 1952)

Hudson, R., *Stolen Time: The History of Tempo Rubato* (Oxford, 1994)

Joachim, J., and Moser, A., *Violinschule* (3 vols., Berlin, 1902–5)

Johnstone, H. D., 'Yet more ornaments for Corelli's Violin Sonatas, Op. 5', *Early Music* 24 (1996), pp. 623–33

Kenyon, N. (ed.), *Authenticity and Early Music* (Oxford, 1988)

Kerman, J., *Musicology* (London, 1985)

Kirkpatrick, R., '18th-century metronomic indications', *Papers of the AMS* (1938), pp. 30–50

Kivy, P., *Authenticities* (Ithaca and London, 1995)

Kolneder, W., *Georg Muffat zur Aufführungspraxis* (Strasbourg, 1970)

Performance Practices in Vivaldi (Leipzig, 1955); trans. A. de Dadelsen (Winterthur, 1979)

Koopman, T., 'One to a part? Who then turns the pages? – More on Bach's chorus', *Early Music* 25 (1997), pp. 541–2

'Bach's choir, an ongoing story', *Early Music* 26 (1998), pp. 109–21

Koury, D. J., *Orchestral Performance Practices in the Nineteenth Century: Size, Proportions and Seating* (Ann Arbor, 1986)

Lasocki, D., see Mather, B. B.

Lawson, C., *Mozart: Clarinet Concerto* (Cambridge, 1996)

Brahms: Clarinet Quintet (Cambridge, 1998)

Lee, D. A., 'Some embellished versions of sonatas by Franz Benda', *Musical Quarterly* 62 (1976), pp. 58–71

Leeson, D. N., and Whitwell, D., 'Concerning Mozart's Serenade in B♭ for thirteen instruments, K361 (370a)', *Mozart-Jahrbuch* (1976–7), pp. 97–130

le Huray, P. G., *Authenticity in Performance: Eighteenth-Century Case Studies* (Cambridge, 1990)

le Huray, P. G., and Day, J., *Music and Aesthetics in the Eighteenth and Early Nineteenth Centuries* (Cambridge, 1981)

Malloch, W., 'Carl Czerny's metronome marks for Haydn and Mozart symphonies', *Early Music* 16 (1988), pp. 72–82

Marshall, R. L., *The Compositional Process of J. S. Bach* (Princeton, 1972)

'Bach's Chorus: a preliminary reply to Joshua Rifkin', *Musical Times* 124 (1983), pp. 19–22

'Tempo and dynamic indications in the Bach sources: a review of the terminology', in P. Williams (ed.), *Bach, Handel, Scarlatti: Tercentenary Essays* (Cambridge, 1985), pp. 259–76

Marty, J.-P., *The Tempo Indications of Mozart* (New Haven, 1988)

'Mozart's tempo indications and the problems of interpretation', in R. L. Todd and P. Williams (eds.), *Perspectives on Mozart Performance* (Cambridge, 1991), pp. 55–73

Marx, H. J., 'Some unknown embellishments of Corelli's violin sonatas', *Musical Quarterly* 61 (1975), pp. 65–76

Mather, B. B., and Lasocki, D., *Free Ornamentation in Woodwind Music* (New York, 1976)

The Classical Woodwind Cadenza (New York, 1978)

Macdonald, H. J., 'Two peculiarities of Berlioz's Notation', *Music and Letters* 50 (1969) pp. 25–32

'Berlioz and the metronome', in P. Bloom (ed.), *Berlioz Studies* (Cambridge, 1992), pp. 17–36

Maunder, R., 'Viennese wind-instrument makers, 1700–1800', *Galpin Society Journal* 51 (1998), pp. 170–91

Mendel, A., 'On the keyboard accompaniments to Bach's Leipzig church music', *Musical Quarterly* 36 (1950), pp. 339–62

'On the pitches in use in Bach's time', *Musical Quarterly* 41 (1955), pp. 332–55 and 466–80

'Pitch in Western music since 1500, a re-examination', Acta *Musicologica* 1 (1978), pp. 1–93

Moens-Haenen, G., *Das Vibrato in der Musik des Barocks: Ein Handbuch zur Aufführungspraxis für Vokalisten und Instrumenten* (Graz, 1988)

Moser, A., see Joachim, J.

Munster, R., 'Authentische Tempi zu den sechs letzten Sinfonien W. A. Mozarts?', *Mozart-Jahrbuch* (1962–3), pp. 185–99

Musgrave, M., *The Music of Brahms* (London, 1985)

Neumann, F., 'The French *Inégales*, Quantz, and Bach', *Journal of the American Musicological Society* 18 (1965), pp. 315–58

'The use of Baroque treatises on musical performance', *Music and Letters* 48 (1967), pp. 315–24

'The dotted note and the so-called French style', *Early Music* 5 (1977), pp. 310–24

Ornamentation in Baroque and Post-Baroque Music with Special Emphasis on J. S. Bach (Princeton, 1978)

Essays in Performance Practice (Ann Arbor, 1982)

Ornamentation and Improvisation in Mozart (Princeton, 1986)

New Essays on Performance Practice (Ann Arbor, 1989)

Performance Practices of the Seventeenth and Eighteenth Centuries (New York, 1993)

O'Donnell, J. O., 'The French style and the overtures of Bach', *Early Music* 7 (1979), pp. 190–6, 336–45

Parrott, A., 'Bach's chorus: a "brief yet highly necessary" reappraisal', *Early Music* 24 (1996), pp. 551–80

'Bach's chorus: who cares?', *Early Music* 26 (1998), pp. 99–107

Philip, R., *Early Recordings and Musical Style* (Cambridge, 1992)

Pincherle, M., 'On the rights of the interpreter in the performance of seventeenth- and eighteenth-century music', *Musical Quarterly* 44 (1958), pp. 145–66

Pont, G., 'Rhythmic alteration and the majestic', *Studies in Music* 12 (1978), pp. 68–100

'French overtures at the keyboard: "How Handel Rendered the Playing of Them"', *Musicology* 6 (1980), pp. 29–50

Poulin, P., 'A view of eighteenth-century musical life and training: Anton Stadler's "Musick Plan"', *Music and Letters* 71 (1990), pp. 215–24

Reilly, E. R., 'Quantz on national styles in music', *Musical Quarterly* 49 (1963), pp. 163–87

Rifkin, J., 'The chronology of Bach's St. Matthew Passion', *Musical Quarterly* 61 (1975), pp. 360–87

'Bach's chorus: a preliminary report', *Musical Times* 123 (1982), pp. 747–54 (revised as 'Bachs Chor – Ein vorläufiger Bericht', *Basler Jahrbuch für historische Musikpraxis* 9 (1985), pp. 141–55)

'Bach's Chorus: a response to Robert Marshall', *Musical Times* 124 (1983), pp. 161–2

'More and less on Bach's orchestra', *Performance Practice Review* 4 (1991), pp. 5–13

'Page turns, players and ripieno parts: more questions of scoring in Bach's vocal music', *Early Music* 25 (1997), pp. 728–34

Robison, J. O., 'The messa di voce as an instrumental ornament in the seventeenth and eighteenth centuries', *Music Review* 43 (1982), pp. 1–14

Rosenblum, S. P., *Performance Practices in Classic Piano Music: Their Principles and Applications* (Bloomington and Indianapolis, 1988)

Rowland, D., *A History of Pianoforte Pedalling* (Cambridge, 1993)

Rushton, J., *The Musical Language of Berlioz* (Cambridge, 1983)

Sadie, S., see Brown, H. M.

Saint-Saëns, C., 'The execution of classical works: notably those of the older masters', *Musical Times* 56 (1915), pp. 474–8, reprinted in *MT* 138 (1997), pp. 31–5

Schulze, H.-J., 'Johann Sebastian Bach's orchestra: some unanswered questions', *Early Music* 17 (1989), pp. 3–15

Scruton, R., *The Aesthetics of Music* (Oxford, 1997)

Seletsky, R. E., '18th-century variations for Corelli's sonatas, Op. 5', *Early Music* 24 (1996), pp. 119–31

Sherman, B., *Inside Early Music* (Oxford, 1997)

'Tempo and proportions in Brahms: period evidence', *Early Music* 25 (1997), pp. 463–77

Smiles, J. E., 'Directions for improvised ornamentation in Italian method books of the late eighteenth century', *Journal of the American Musicological Society* 31 (1978), pp. 459–509

Spitzer, J., and Zaslaw, N., 'Improvised ornamentation in eighteenth-century orchestras', *Journal of the American Musicological Society* 39 (1986), pp. 524–77

Stadlen, P., 'Beethoven and the metronome', *Music and Letters* 48 (1967), pp. 330–49

Steblin, R., *A History of Key Characteristics in the Eighteenth and Early Nineteenth Centuries* (Ann Arbor, 1983)

Stowell, R., *Violin Technique and Performance Practice in the Late Eighteenth and Early Nineteenth Centuries* (Cambridge, 1985)

'Good execution and other necessary skills: the role of the concertmaster in the late 18th century', *Early Music* 16 (1988), pp. 21–33

Stowell, R. (ed.), *Performing Beethoven* (Cambridge, 1994)

Strunk, O., *Source Readings in Music History* (New York 1950/R1965)

Taruskin, R., *Text and Act* (Oxford, 1995)

Temperley, N. 'The Symphonie Fantastique and its programme', *Musical Quarterly* 57 (1971), pp. 593–608

'Berlioz and the slur', *Music and Letters* 50 (1969), pp. 388–92

Weber, W., 'Did people listen in the eighteenth century?', *Early Music* 25 (1997), pp. 678–91

Weingartner, F., *Über das Dirigieren* (Leipzig 1895, rev. 3rd edn. 1905, trans. 1906)

Westrup, J. A., 'The continuo in the "St. Matthew Passion"', *Bach-Gedenkschrift 1950* (Zurich, 1950), pp. 103–17

Whitmore, P., *Unpremeditated Art – The Cadenza in the Classical Keyboard Concerto* (Oxford, 1991)

Williams, P., *Figured Bass Accompaniment* (Edinburgh, 1970)

'Basso continuo on the Organ', *Music and Letters* 50 (1969), pp. 136–52 and 230–45

Wilson, J. (ed.), *Roger North on Music* (London, 1959)

Zaslaw, N., 'Mozart's tempo conventions', in H. Glahn, S. Sørensen, P. Ryan (eds.), *International Musicological Society: Report of the Eleventh Congress, Copenhagen 1972* (Copenhagen, 1974), vol. II, pp. 720–33

'Toward the revival of the classical orchestra', *Proceedings of the Royal Musical Association* 103 (1976–7), pp. 158–87

Mozart's Symphonies: Context, Performance Practice, Reception (Oxford, 1989)

see also Spitzer, J. D.

Index